ERIC HENSON'S

EDEN

ALTERNA

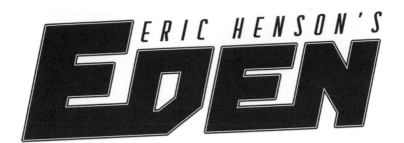

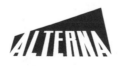

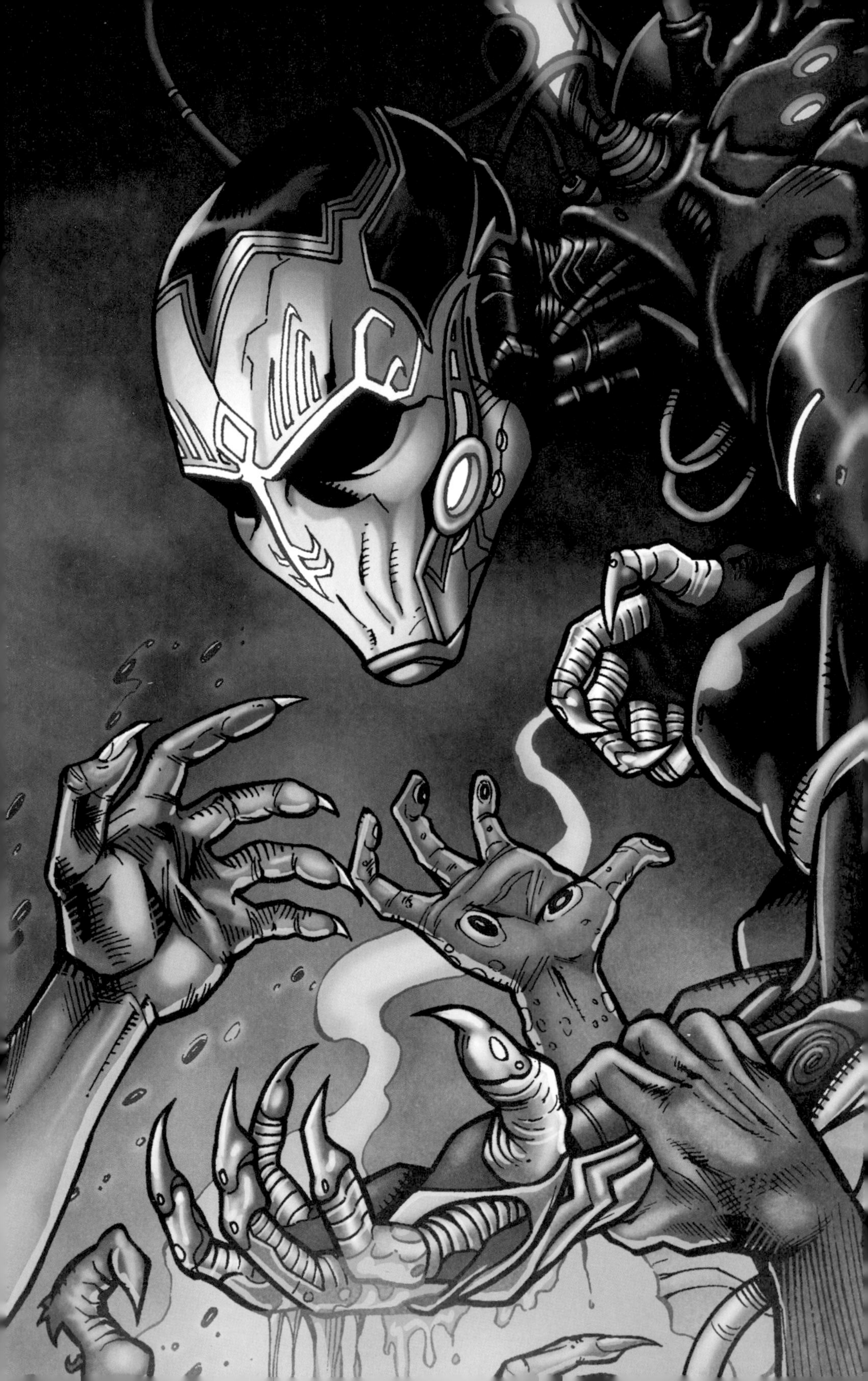

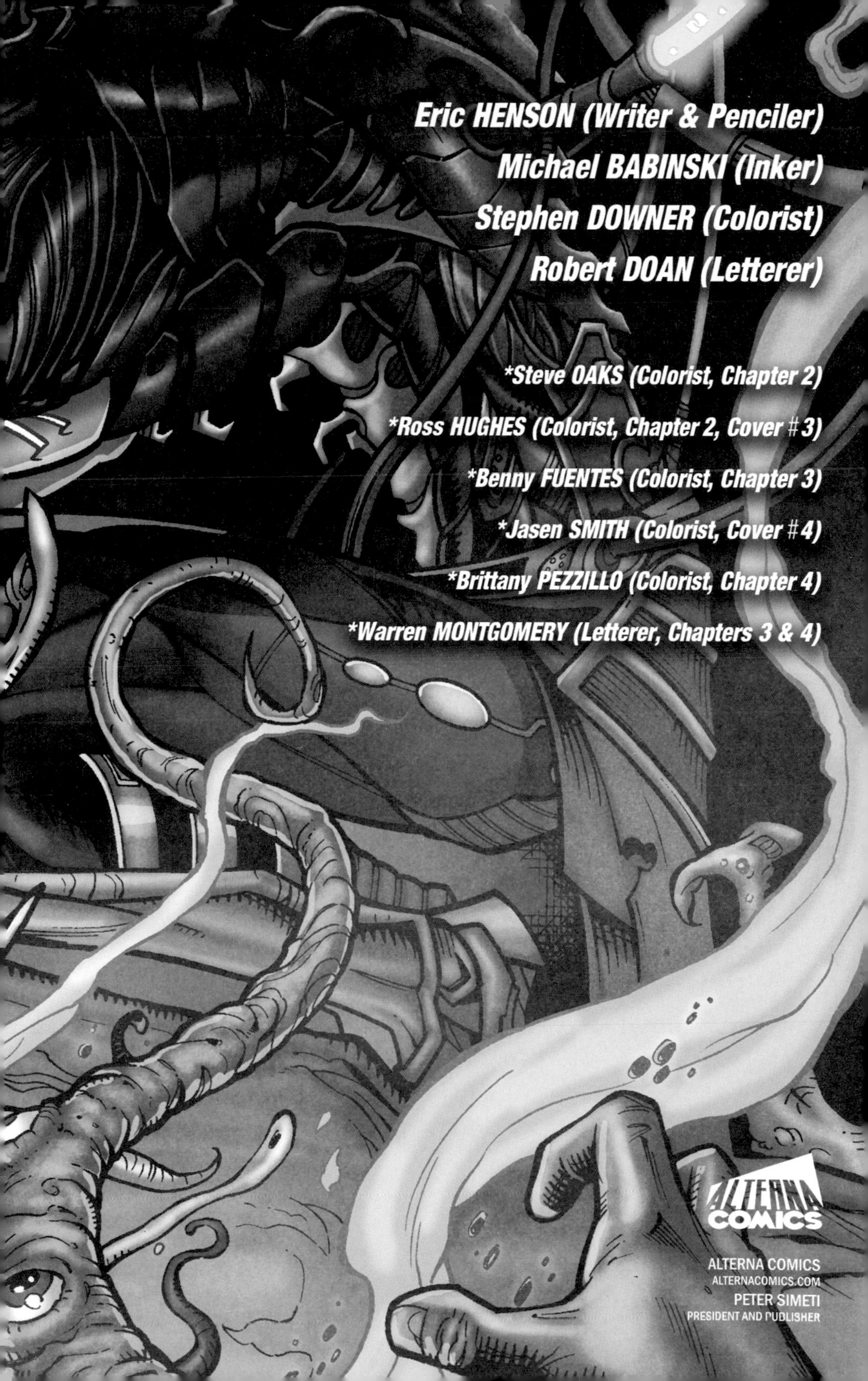

Eric HENSON (Writer & Penciler)

Michael BABINSKI (Inker)

Stephen DOWNER (Colorist)

Robert DOAN (Letterer)

*Steve OAKS (Colorist, Chapter 2)

*Ross HUGHES (Colorist, Chapter 2, Cover #3)

*Benny FUENTES (Colorist, Chapter 3)

*Jasen SMITH (Colorist, Cover #4)

*Brittany PEZZILLO (Colorist, Chapter 4)

*Warren MONTGOMERY (Letterer, Chapters 3 & 4)

ALTERNA COMICS
ALTERNACOMICS.COM
PETER SIMETI
PRESIDENT AND PUBLISHER

EDEN
9781945762727
2019 FIRST PRINTING; 1ST EDITION
Published by Alterna Comics, Inc.
Alterna Comics and its logos are ™ and © 2007-2019 Alterna Comics,
Inc. All Rights Reserved. EDEN and all related characters are ™ and
© 2019 Eric Henson. All Rights Reserved. The story presented in this
publication is fictional. Any similarities to events or persons living or
dead is purely coincidental. With the exception of artwork used for
review purposes, no portion of this publication may be reproduced
by any means without the expressed written consent of the
copyright holder. PRINTED IN THE USA.

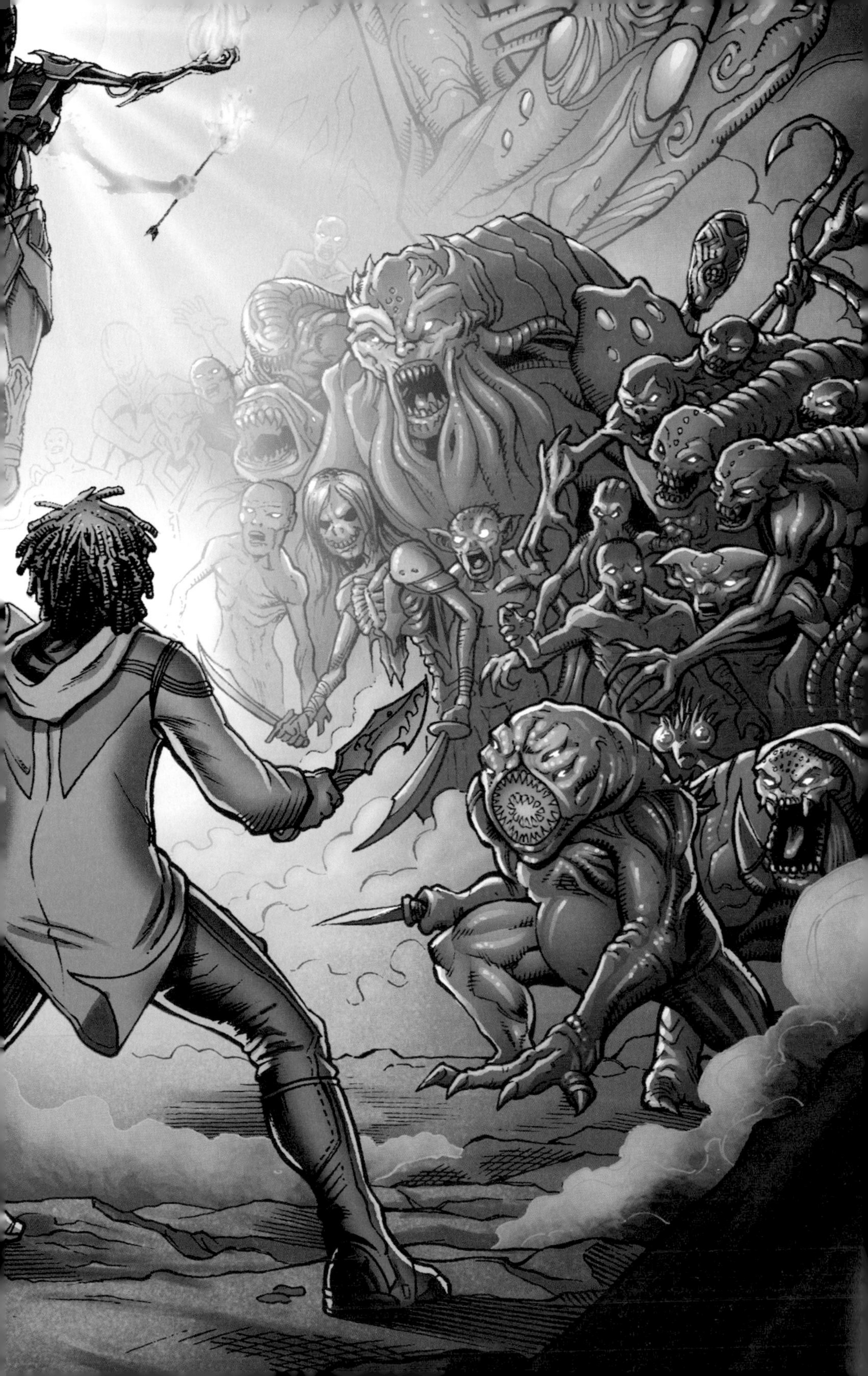

FOREWORDS are tricky.

Right...?

I mean, you wanna use the opportunity to go off on just how truly sensational the story is, while at the same time, not reveal anything about the story at hand. And spoil it.

That is, if anyone reads the Forewords first.

Which we don't. I mean, I do, but I think I'm weird like that.

So I'll make the promise right up front here and say that I will not be discussing anything about the story that will ruin any details for you. I'll keep things very general and try to keep this short. I see you looking now to see how long this is... Not too bad, right?

So I'll talk about Eric.

First though— Who am I? Okay, fair question. My name is Todd Dezago and I write comics. Among other things. I've written for Marvel and DC, Image and Dark Horse, Spider-Man, X-Factor, Impulse, and The Super Hero Squad. I've co-created several comics of my own called Tellos and The Perhapanauts.

And The Perhapanauts is how Eric and I first met; a friend of mine forwarded me a couple spec pages Eric had written and drawn for his portfolio claiming that he was a big fan of the comic. Well, so was I, so we had that in common. I reached out, we talked, and found that we had much, much more in common, our love of comics and the art of storytelling being one of our favorite subjects.

Eric was soon drawing a back-up story for us on The Perhapanauts and, eventually — when that story bled into our main story — was contributing some absolutely gorgeous pages that made up one of the two major plots that drove our graphic novel titled Danger Down Under.

So I knew Eric to be fast, professional, and attentive as an artist, passionate, insightful, and creative as a storyteller, and kind, funny, and compassionate as an Airmen, a father, a friend.

When Eric started bouncing his ideas, designs, and early scripts off me for his dream project, EDEN, I saw that he was more than a pencil monkey — his story was emotional and thrilling, vibrant and fantastic, layered and evocative. I was stunned. Not because I didn't think he was capable of those things, but he made it look so effortless. Damn him.

His protagonists were flawed, his antagonists, relatable. They remind you of people you know or — even better praise for a writer — yourself.
I promised I wouldn't go too far here, but I think I can comfortably say that, each of these characters, be they alien or otherwise, are all imbued with a rich, textured humanity, making their triumphs and challenges familiar, their choices, understandable.

What struck me more than anything though, as I watched Eric move through this experience, was that he was staying so true to himself, his vision — this is his pure and unfiltered creation. Eric is an auteur ... and that's a word I never thought I'd ever need in my toolbox. But that's him.

You've done an amazing job, Brother.

And you, Kind Reader, throw yourself into this world that Eric has created for us. Immerse yourself. You'll be glad you did.

Todd Dezago
Rhinebeck 2019

CHAPTER ONE

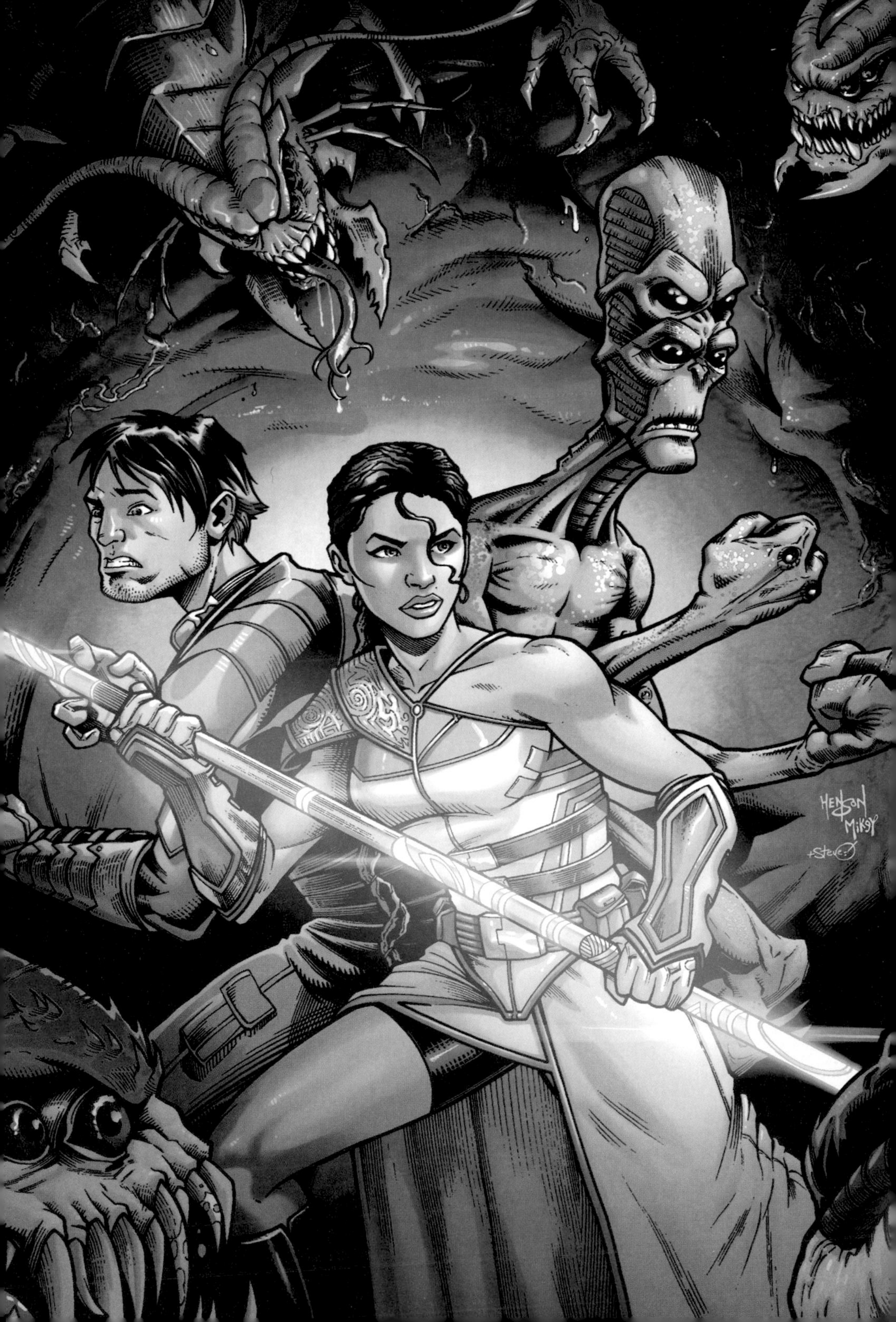

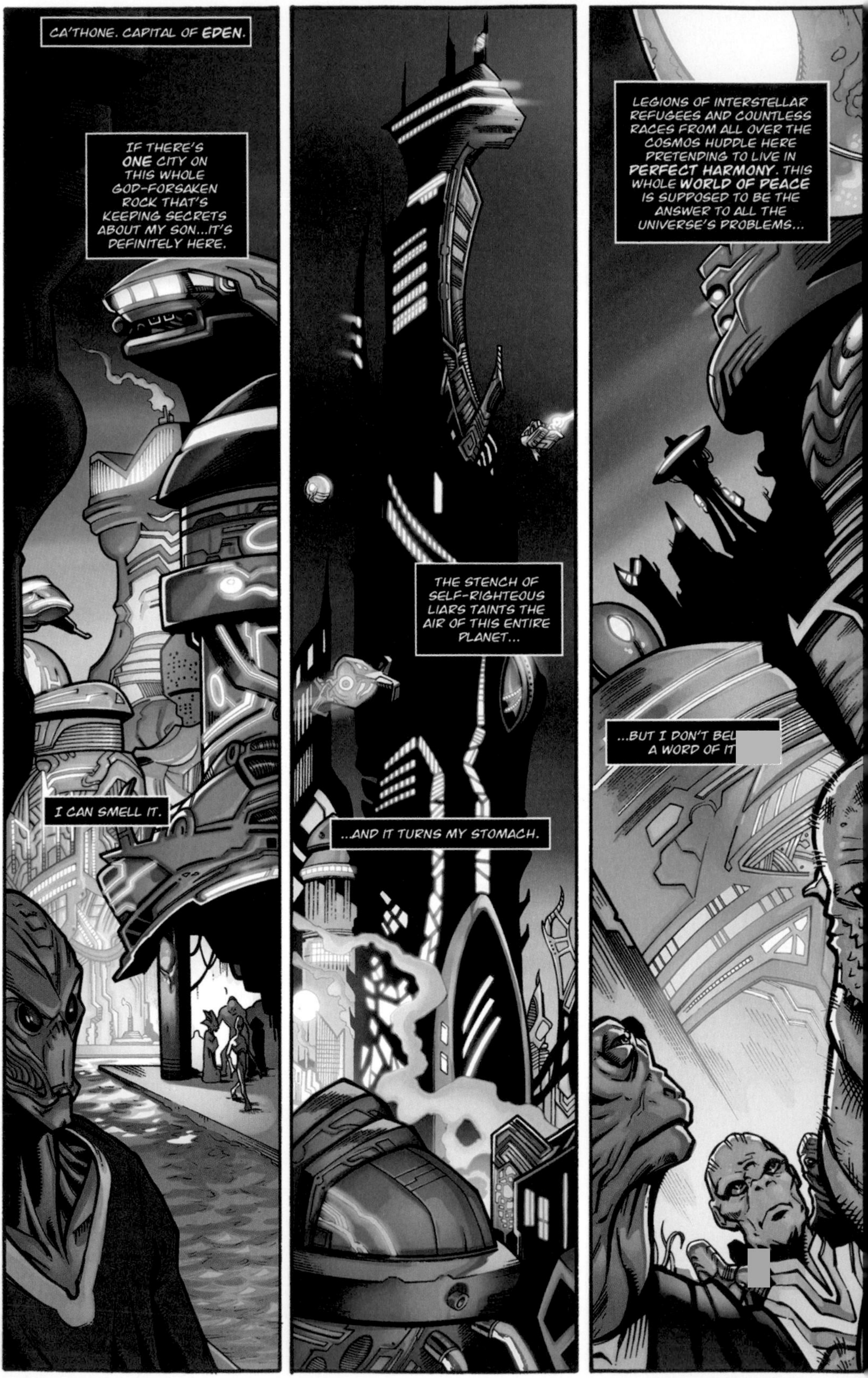
CA'THONE. CAPITAL OF EDEN.
IF THERE'S ONE CITY ON THIS WHOLE GOD-FORSAKEN ROCK THAT'S KEEPING SECRETS ABOUT MY SON...IT'S DEFINITELY HERE.
I CAN SMELL IT.
THE STENCH OF SELF-RIGHTEOUS LIARS TAINTS THE AIR OF THIS ENTIRE PLANET...
...AND IT TURNS MY STOMACH.
LEGIONS OF INTERSTELLAR REFUGEES AND COUNTLESS RACES FROM ALL OVER THE COSMOS HUDDLE HERE PRETENDING TO LIVE IN PERFECT HARMONY. THIS WHOLE WORLD OF PEACE IS SUPPOSED TO BE THE ANSWER TO ALL THE UNIVERSE'S PROBLEMS...
...BUT I DON'T BEL
A WORD OF IT

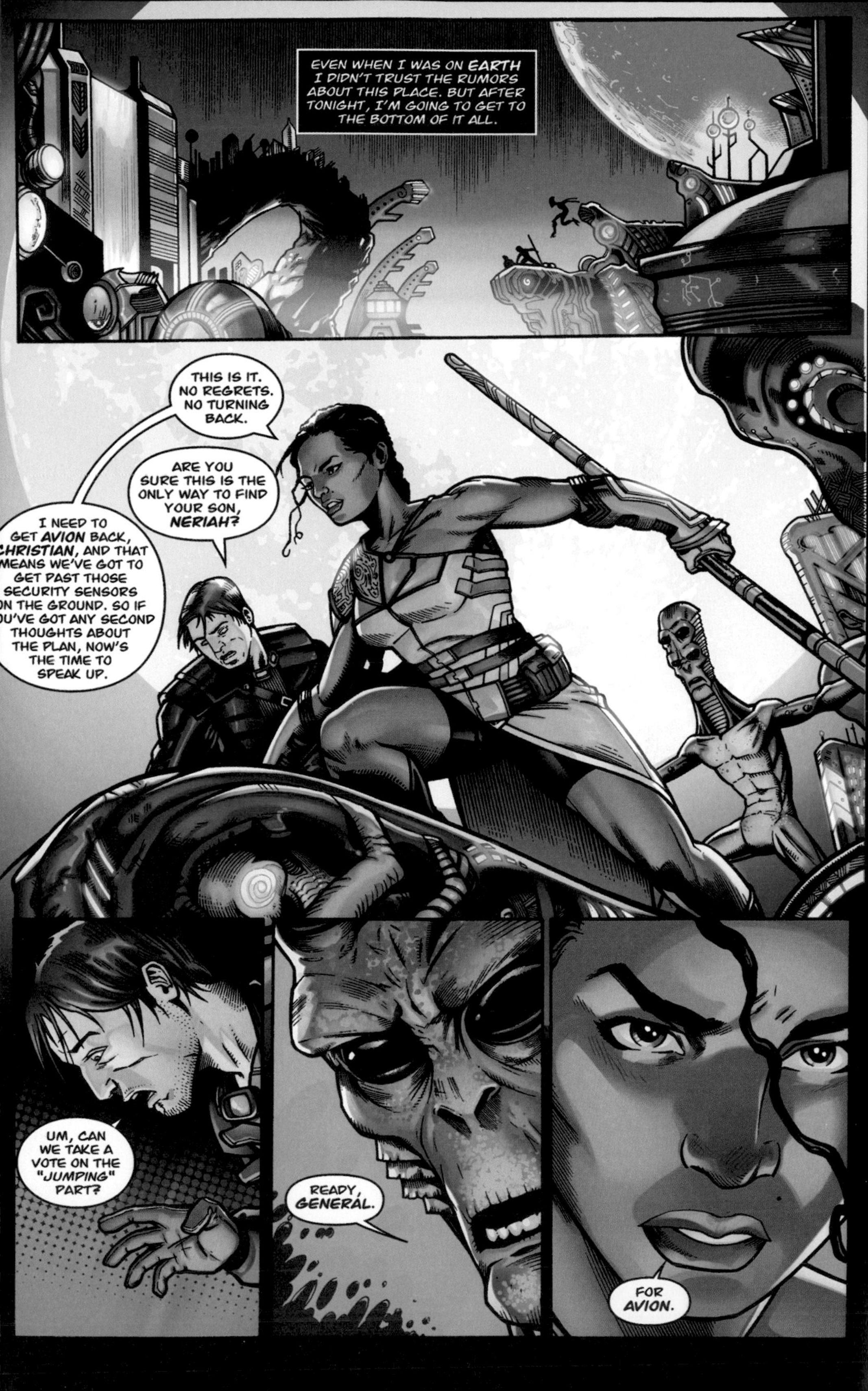
EVEN WHEN I WAS ON EARTH I DIDN'T TRUST THE RUMORS ABOUT THIS PLACE. BUT AFTER TONIGHT, I'M GOING TO GET TO THE BOTTOM OF IT ALL.
THIS IS IT. NO REGRETS. NO TURNING BACK.
ARE YOU SURE THIS IS THE ONLY WAY TO FIND YOUR SON, NERIAH?
I NEED TO GET AVION BACK, CHRISTIAN, AND THAT MEANS WE'VE GOT TO GET PAST THOSE SECURITY SENSORS ON THE GROUND. SO IF YOU'VE GOT ANY SECOND THOUGHTS ABOUT THE PLAN, NOW'S THE TIME TO SPEAK UP.
UM, CAN WE TAKE A VOTE ON THE "JUMPING" PART?
READY, GENERAL.
FOR AVION.

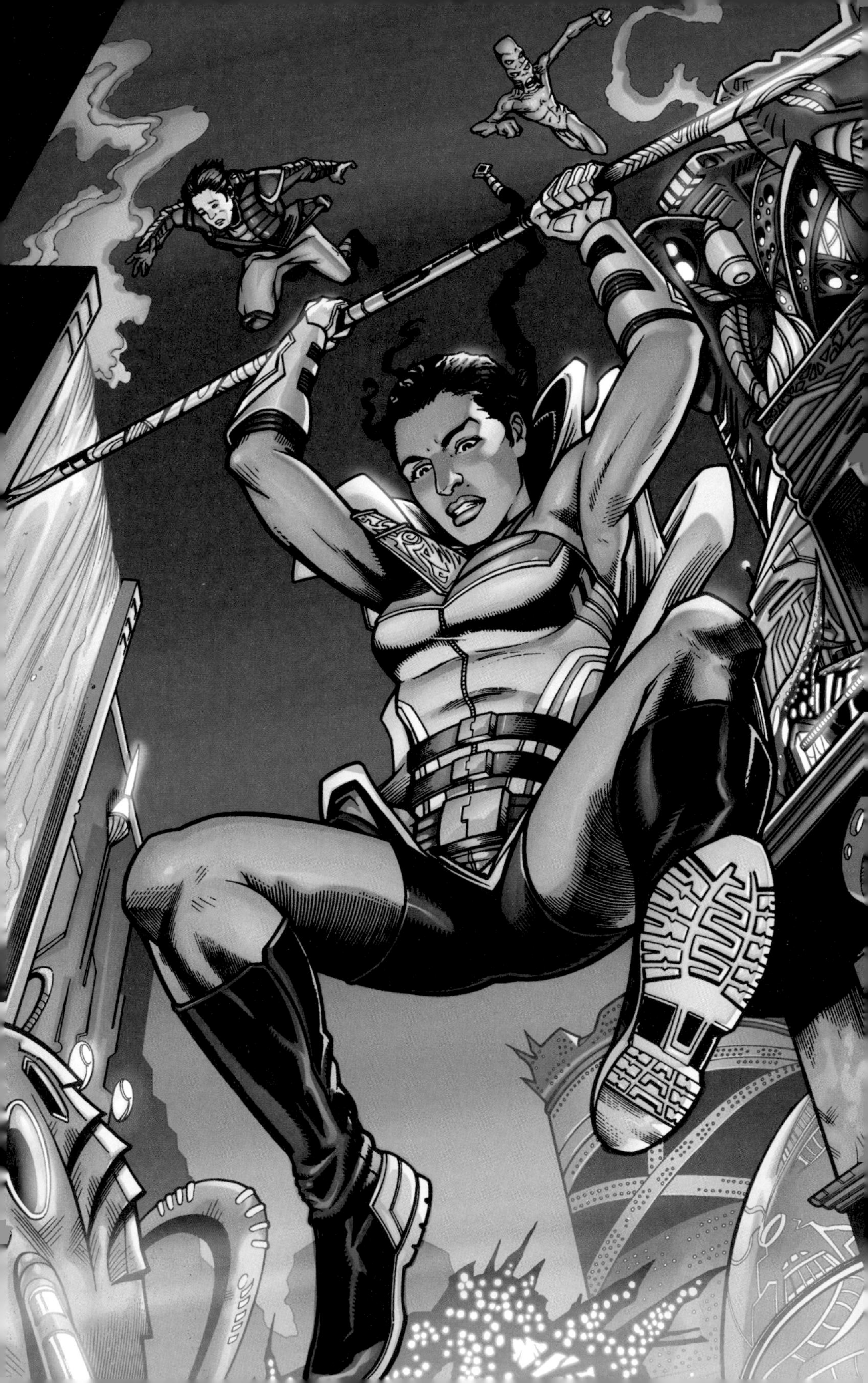

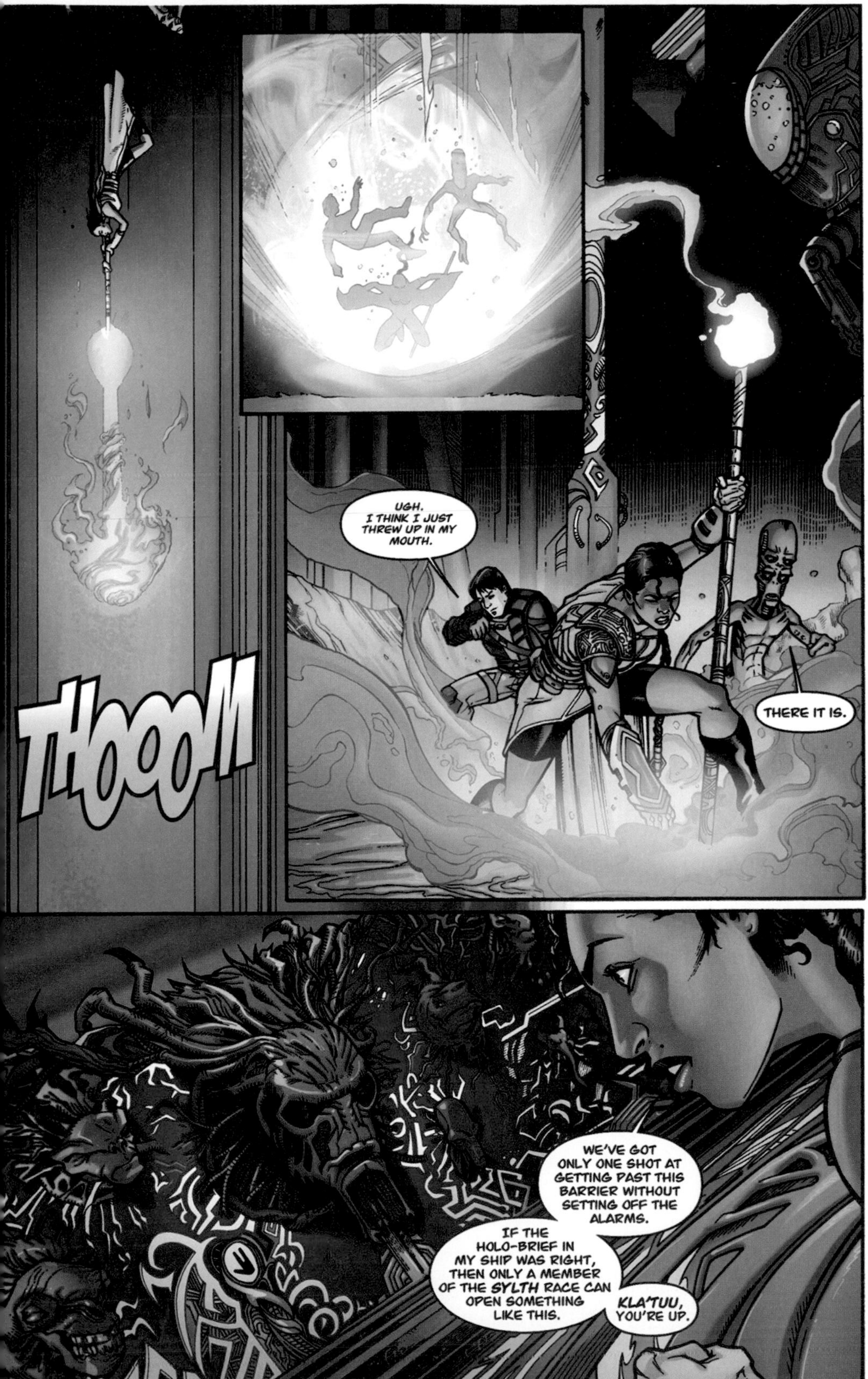
THOOOM
UGH. I THINK I JUST THREW UP IN MY MOUTH.
THERE IT IS.
WE'VE GOT ONLY ONE SHOT AT GETTING PAST THIS BARRIER WITHOUT SETTING OFF THE ALARMS.
IF THE HOLO-BRIEF IN MY SHIP WAS RIGHT, THEN ONLY A MEMBER OF THE SYLTH RACE CAN OPEN SOMETHING LIKE THIS.
KLA'TUU, YOU'RE UP.

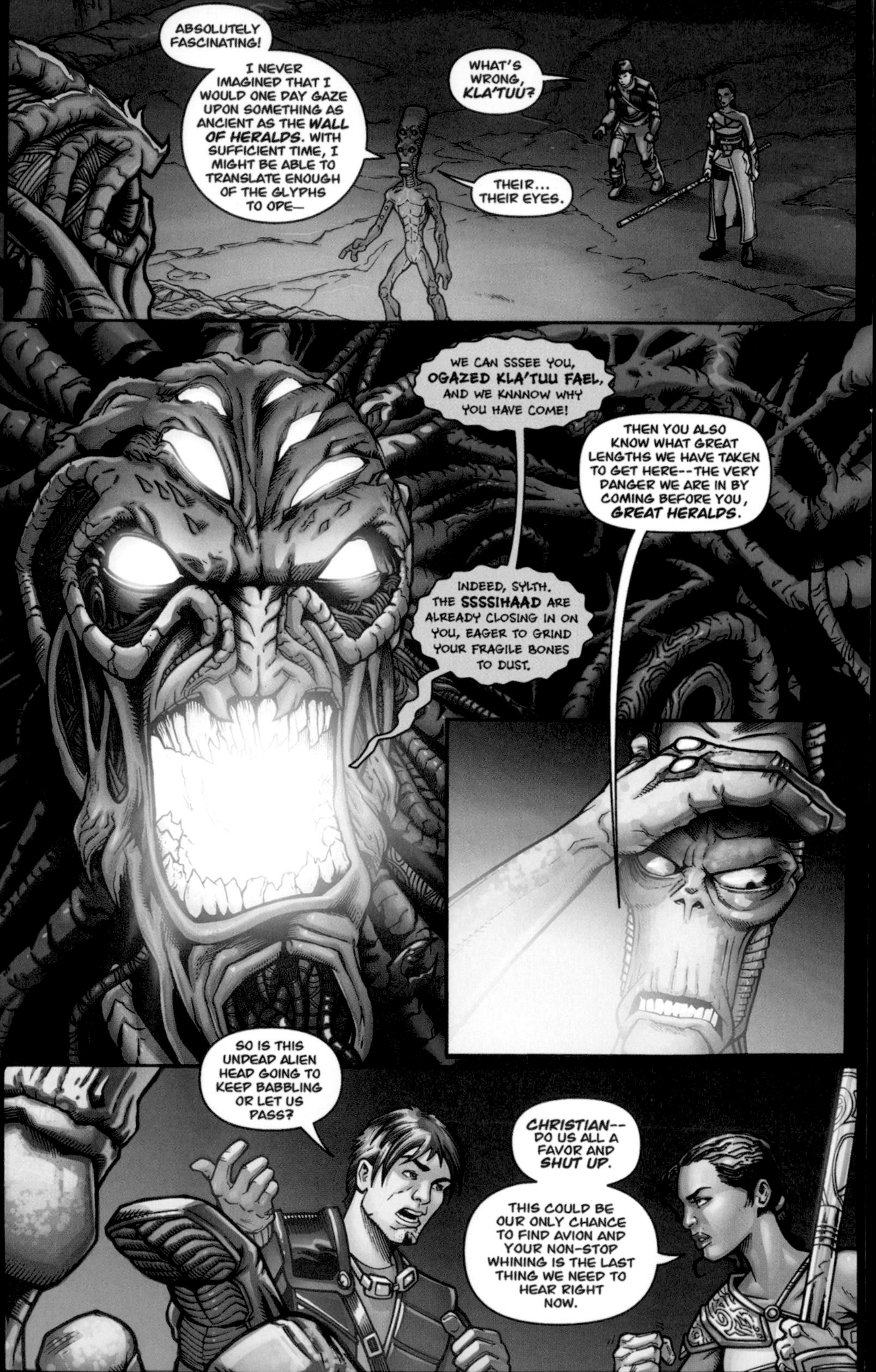
ABSOLUTELY FASCINATING!
I NEVER IMAGINED THAT I WOULD ONE DAY GAZE UPON SOMETHING AS ANCIENT AS THE WALL OF HERALDS. WITH SUFFICIENT TIME, I MIGHT BE ABLE TO TRANSLATE ENOUGH OF THE GLYPHS TO OPE—
WHAT'S WRONG, KLA'TUU?
THEIR... THEIR EYES.
WE CAN SSSEE YOU, OGAZED KLA'TUU FAEL, AND WE KNNOW WHY YOU HAVE COME!
THEN YOU ALSO KNOW WHAT GREAT LENGTHS WE HAVE TAKEN TO GET HERE--THE VERY DANGER WE ARE IN BY COMING BEFORE YOU, GREAT HERALDS.
INDEED, SYLTH. THE SSSSIHAAD ARE ALREADY CLOSING IN ON YOU, EAGER TO GRIND YOUR FRAGILE BONES TO DUST.
SO IS THIS UNDEAD ALIEN HEAD GOING TO KEEP BABBLING OR LET US PASS?
CHRISTIAN-- DO US ALL A FAVOR AND SHUT UP.
THIS COULD BE OUR ONLY CHANCE TO FIND AVION AND YOUR NON-STOP WHINING IS THE LAST THING WE NEED TO HEAR RIGHT NOW.

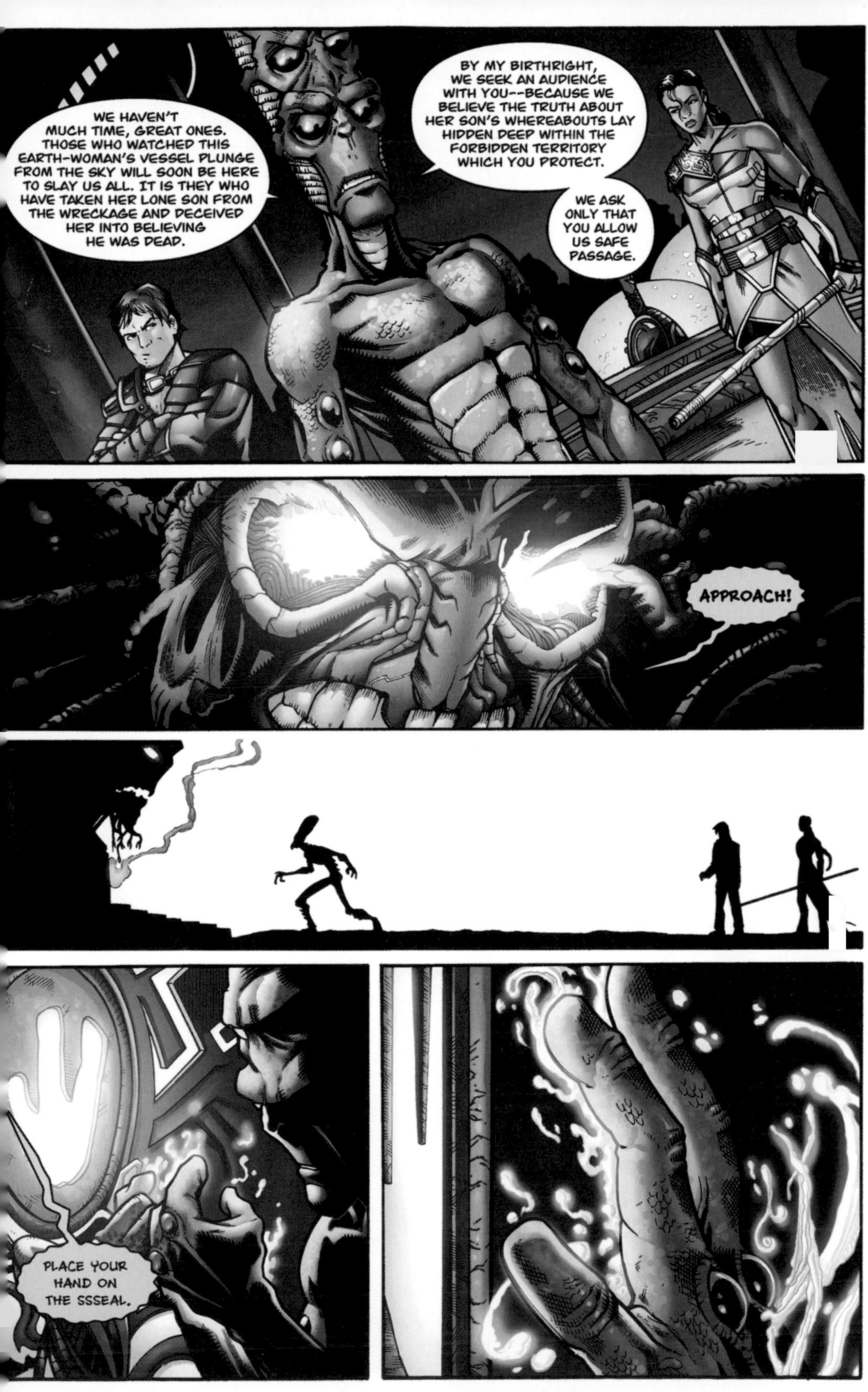
WE HAVEN'T MUCH TIME, GREAT ONES. THOSE WHO WATCHED THIS EARTH-WOMAN'S VESSEL PLUNGE FROM THE SKY WILL SOON BE HERE TO SLAY US ALL. IT IS THEY WHO HAVE TAKEN HER LONE SON FROM THE WRECKAGE AND DECEIVED HER INTO BELIEVING HE WAS DEAD.
BY MY BIRTHRIGHT, WE SEEK AN AUDIENCE WITH YOU--BECAUSE WE BELIEVE THE TRUTH ABOUT HER SON'S WHEREABOUTS LAY HIDDEN DEEP WITHIN THE FORBIDDEN TERRITORY WHICH YOU PROTECT.
WE ASK ONLY THAT YOU ALLOW US SAFE PASSAGE.
APPROACH!
PLACE YOUR HAND ON THE SSSEAL.

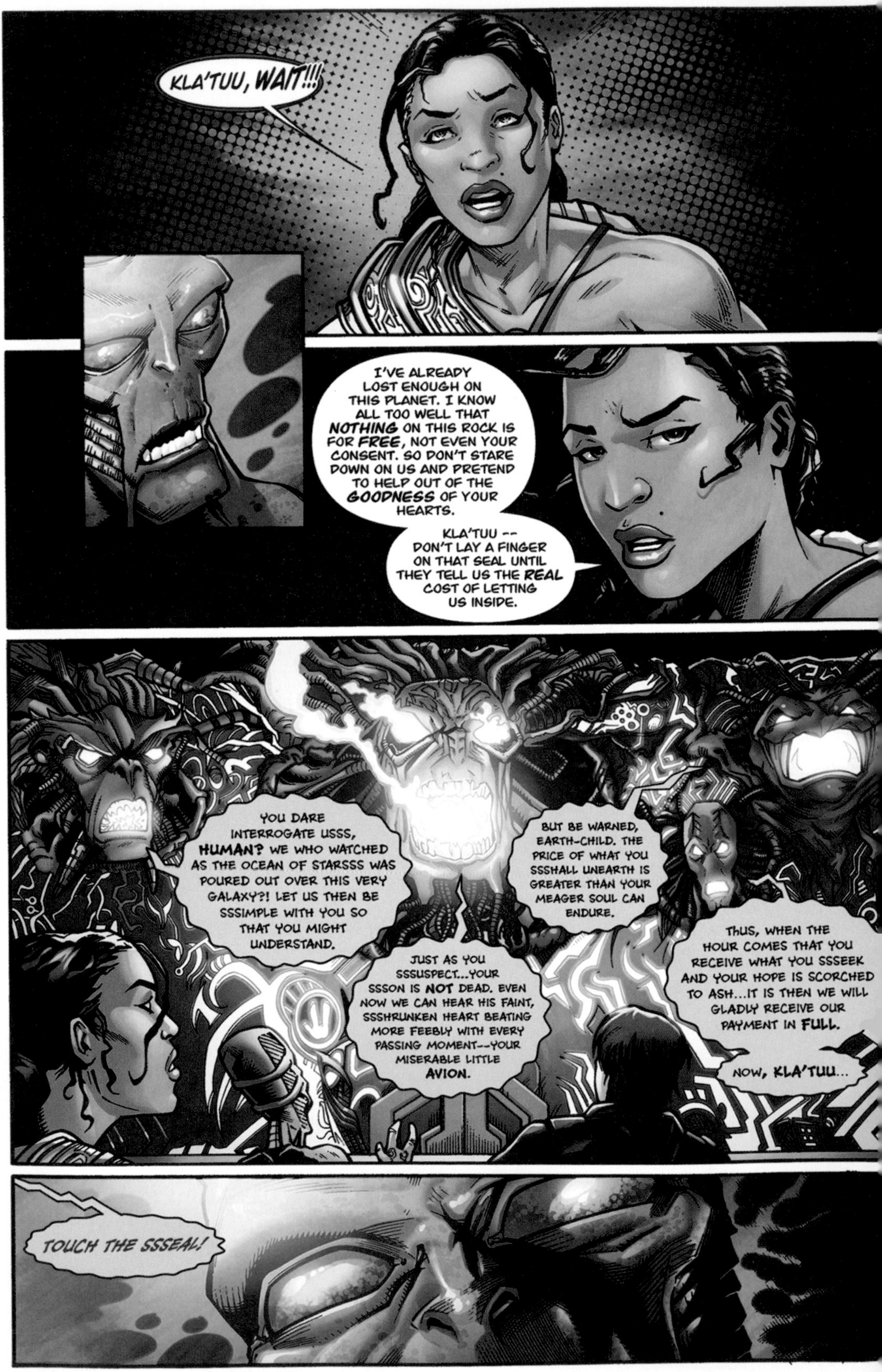
KLA'TUU, WAIT!!!
I'VE ALREADY LOST ENOUGH ON THIS PLANET. I KNOW ALL TOO WELL THAT NOTHING ON THIS ROCK IS FOR FREE, NOT EVEN YOUR CONSENT. SO DON'T STARE DOWN ON US AND PRETEND TO HELP OUT OF THE GOODNESS OF YOUR HEARTS.
KLA'TUU -- DON'T LAY A FINGER ON THAT SEAL UNTIL THEY TELL US THE REAL COST OF LETTING US INSIDE.
YOU DARE INTERROGATE USSS, HUMAN? WE WHO WATCHED AS THE OCEAN OF STARSSS WAS POURED OUT OVER THIS VERY GALAXY?! LET US THEN BE SSSIMPLE WITH YOU SO THAT YOU MIGHT UNDERSTAND.
JUST AS YOU SSSUSPECT...YOUR SSSON IS NOT DEAD. EVEN NOW WE CAN HEAR HIS FAINT, SSSHRUNKEN HEART BEATING MORE FEEBLY WITH EVERY PASSING MOMENT--YOUR MISERABLE LITTLE AVION.
BUT BE WARNED, EARTH-CHILD. THE PRICE OF WHAT YOU SSSHALL UNEARTH IS GREATER THAN YOUR MEAGER SOUL CAN ENDURE.
THUS, WHEN THE HOUR COMES THAT YOU RECEIVE WHAT YOU SSSEEK AND YOUR HOPE IS SCORCHED TO ASH...IT IS THEN WE WILL GLADLY RECEIVE OUR PAYMENT IN FULL.
NOW, KLA'TUU...
TOUCH THE SSSEAL!

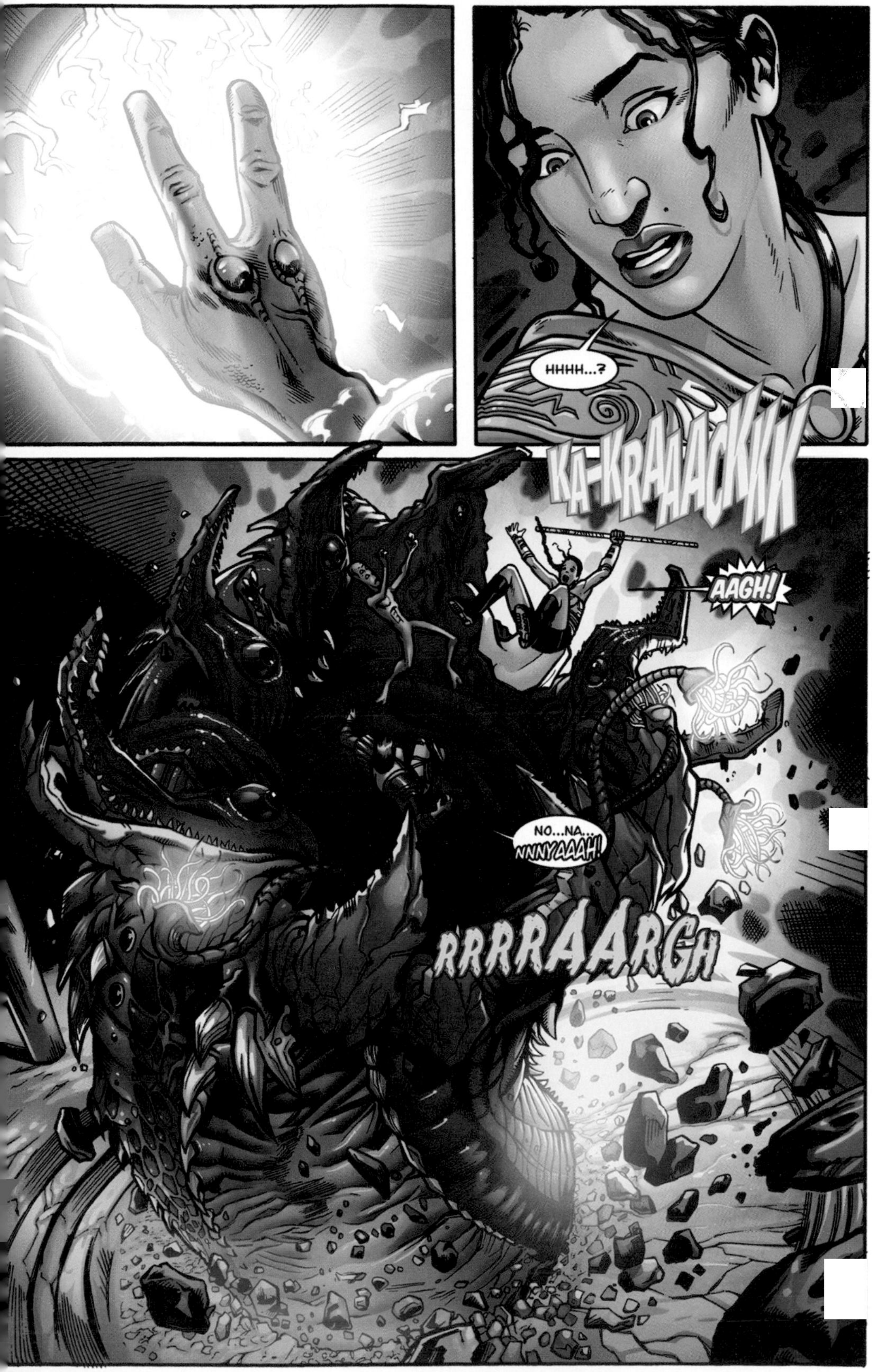
HHHH...?
KA-KRAAACKKK
AAGH!
NO...NA...
NNNYAAAH!
RRRRAARGH

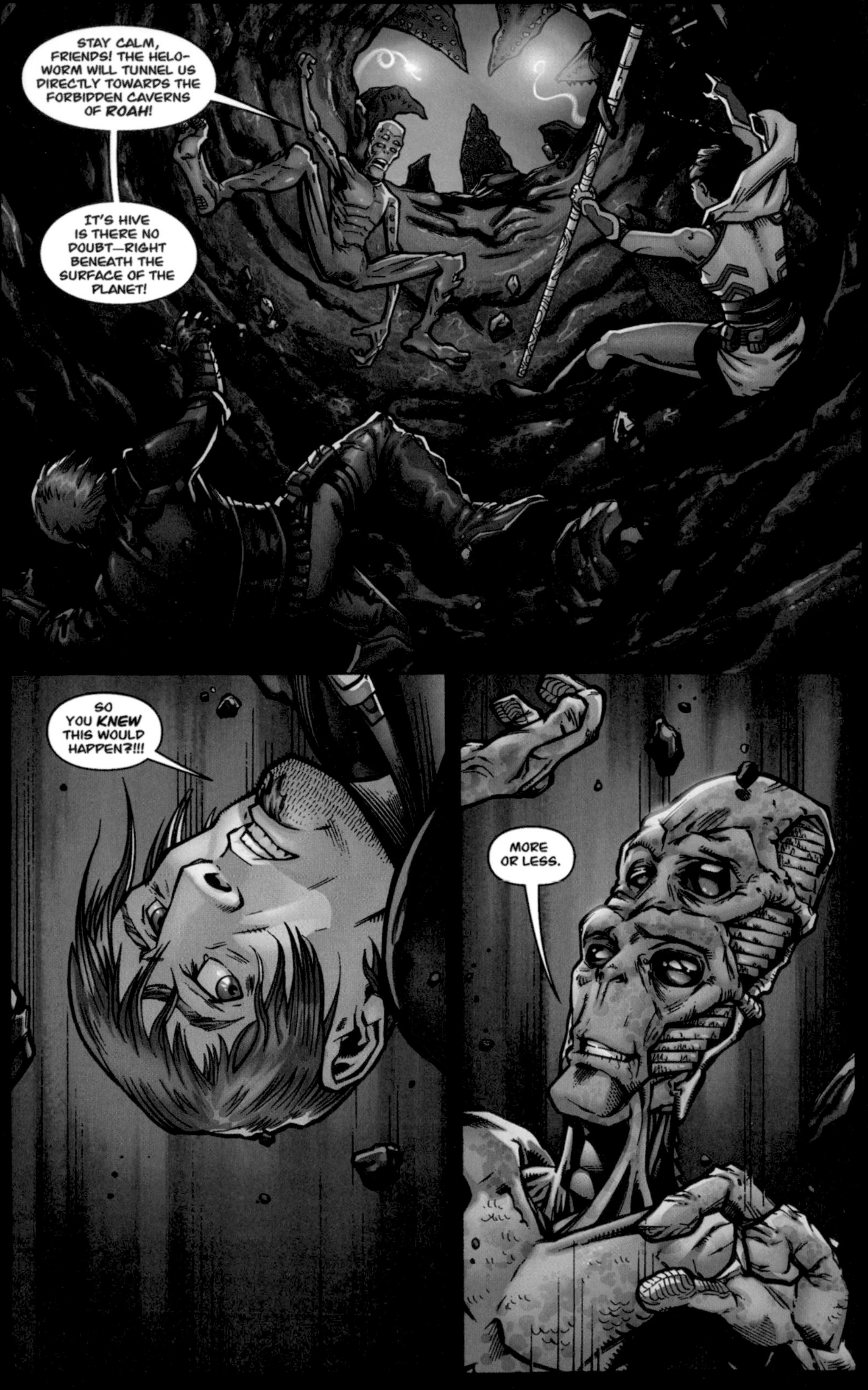
STAY CALM, FRIENDS! THE HELO-WORM WILL TUNNEL US DIRECTLY TOWARDS THE FORBIDDEN CAVERNS OF ROAH!
IT'S HIVE IS THERE NO DOUBT—RIGHT BENEATH THE SURFACE OF THE PLANET!
SO YOU KNEW THIS WOULD HAPPEN?!!!
MORE OR LESS.

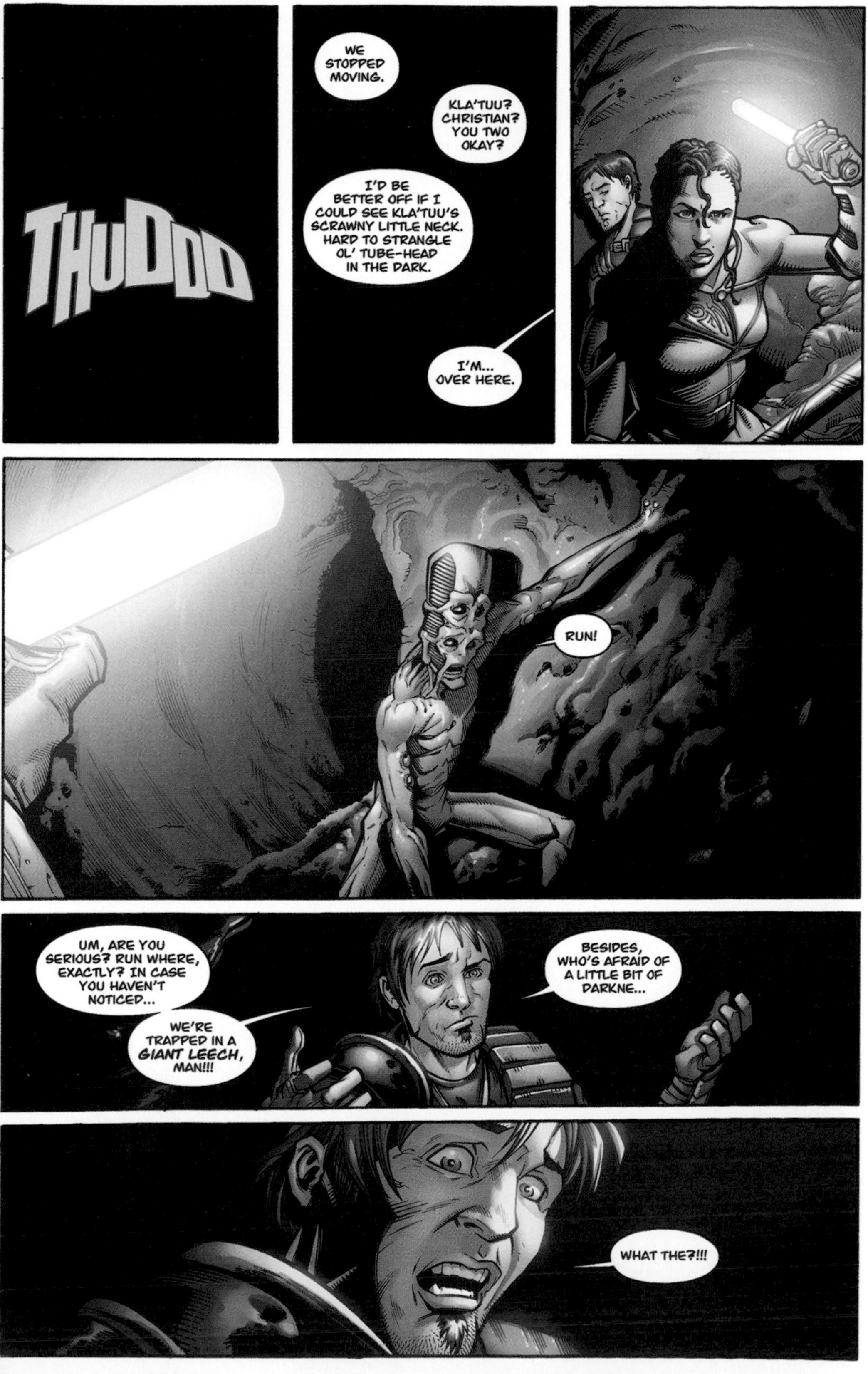
THUDDD
WE STOPPED MOVING.
KLA'TUU? CHRISTIAN? YOU TWO OKAY?
I'D BE BETTER OFF IF I COULD SEE KLA'TUU'S SCRAWNY LITTLE NECK. HARD TO STRANGLE OL' TUBE-HEAD IN THE DARK.
I'M... OVER HERE.
RUN!
UM, ARE YOU SERIOUS? RUN WHERE, EXACTLY? IN CASE YOU HAVEN'T NOTICED...
WE'RE TRAPPED IN A GIANT LEECH, MAN!!!
BESIDES, WHO'S AFRAID OF A LITTLE BIT OF DARKNE...
WHAT THE?!!!

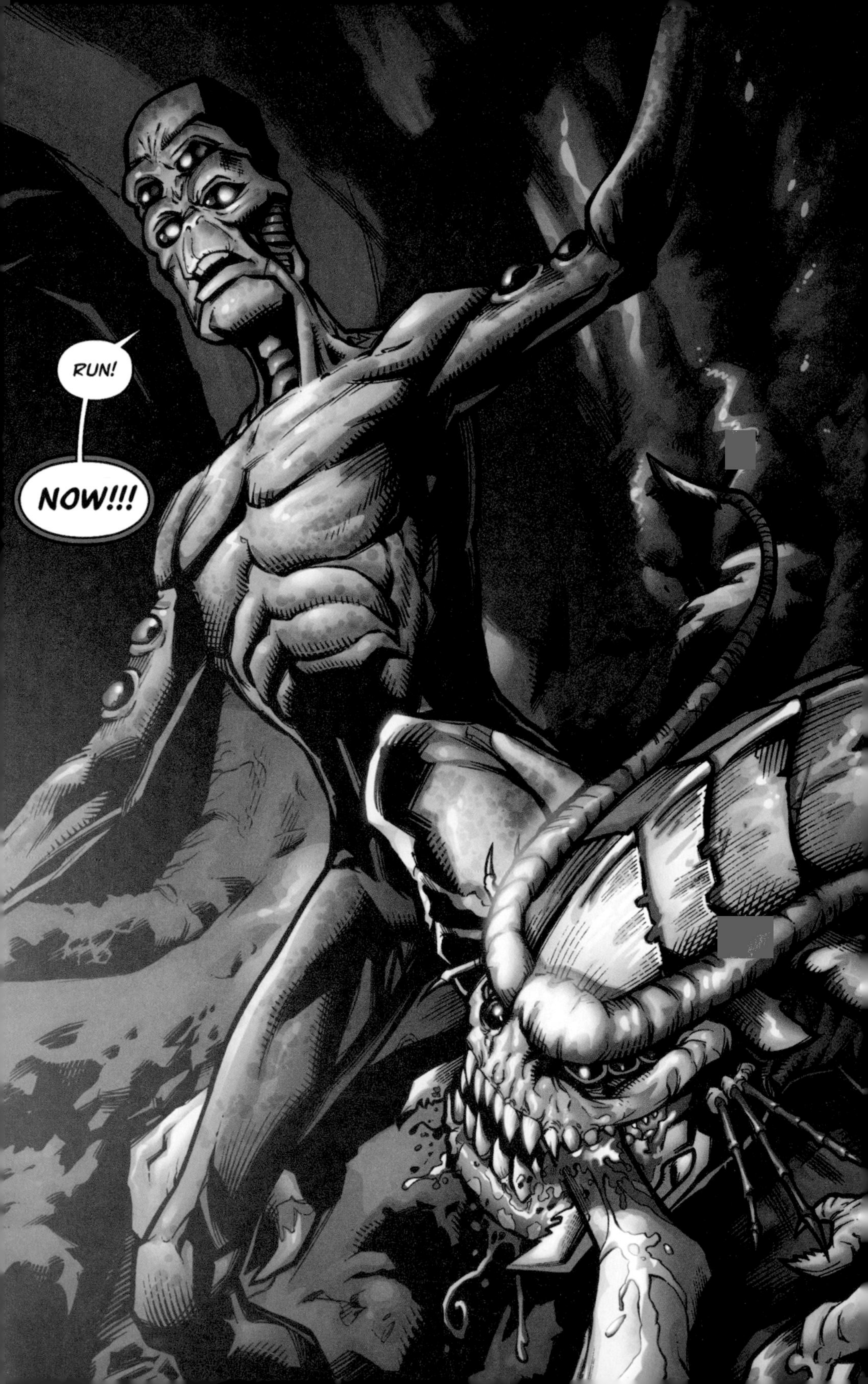
RUN!
NOW!!!

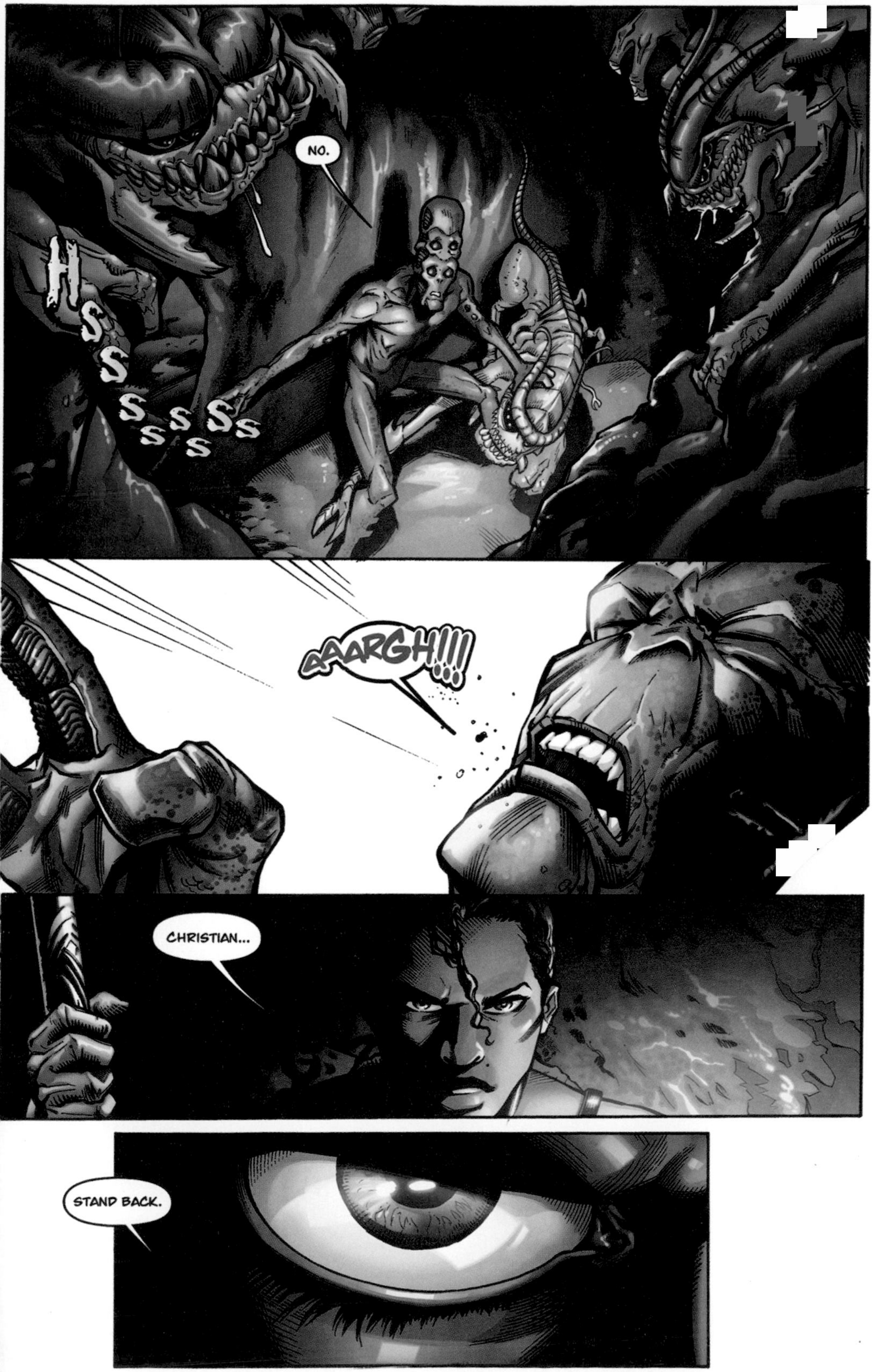
NO.
HSSSSSSSSS
AAARGH!!!!
CHRISTIAN...
STAND BACK.

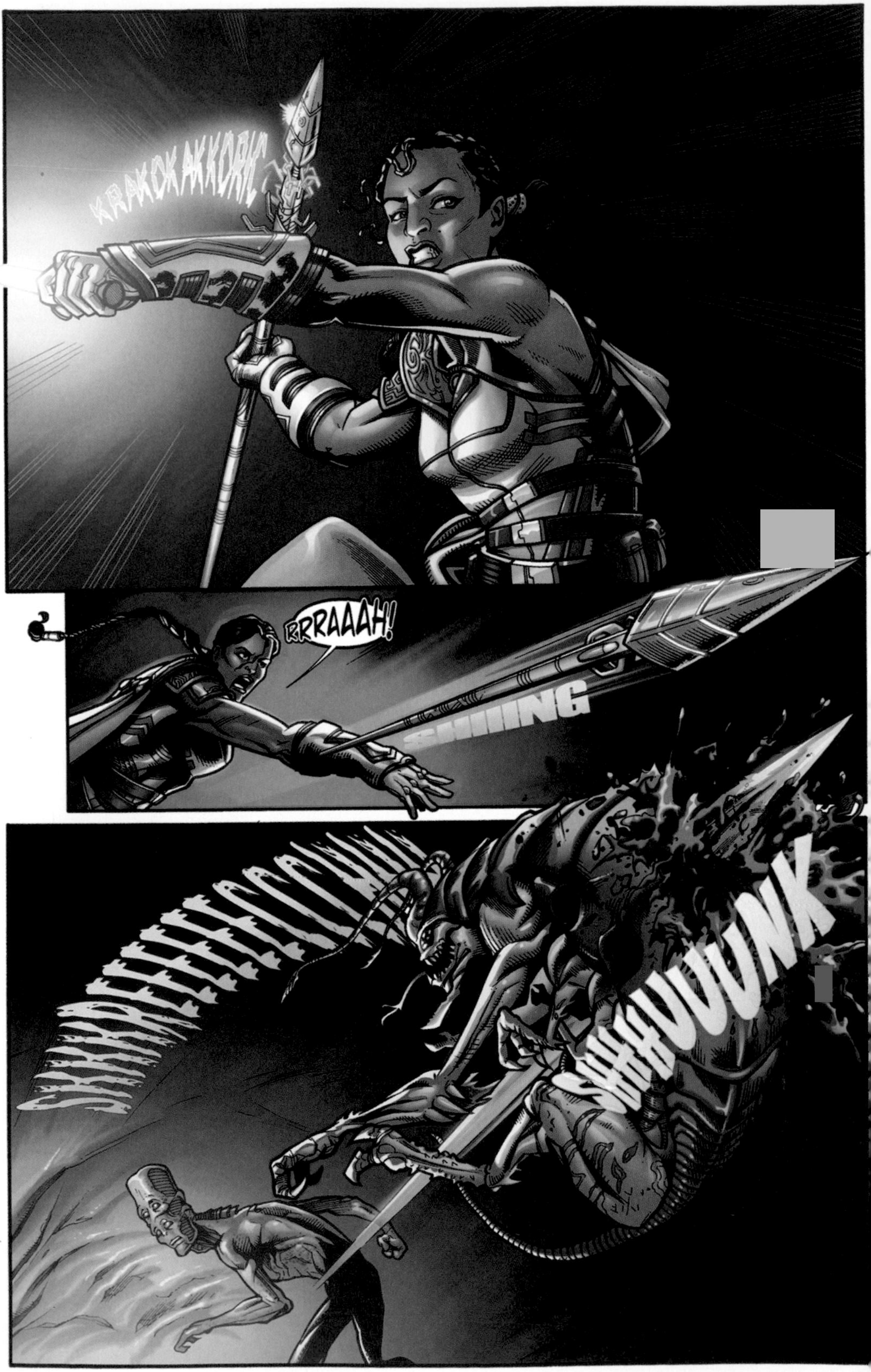
RRRAAAH!

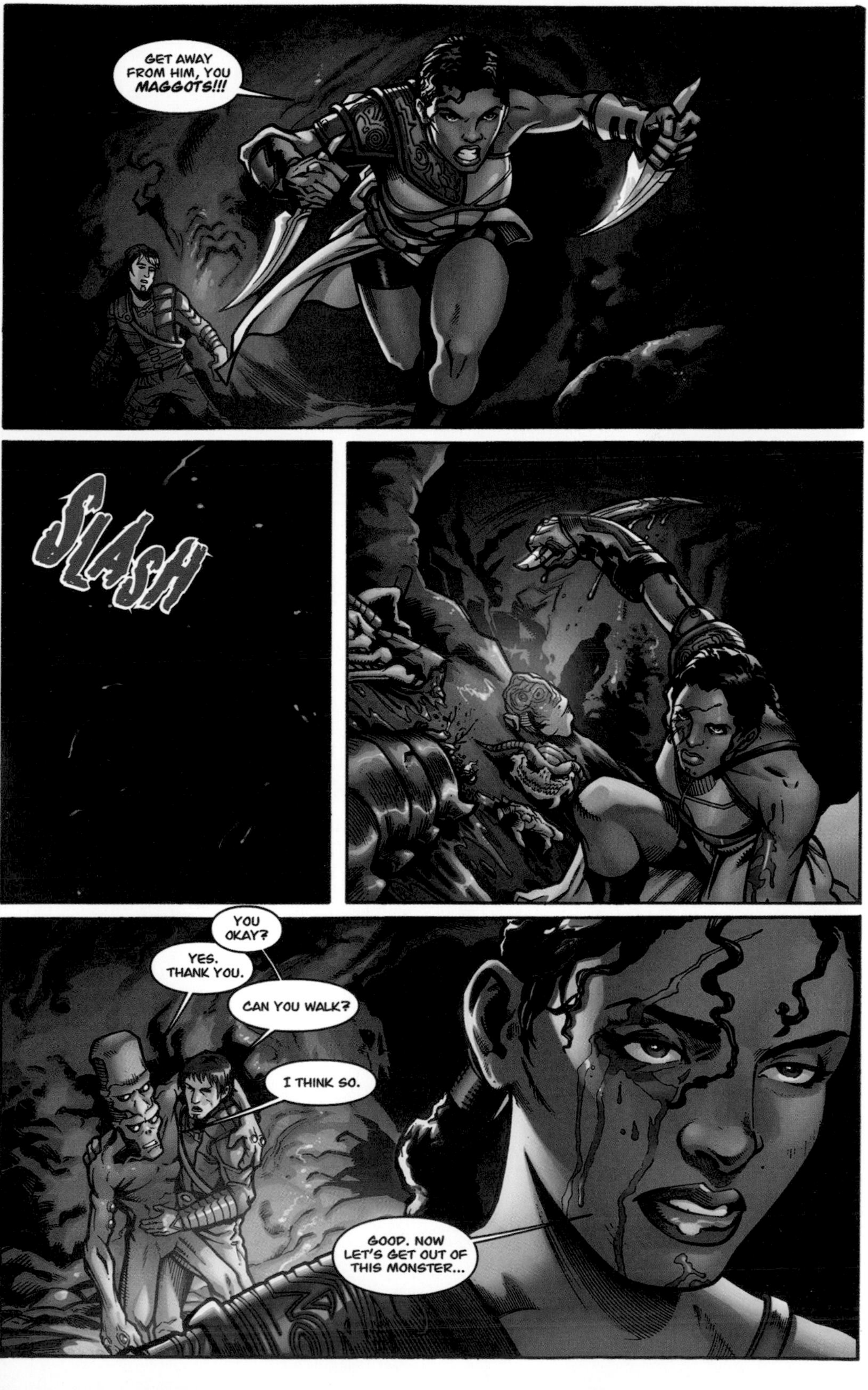
GET AWAY FROM HIM, YOU MAGGOTS!!!
SLASH
YOU OKAY?
YES. THANK YOU.
CAN YOU WALK?
I THINK SO.
GOOD. NOW LET'S GET OUT OF THIS MONSTER...

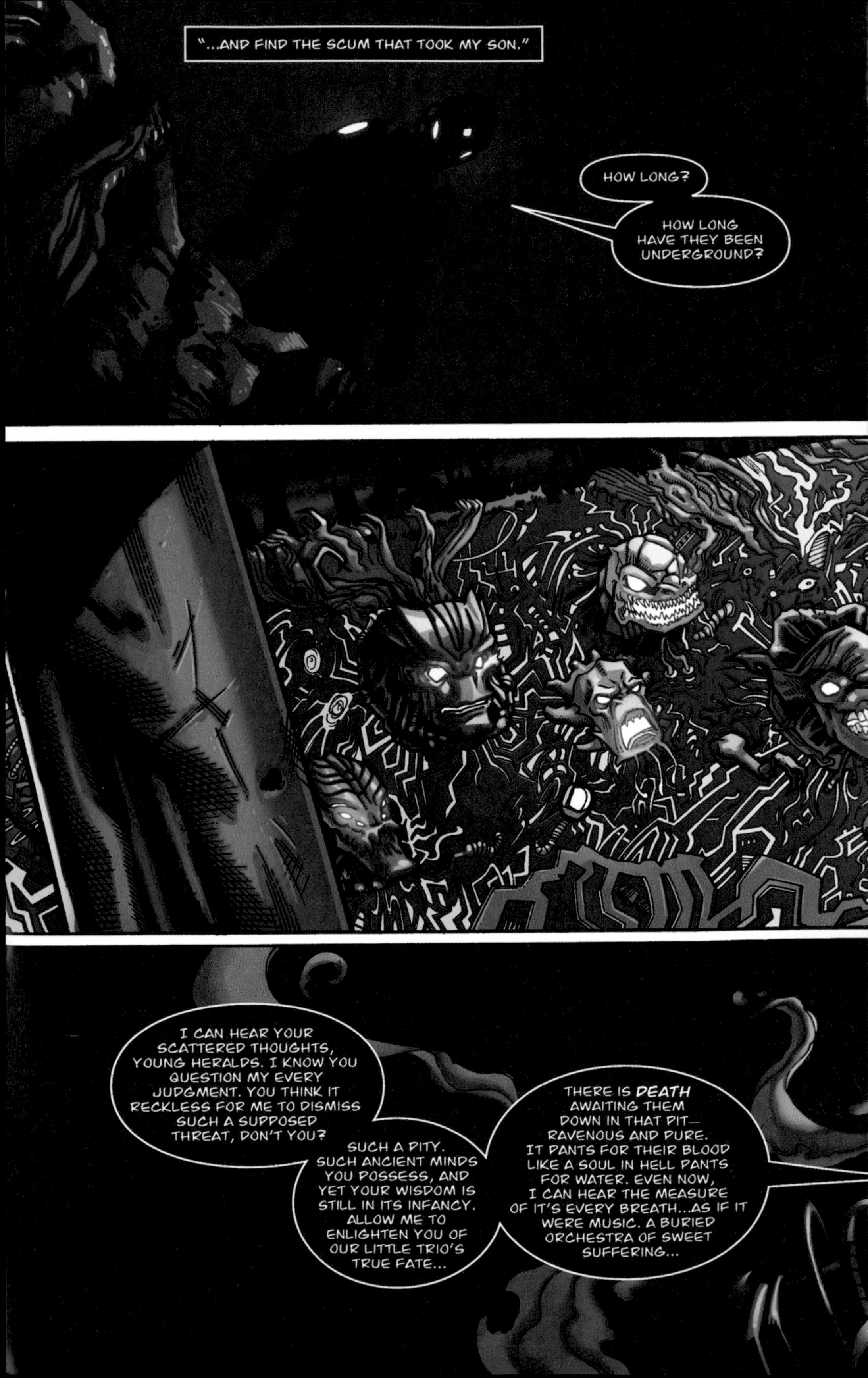
"...AND FIND THE SCUM THAT TOOK MY SON."
HOW LONG?
HOW LONG HAVE THEY BEEN UNDERGROUND?
I CAN HEAR YOUR SCATTERED THOUGHTS, YOUNG HERALDS. I KNOW YOU QUESTION MY EVERY JUDGMENT. YOU THINK IT RECKLESS FOR ME TO DISMISS SUCH A SUPPOSED THREAT, DON'T YOU?
SUCH A PITY. SUCH ANCIENT MINDS YOU POSSESS, AND YET YOUR WISDOM IS STILL IN ITS INFANCY. ALLOW ME TO ENLIGHTEN YOU OF OUR LITTLE TRIO'S TRUE FATE...
THERE IS **DEATH** AWAITING THEM DOWN IN THAT PIT—RAVENOUS AND PURE. IT PANTS FOR THEIR BLOOD LIKE A SOUL IN HELL PANTS FOR WATER. EVEN NOW, I CAN HEAR THE MEASURE OF IT'S EVERY BREATH...AS IF IT WERE MUSIC. A BURIED ORCHESTRA OF SWEET SUFFERING...

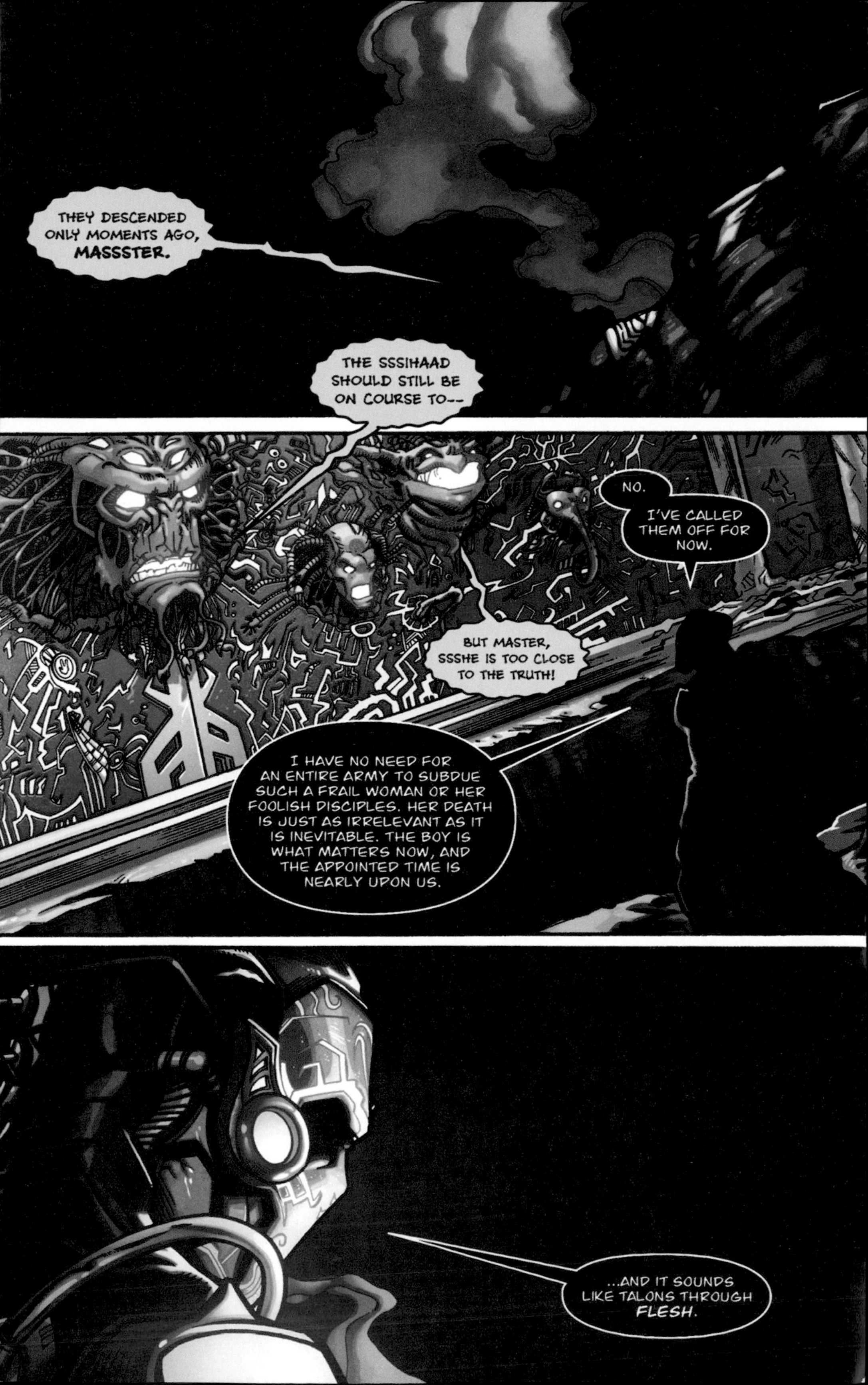
THEY DESCENDED ONLY MOMENTS AGO, MASSSTER.
THE SSSIHAAD SHOULD STILL BE ON COURSE TO--
NO.
I'VE CALLED THEM OFF FOR NOW.
BUT MASTER, SSSHE IS TOO CLOSE TO THE TRUTH!
I HAVE NO NEED FOR AN ENTIRE ARMY TO SUBDUE SUCH A FRAIL WOMAN OR HER FOOLISH DISCIPLES. HER DEATH IS JUST AS IRRELEVANT AS IT IS INEVITABLE. THE BOY IS WHAT MATTERS NOW, AND THE APPOINTED TIME IS NEARLY UPON US.
...AND IT SOUNDS LIKE TALONS THROUGH FLESH.

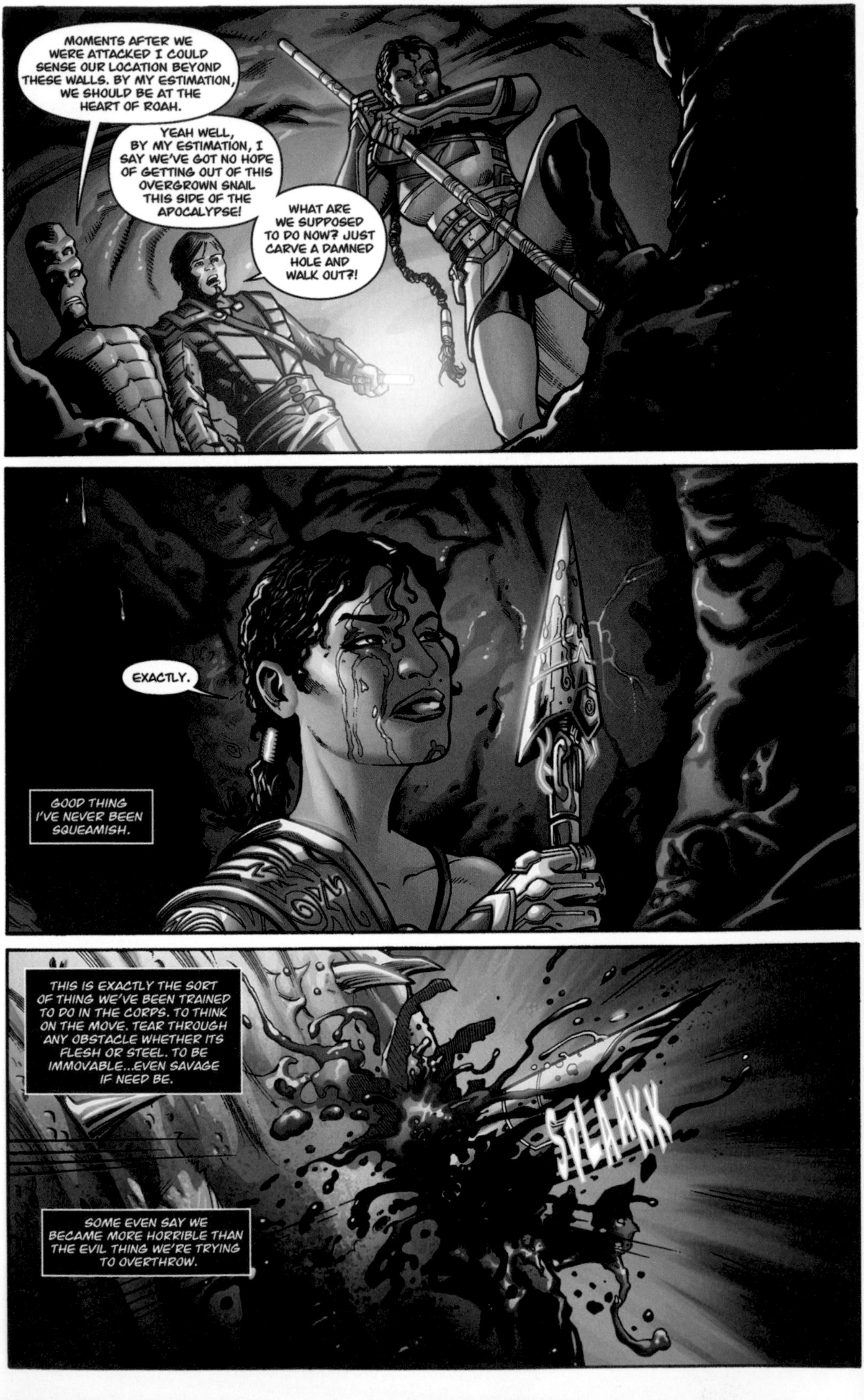
MOMENTS AFTER WE WERE ATTACKED I COULD SENSE OUR LOCATION BEYOND THESE WALLS. BY MY ESTIMATION, WE SHOULD BE AT THE HEART OF ROAH.
YEAH WELL, BY MY ESTIMATION, I SAY WE'VE GOT NO HOPE OF GETTING OUT OF THIS OVERGROWN SNAIL THIS SIDE OF THE APOCALYPSE!
WHAT ARE WE SUPPOSED TO DO NOW? JUST CARVE A DAMNED HOLE AND WALK OUT?!
EXACTLY.
GOOD THING I'VE NEVER BEEN SQUEAMISH.
THIS IS EXACTLY THE SORT OF THING WE'VE BEEN TRAINED TO DO IN THE CORPS. TO THINK ON THE MOVE. TEAR THROUGH ANY OBSTACLE WHETHER ITS FLESH OR STEEL. TO BE IMMOVABLE...EVEN SAVAGE IF NEED BE.
SPLAAKK
SOME EVEN SAY WE BECAME MORE HORRIBLE THAN THE EVIL THING WE'RE TRYING TO OVERTHROW.

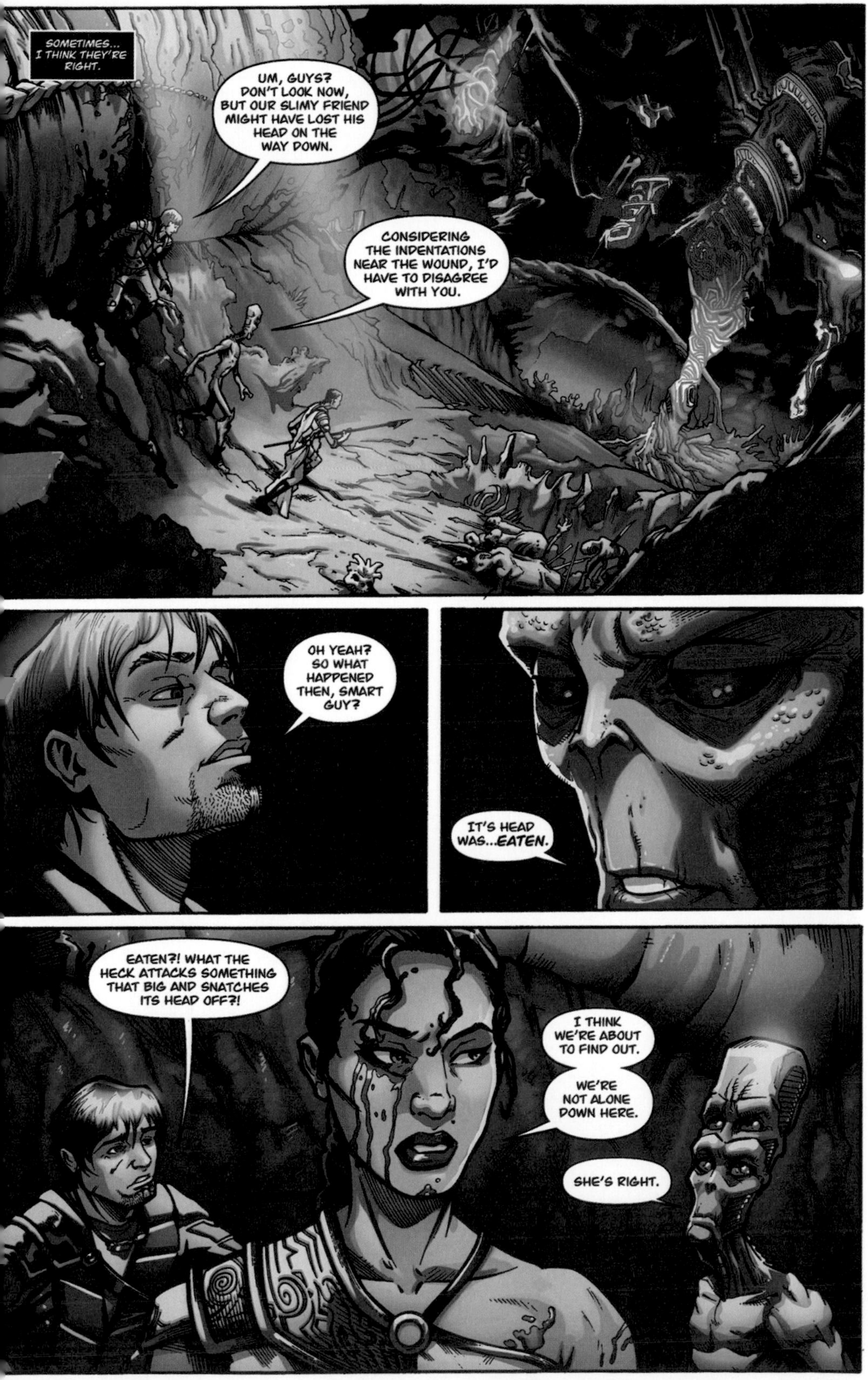
SOMETIMES... I THINK THEY'RE RIGHT.
UM, GUYS? DON'T LOOK NOW, BUT OUR SLIMY FRIEND MIGHT HAVE LOST HIS HEAD ON THE WAY DOWN.
CONSIDERING THE INDENTATIONS NEAR THE WOUND, I'D HAVE TO DISAGREE WITH YOU.
OH YEAH? SO WHAT HAPPENED THEN, SMART GUY?
IT'S HEAD WAS...EATEN.
EATEN?! WHAT THE HECK ATTACKS SOMETHING THAT BIG AND SNATCHES ITS HEAD OFF?!
I THINK WE'RE ABOUT TO FIND OUT.
WE'RE NOT ALONE DOWN HERE.
SHE'S RIGHT.

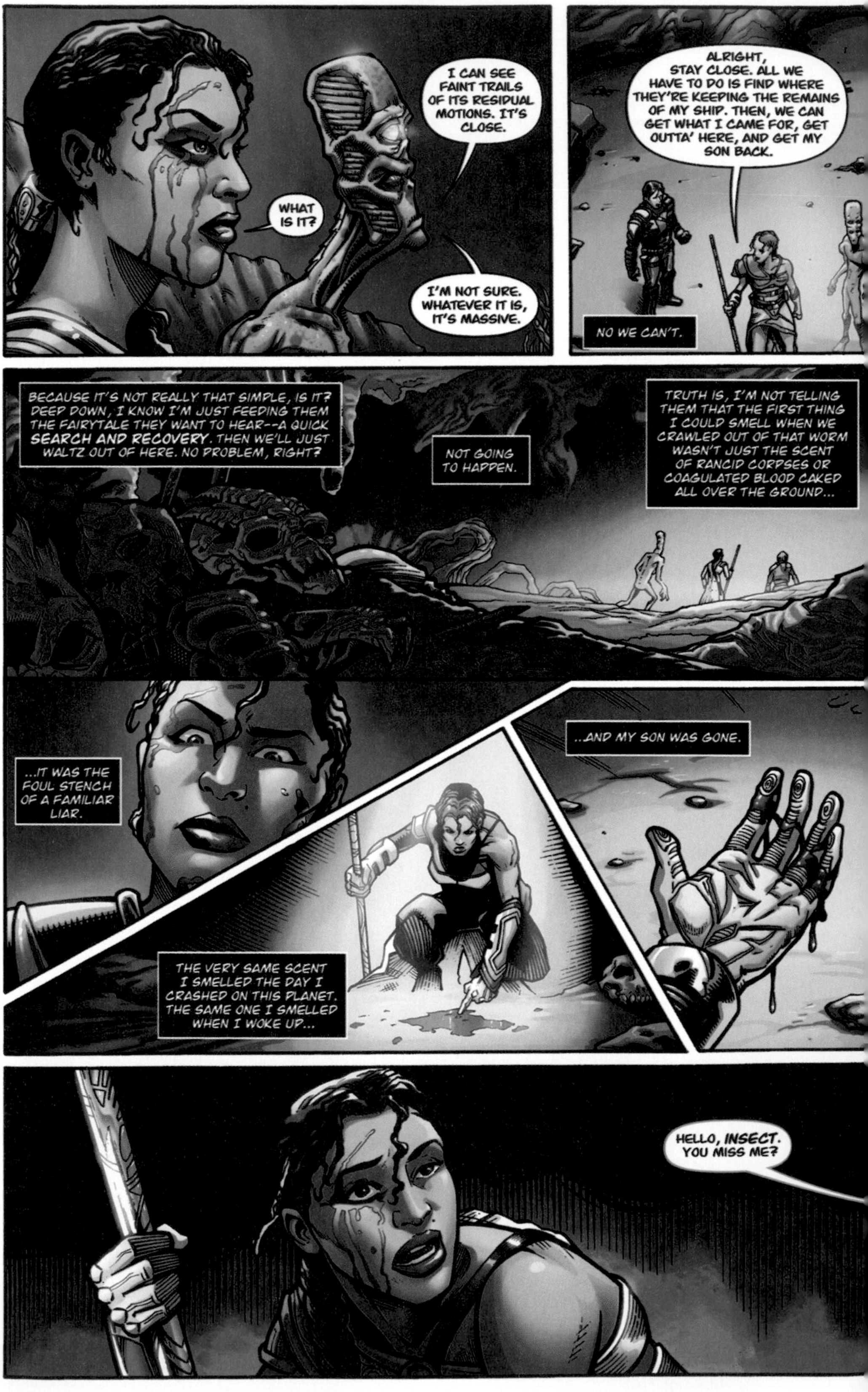
I CAN SEE FAINT TRAILS OF ITS RESIDUAL MOTIONS. IT'S CLOSE.
WHAT IS IT?
I'M NOT SURE. WHATEVER IT IS, IT'S MASSIVE.
ALRIGHT, STAY CLOSE. ALL WE HAVE TO DO IS FIND WHERE THEY'RE KEEPING THE REMAINS OF MY SHIP. THEN, WE CAN GET WHAT I CAME FOR, GET OUTTA' HERE, AND GET MY SON BACK.
NO WE CAN'T.
BECAUSE IT'S NOT REALLY THAT SIMPLE, IS IT? DEEP DOWN, I KNOW I'M JUST FEEDING THEM THE FAIRYTALE THEY WANT TO HEAR--A QUICK SEARCH AND RECOVERY. THEN WE'LL JUST WALTZ OUT OF HERE. NO PROBLEM, RIGHT?
NOT GOING TO HAPPEN.
TRUTH IS, I'M NOT TELLING THEM THAT THE FIRST THING I COULD SMELL WHEN WE CRAWLED OUT OF THAT WORM WASN'T JUST THE SCENT OF RANCID CORPSES OR COAGULATED BLOOD CAKED ALL OVER THE GROUND...
...IT WAS THE FOUL STENCH OF A FAMILIAR LIAR.
THE VERY SAME SCENT I SMELLED THE DAY I CRASHED ON THIS PLANET. THE SAME ONE I SMELLED WHEN I WOKE UP...
...AND MY SON WAS GONE.
HELLO, INSECT. YOU MISS ME?

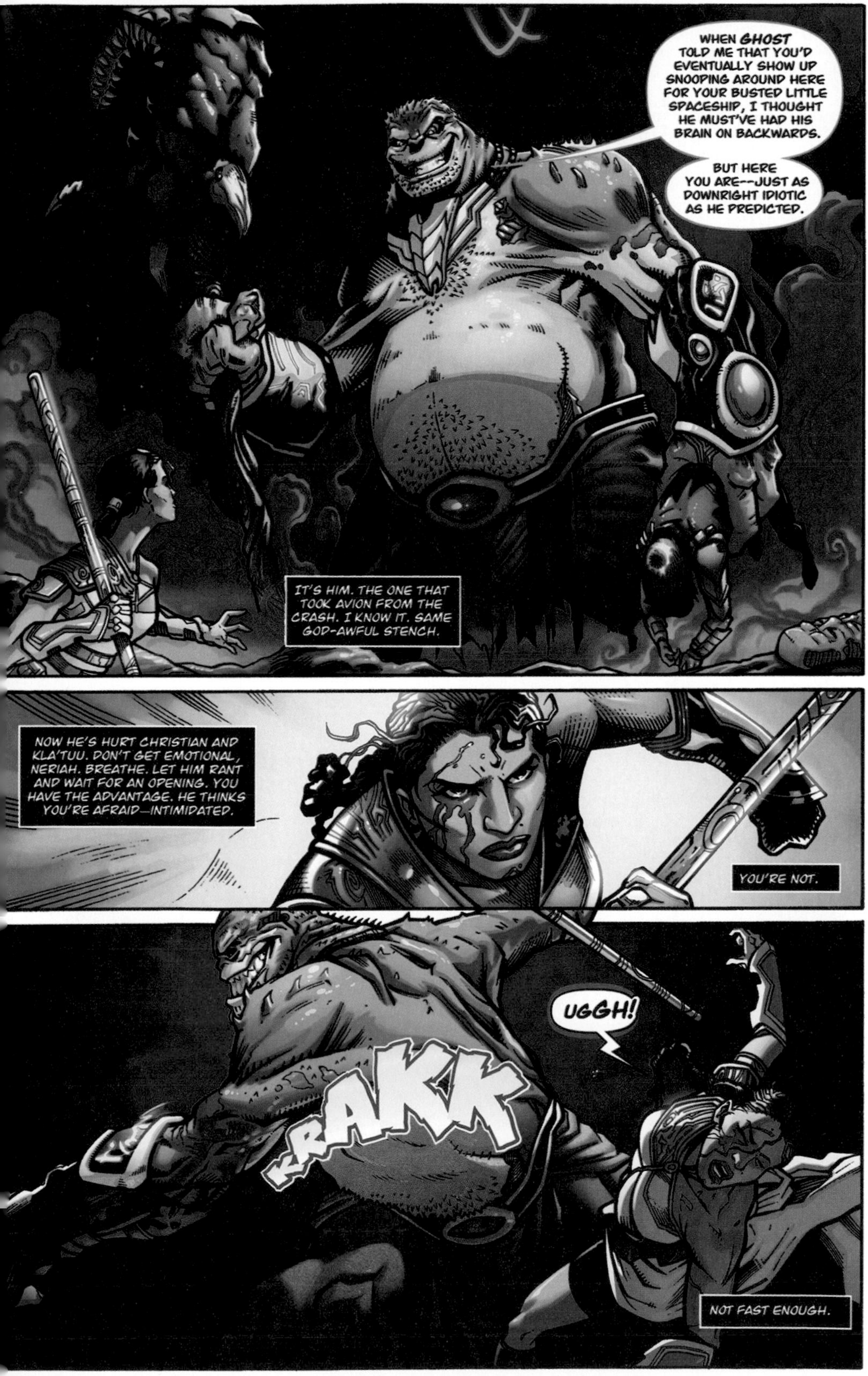
WHEN GHOST TOLD ME THAT YOU'D EVENTUALLY SHOW UP SNOOPING AROUND HERE FOR YOUR BUSTED LITTLE SPACESHIP, I THOUGHT HE MUST'VE HAD HIS BRAIN ON BACKWARDS.
BUT HERE YOU ARE--JUST AS DOWNRIGHT IDIOTIC AS HE PREDICTED.
IT'S HIM. THE ONE THAT TOOK AVION FROM THE CRASH. I KNOW IT. SAME GOD-AWFUL STENCH.
NOW HE'S HURT CHRISTIAN AND KLA'TUU. DON'T GET EMOTIONAL, NERIAH. BREATHE. LET HIM RANT AND WAIT FOR AN OPENING. YOU HAVE THE ADVANTAGE. HE THINKS YOU'RE AFRAID—INTIMIDATED.
YOU'RE NOT.
UGGH!
KRAKK
NOT FAST ENOUGH.

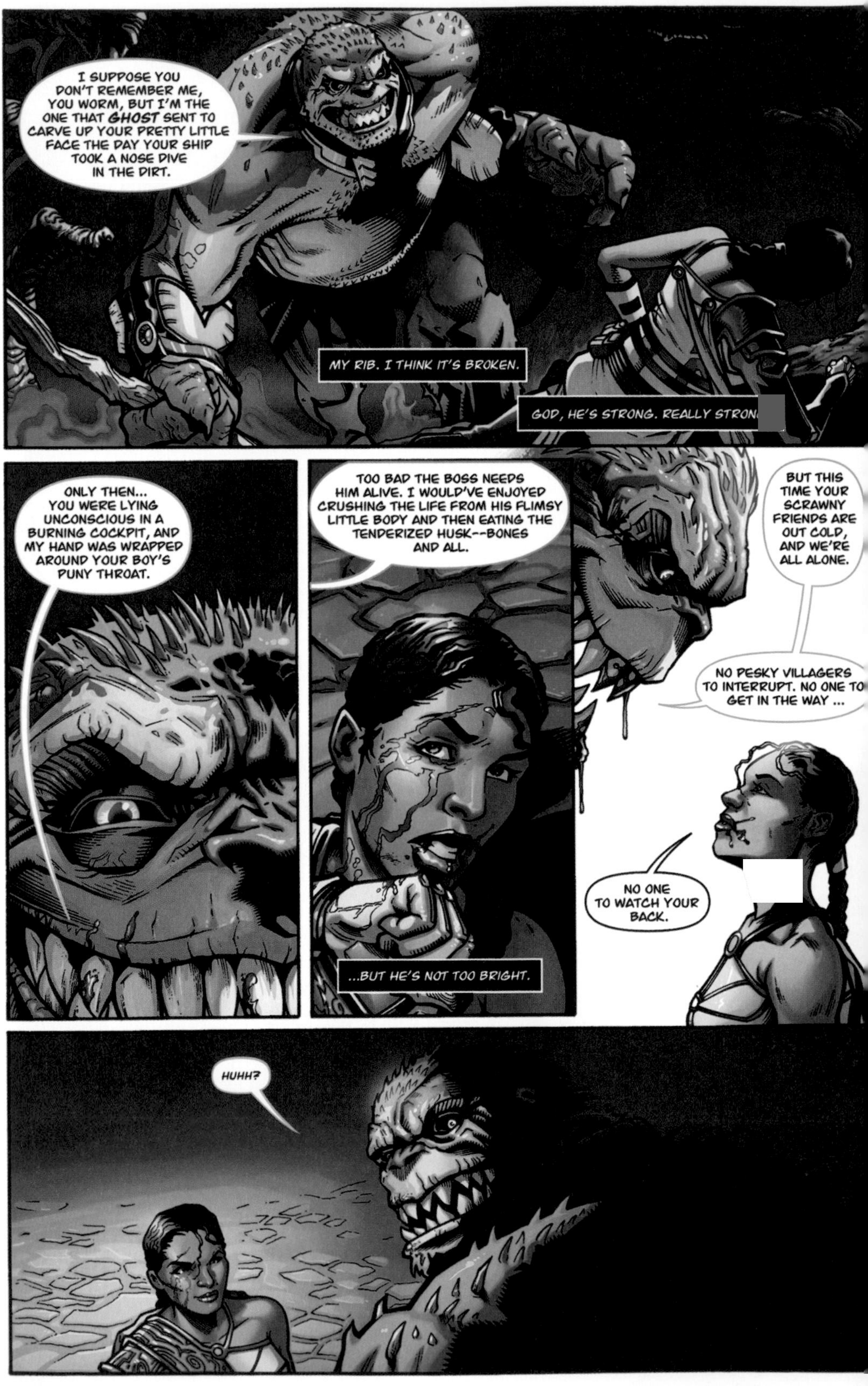
I SUPPOSE YOU DON'T REMEMBER ME, YOU WORM, BUT I'M THE ONE THAT GHOST SENT TO CARVE UP YOUR PRETTY LITTLE FACE THE DAY YOUR SHIP TOOK A NOSE DIVE IN THE DIRT.
MY RIB. I THINK IT'S BROKEN.
GOD, HE'S STRONG. REALLY STRON
ONLY THEN... YOU WERE LYING UNCONSCIOUS IN A BURNING COCKPIT, AND MY HAND WAS WRAPPED AROUND YOUR BOY'S PUNY THROAT.
TOO BAD THE BOSS NEEDS HIM ALIVE. I WOULD'VE ENJOYED CRUSHING THE LIFE FROM HIS FLIMSY LITTLE BODY AND THEN EATING THE TENDERIZED HUSK--BONES AND ALL.
...BUT HE'S NOT TOO BRIGHT.
BUT THIS TIME YOUR SCRAWNY FRIENDS ARE OUT COLD, AND WE'RE ALL ALONE.
NO PESKY VILLAGERS TO INTERRUPT. NO ONE TO GET IN THE WAY ...
NO ONE TO WATCH YOUR BACK.
HUHH?

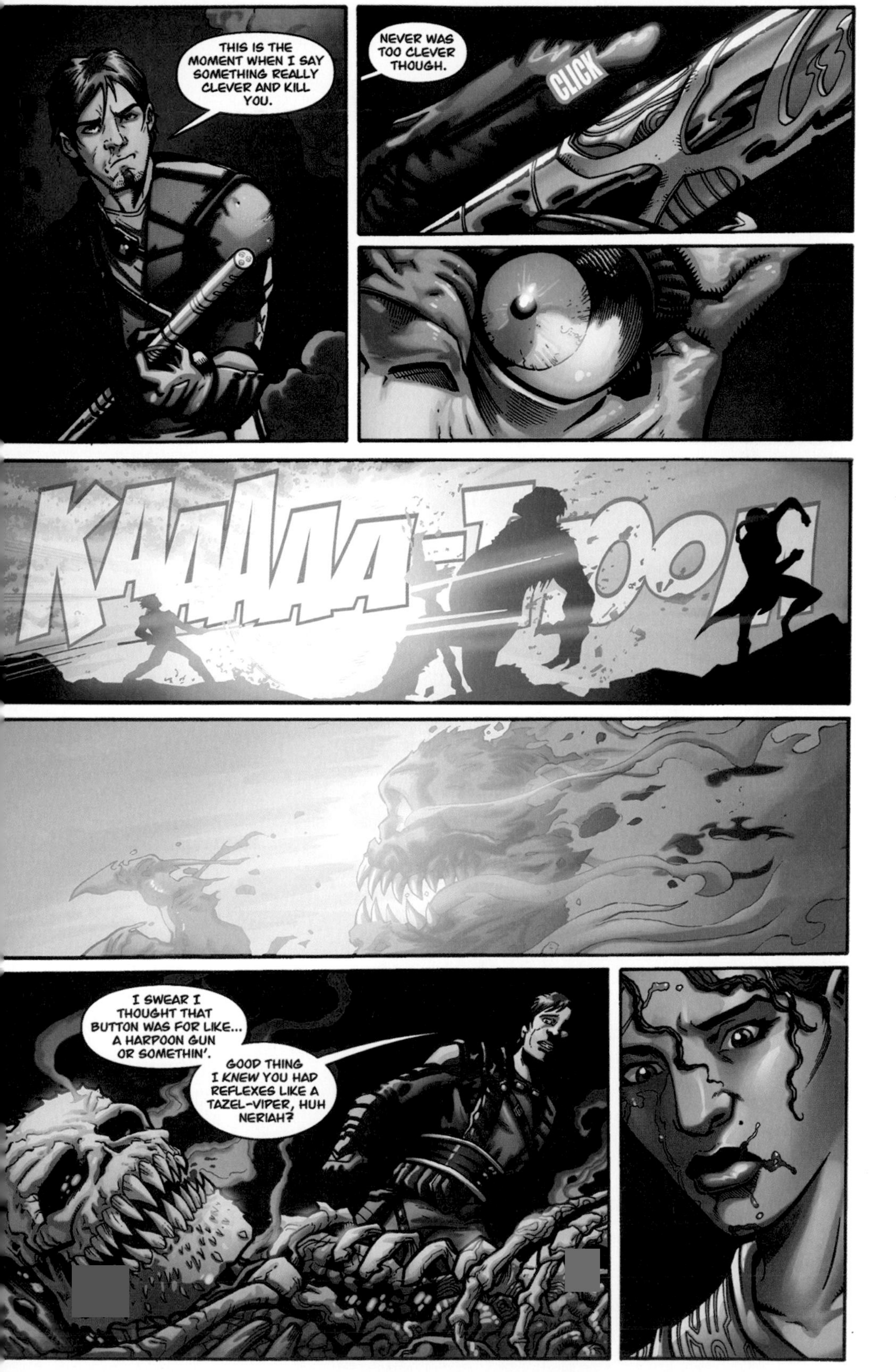
THIS IS THE MOMENT WHEN I SAY SOMETHING REALLY CLEVER AND KILL YOU.
NEVER WAS TOO CLEVER THOUGH.
CLICK
I SWEAR I THOUGHT THAT BUTTON WAS FOR LIKE... A HARPOON GUN OR SOMETHIN'.
GOOD THING I KNEW YOU HAD REFLEXES LIKE A TAZEL-VIPER, HUH NERIAH?

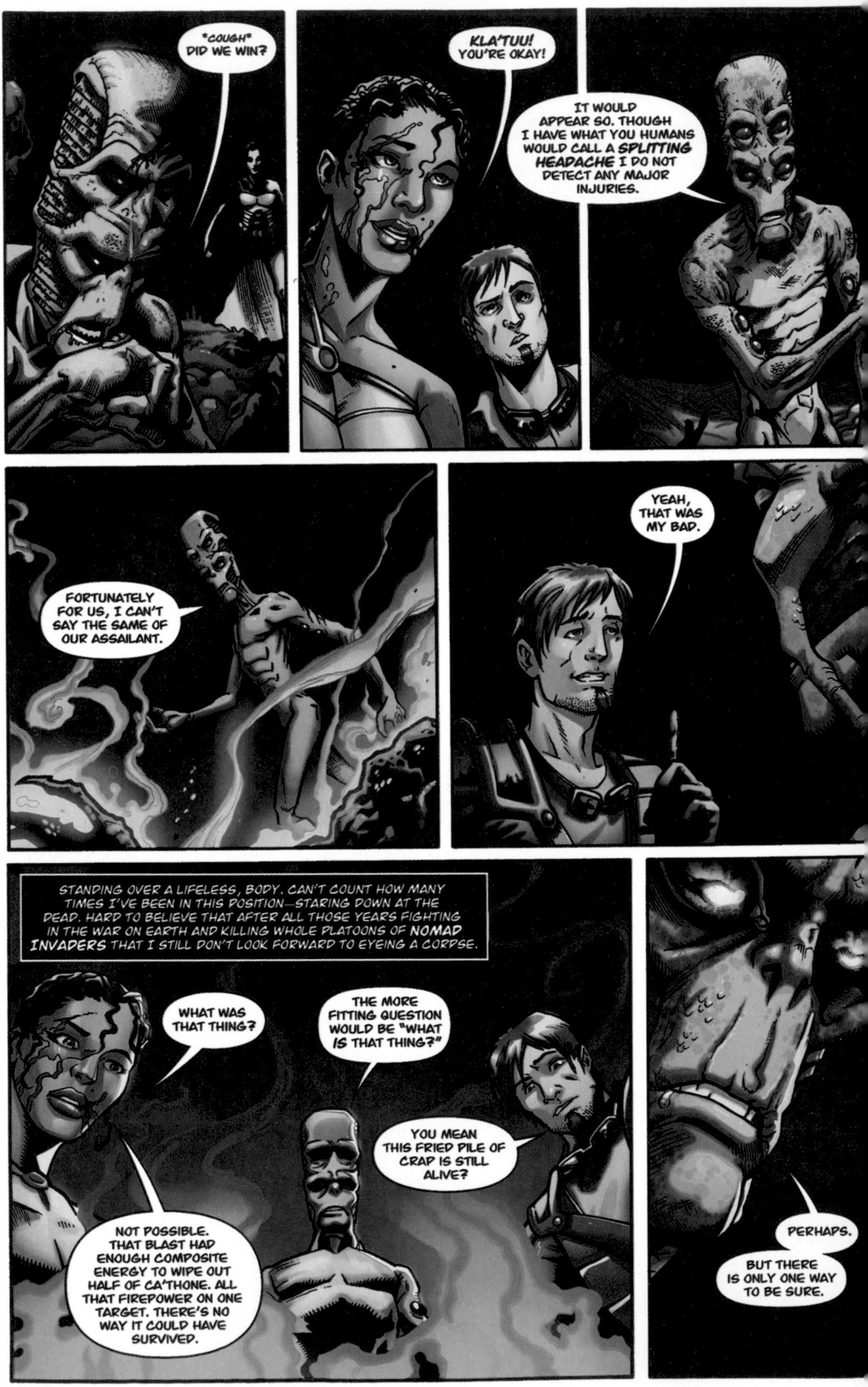
COUGH DID WE WIN?
KLA'TUU! YOU'RE OKAY!
IT WOULD APPEAR SO. THOUGH I HAVE WHAT YOU HUMANS WOULD CALL A SPLITTING HEADACHE I DO NOT DETECT ANY MAJOR INJURIES.
FORTUNATELY FOR US, I CAN'T SAY THE SAME OF OUR ASSAILANT.
YEAH, THAT WAS MY BAD.
STANDING OVER A LIFELESS, BODY. CAN'T COUNT HOW MANY TIMES I'VE BEEN IN THIS POSITION—STARING DOWN AT THE DEAD. HARD TO BELIEVE THAT AFTER ALL THOSE YEARS FIGHTING IN THE WAR ON EARTH AND KILLING WHOLE PLATOONS OF NOMAD INVADERS THAT I STILL DON'T LOOK FORWARD TO EYEING A CORPSE.
WHAT WAS THAT THING?
THE MORE FITTING QUESTION WOULD BE "WHAT IS THAT THING?"
YOU MEAN THIS FRIED PILE OF CRAP IS STILL ALIVE?
NOT POSSIBLE. THAT BLAST HAD ENOUGH COMPOSITE ENERGY TO WIPE OUT HALF OF CA'THONE. ALL THAT FIREPOWER ON ONE TARGET. THERE'S NO WAY IT COULD HAVE SURVIVED.
PERHAPS.
BUT THERE IS ONLY ONE WAY TO BE SURE.

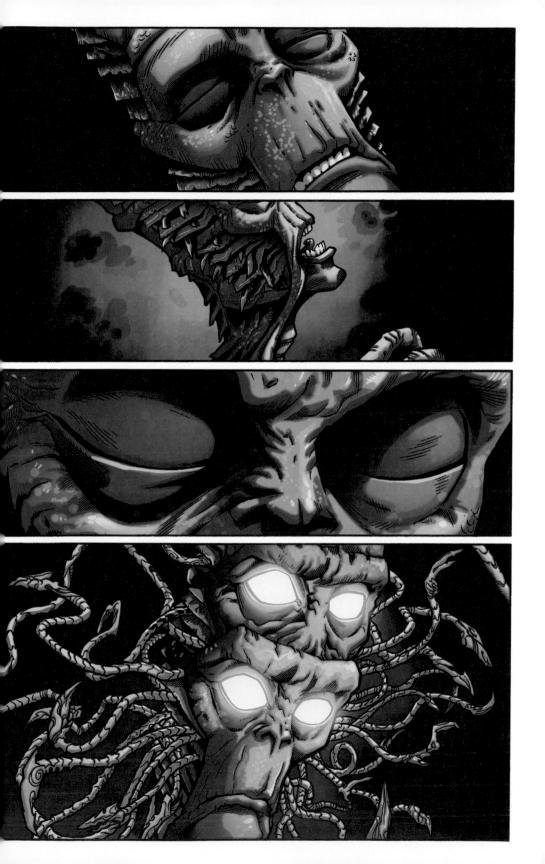

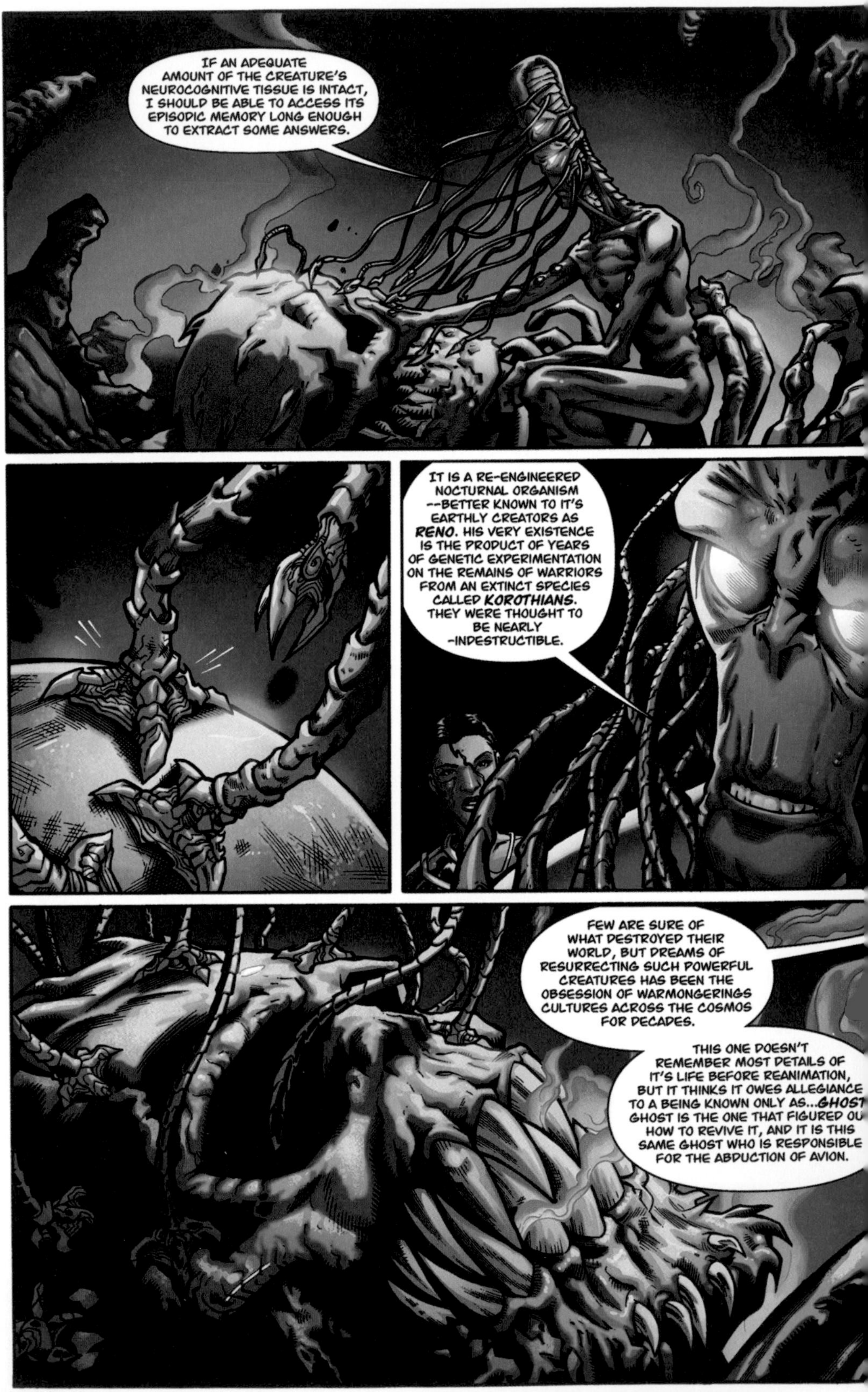
IF AN ADEQUATE AMOUNT OF THE CREATURE'S NEUROCOGNITIVE TISSUE IS INTACT, I SHOULD BE ABLE TO ACCESS ITS EPISODIC MEMORY LONG ENOUGH TO EXTRACT SOME ANSWERS.
IT IS A RE-ENGINEERED NOCTURNAL ORGANISM --BETTER KNOWN TO IT'S EARTHLY CREATORS AS ***RENO***. HIS VERY EXISTENCE IS THE PRODUCT OF YEARS OF GENETIC EXPERIMENTATION ON THE REMAINS OF WARRIORS FROM AN EXTINCT SPECIES CALLED ***KOROTHIANS***. THEY WERE THOUGHT TO BE NEARLY -INDESTRUCTIBLE.
FEW ARE SURE OF WHAT DESTROYED THEIR WORLD, BUT DREAMS OF RESURRECTING SUCH POWERFUL CREATURES HAS BEEN THE OBSESSION OF WARMONGERINGS CULTURES ACROSS THE COSMOS FOR DECADES.
THIS ONE DOESN'T REMEMBER MOST DETAILS OF IT'S LIFE BEFORE REANIMATION, BUT IT THINKS IT OWES ALLEGIANCE TO A BEING KNOWN ONLY AS...***GHOST*** GHOST IS THE ONE THAT FIGURED OU HOW TO REVIVE IT, AND IT IS THIS SAME GHOST WHO IS RESPONSIBLE FOR THE ABDUCTION OF AVION.

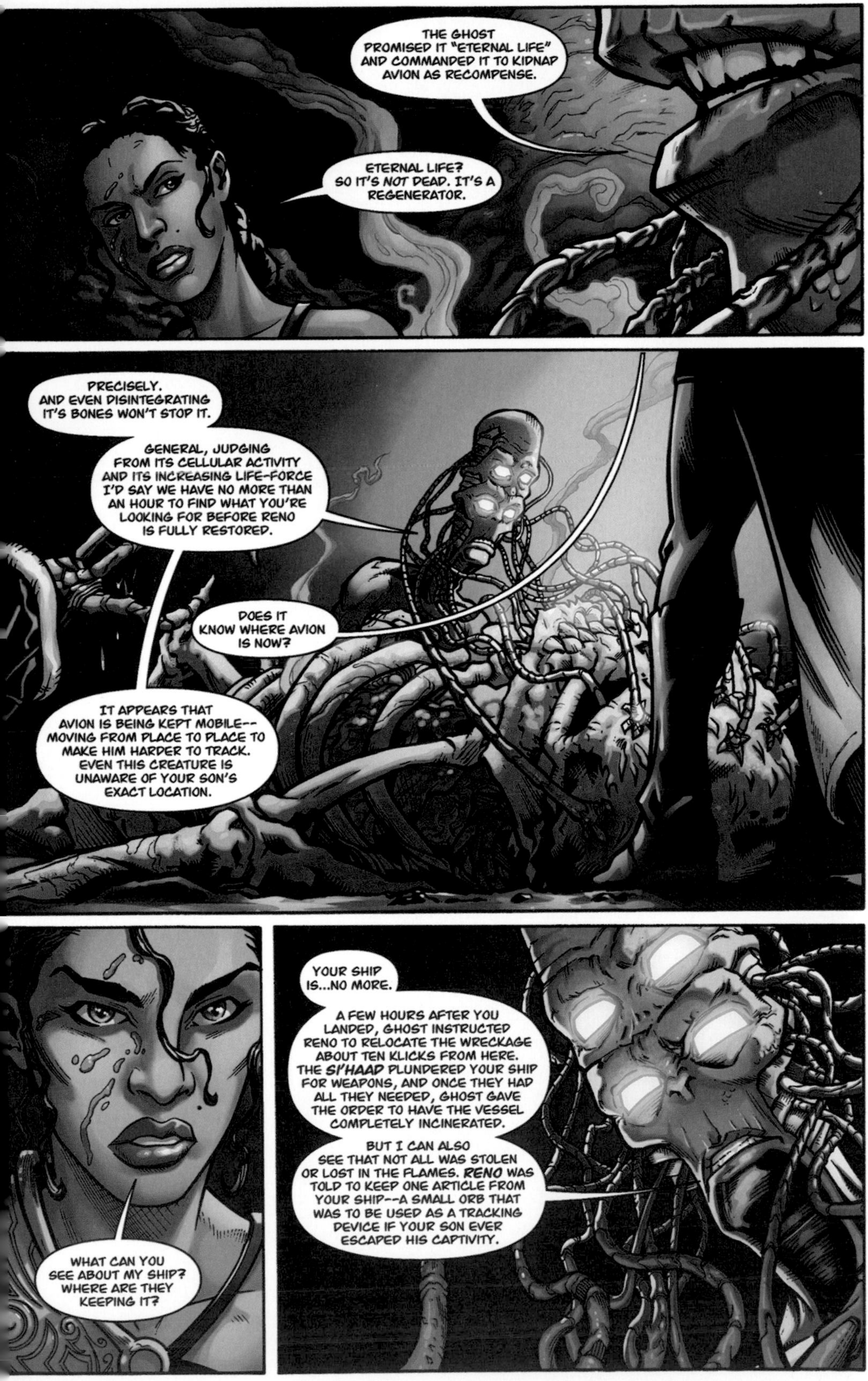
THE GHOST PROMISED IT "ETERNAL LIFE" AND COMMANDED IT TO KIDNAP AVION AS RECOMPENSE.
ETERNAL LIFE? SO IT'S NOT DEAD. IT'S A REGENERATOR.
PRECISELY. AND EVEN DISINTEGRATING IT'S BONES WON'T STOP IT.
GENERAL, JUDGING FROM ITS CELLULAR ACTIVITY AND ITS INCREASING LIFE-FORCE I'D SAY WE HAVE NO MORE THAN AN HOUR TO FIND WHAT YOU'RE LOOKING FOR BEFORE RENO IS FULLY RESTORED.
DOES IT KNOW WHERE AVION IS NOW?
IT APPEARS THAT AVION IS BEING KEPT MOBILE--MOVING FROM PLACE TO PLACE TO MAKE HIM HARDER TO TRACK. EVEN THIS CREATURE IS UNAWARE OF YOUR SON'S EXACT LOCATION.
WHAT CAN YOU SEE ABOUT MY SHIP? WHERE ARE THEY KEEPING IT?
YOUR SHIP IS...NO MORE.
A FEW HOURS AFTER YOU LANDED, GHOST INSTRUCTED RENO TO RELOCATE THE WRECKAGE ABOUT TEN KLICKS FROM HERE. THE SI'HAAD PLUNDERED YOUR SHIP FOR WEAPONS, AND ONCE THEY HAD ALL THEY NEEDED, GHOST GAVE THE ORDER TO HAVE THE VESSEL COMPLETELY INCINERATED.
BUT I CAN ALSO SEE THAT NOT ALL WAS STOLEN OR LOST IN THE FLAMES. RENO WAS TOLD TO KEEP ONE ARTICLE FROM YOUR SHIP--A SMALL ORB THAT WAS TO BE USED AS A TRACKING DEVICE IF YOUR SON EVER ESCAPED HIS CAPTIVITY.

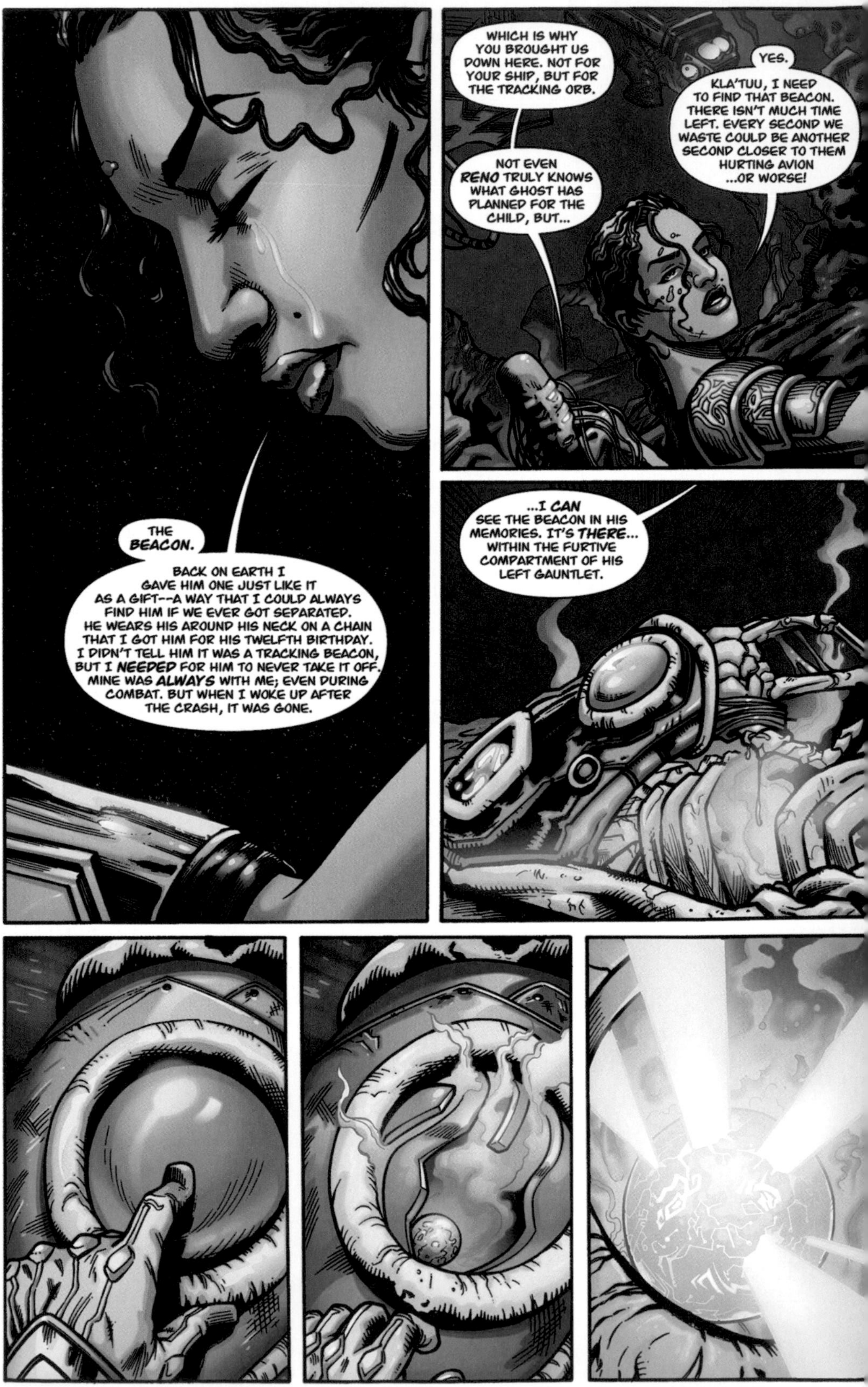
THE BEACON.
BACK ON EARTH I GAVE HIM ONE JUST LIKE IT AS A GIFT--A WAY THAT I COULD ALWAYS FIND HIM IF WE EVER GOT SEPARATED. HE WEARS HIS AROUND HIS NECK ON A CHAIN THAT I GOT HIM FOR HIS TWELFTH BIRTHDAY. I DIDN'T TELL HIM IT WAS A TRACKING BEACON, BUT I NEEDED FOR HIM TO NEVER TAKE IT OFF. MINE WAS ALWAYS WITH ME; EVEN DURING COMBAT. BUT WHEN I WOKE UP AFTER THE CRASH, IT WAS GONE.
WHICH IS WHY YOU BROUGHT US DOWN HERE. NOT FOR YOUR SHIP, BUT FOR THE TRACKING ORB.
NOT EVEN RENO TRULY KNOWS WHAT GHOST HAS PLANNED FOR THE CHILD, BUT...
YES.
KLA'TUU, I NEED TO FIND THAT BEACON. THERE ISN'T MUCH TIME LEFT. EVERY SECOND WE WASTE COULD BE ANOTHER SECOND CLOSER TO THEM HURTING AVION ...OR WORSE!
...I CAN SEE THE BEACON IN HIS MEMORIES. IT'S THERE... WITHIN THE FURTIVE COMPARTMENT OF HIS LEFT GAUNTLET.

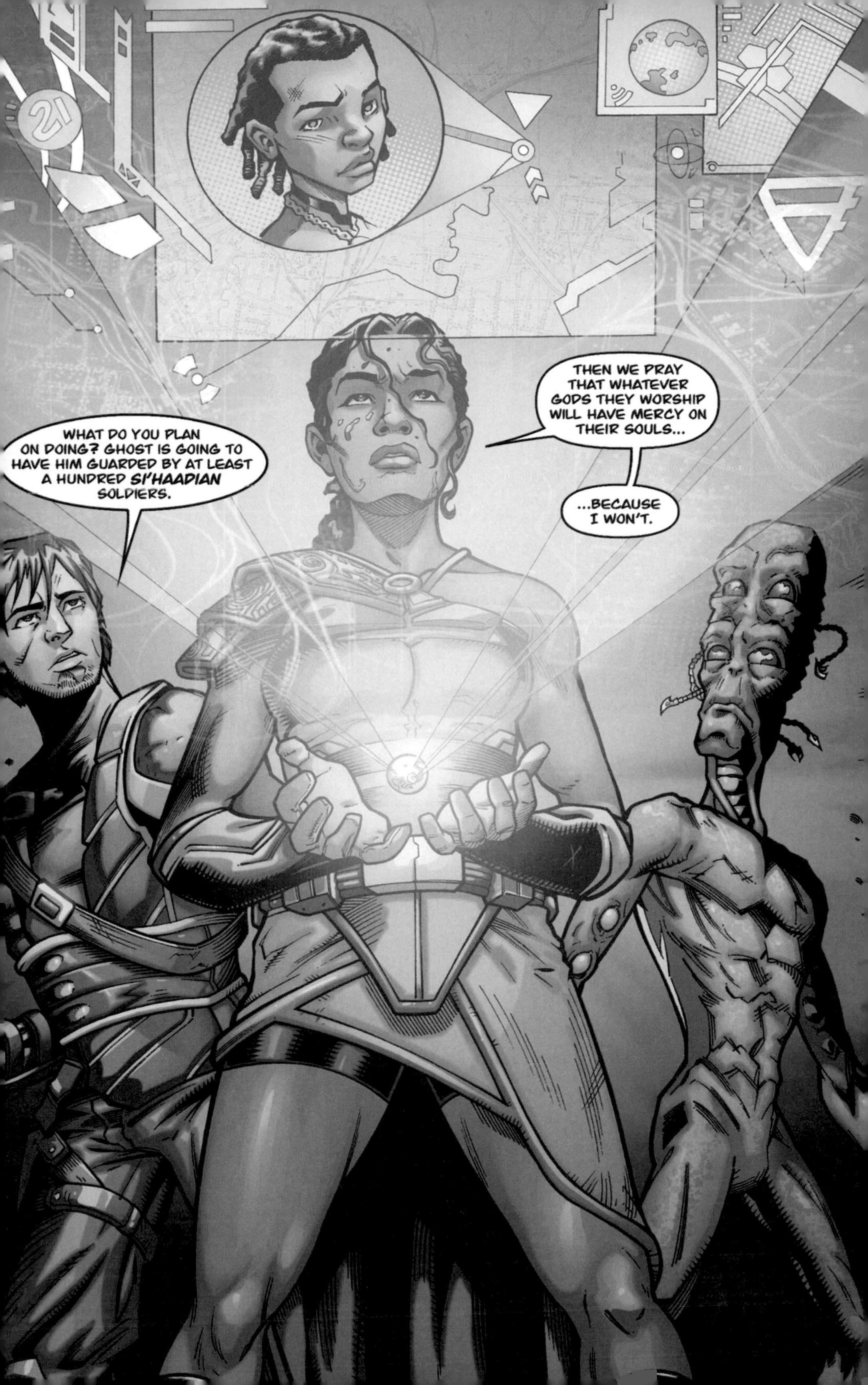
WHAT DO YOU PLAN ON DOING? GHOST IS GOING TO HAVE HIM GUARDED BY AT LEAST A HUNDRED SI'HAADIAN SOLDIERS.
THEN WE PRAY THAT WHATEVER GODS THEY WORSHIP WILL HAVE MERCY ON THEIR SOULS...
...BECAUSE I WON'T.

CHAPTER TWO

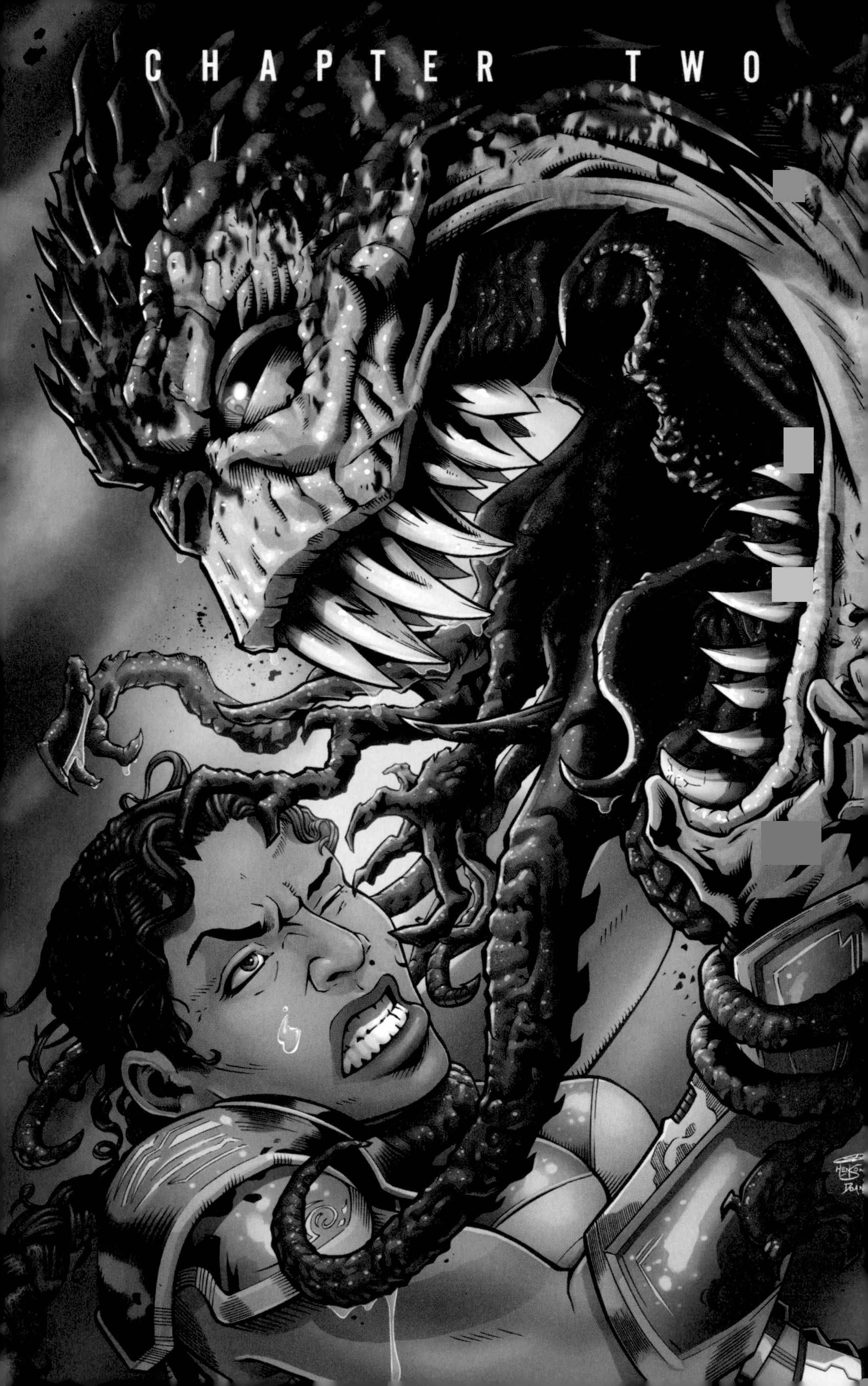

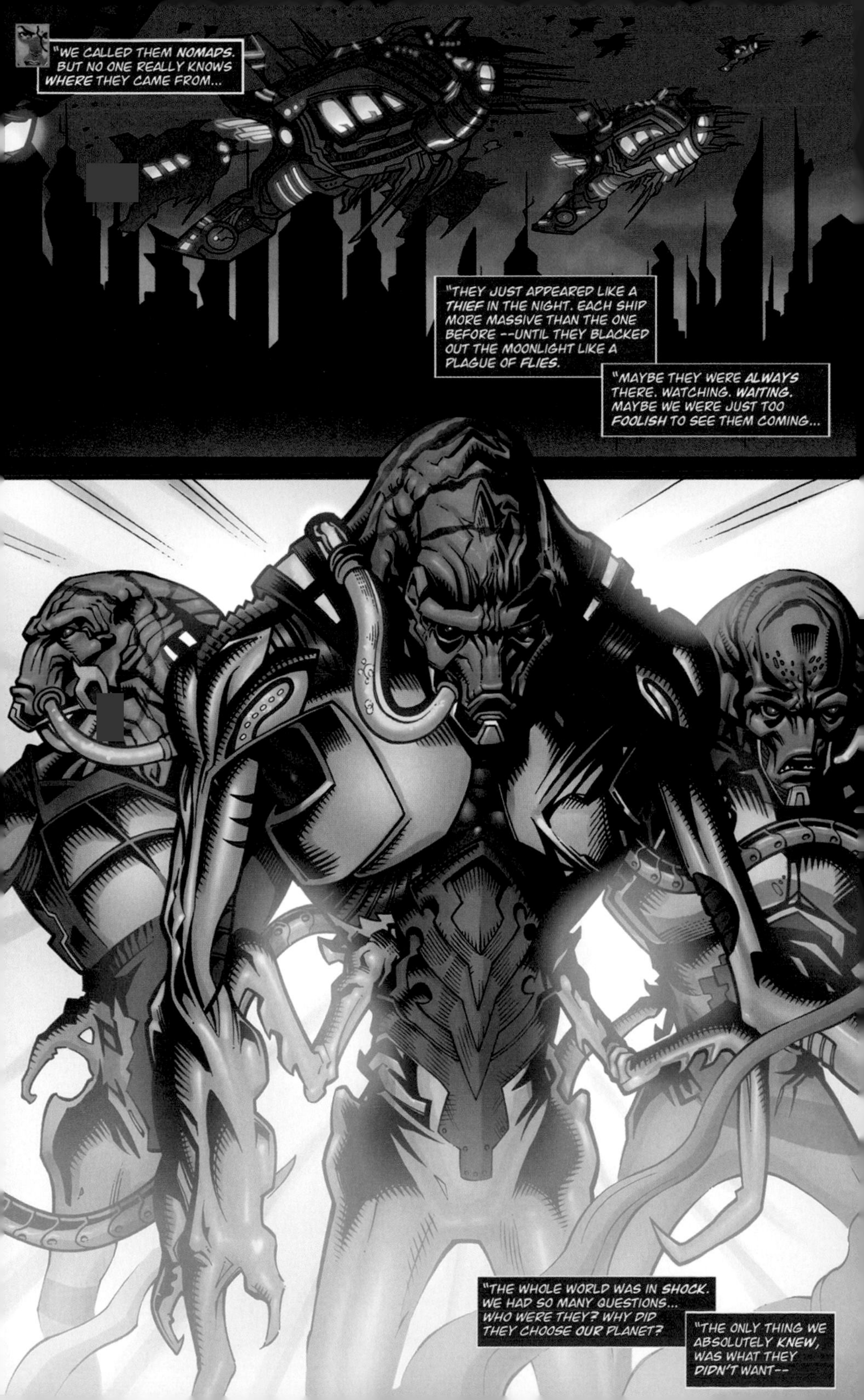
"WE CALLED THEM NOMADS. BUT NO ONE REALLY KNOWS WHERE THEY CAME FROM...
"THEY JUST APPEARED LIKE A THIEF IN THE NIGHT. EACH SHIP MORE MASSIVE THAN THE ONE BEFORE --UNTIL THEY BLACKED OUT THE MOONLIGHT LIKE A PLAGUE OF FLIES.
"MAYBE THEY WERE ALWAYS THERE. WATCHING. WAITING. MAYBE WE WERE JUST TOO FOOLISH TO SEE THEM COMING...
"THE WHOLE WORLD WAS IN SHOCK. WE HAD SO MANY QUESTIONS... WHO WERE THEY? WHY DID THEY CHOOSE OUR PLANET?
"THE ONLY THING WE ABSOLUTELY KNEW, WAS WHAT THEY DIDN'T WANT--

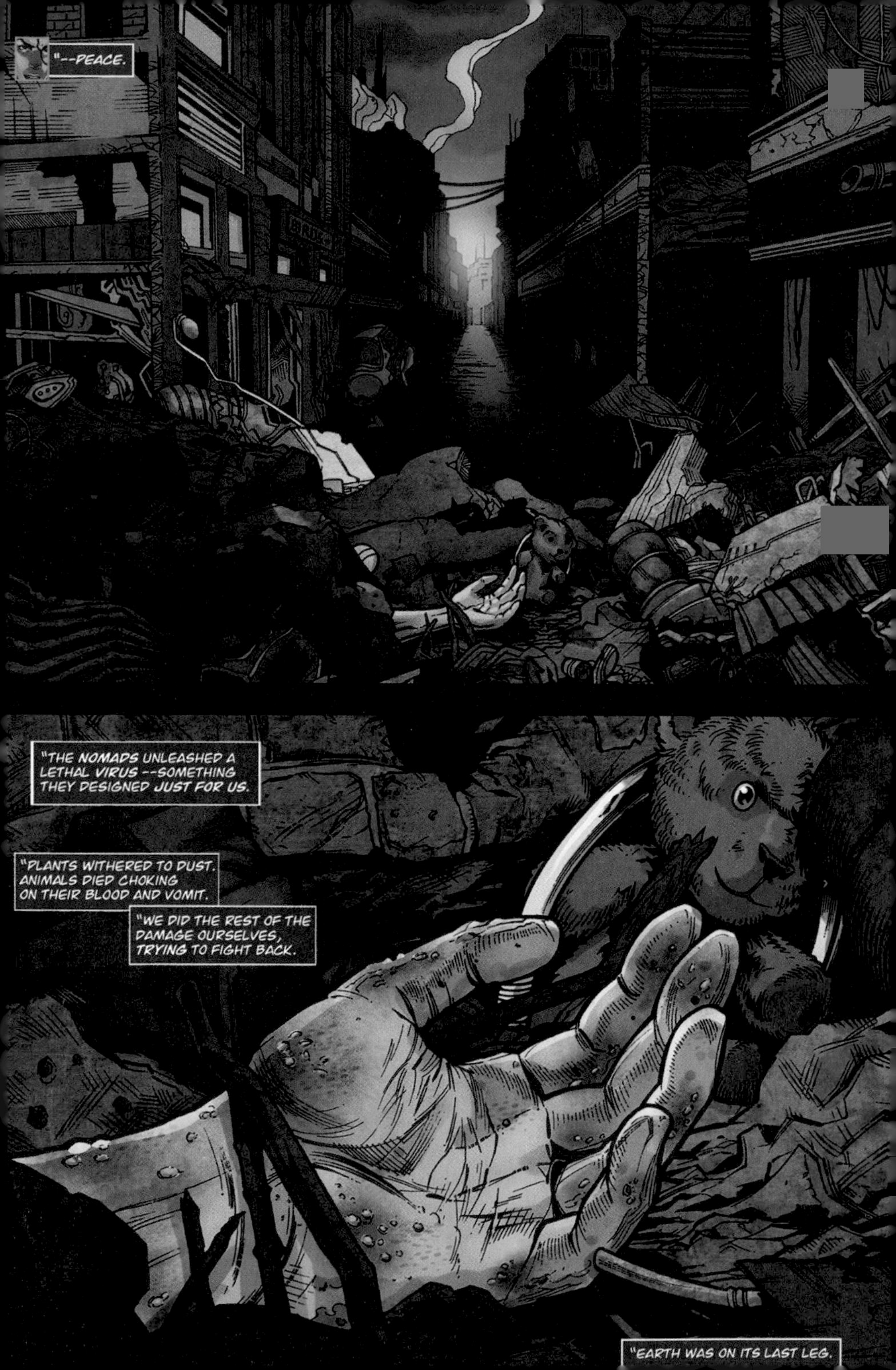
"--PEACE.
"THE NOMADS UNLEASHED A LETHAL VIRUS --SOMETHING THEY DESIGNED JUST FOR US.
"PLANTS WITHERED TO DUST. ANIMALS DIED CHOKING ON THEIR BLOOD AND VOMIT.
"WE DID THE REST OF THE DAMAGE OURSELVES, TRYING TO FIGHT BACK.
"EARTH WAS ON ITS LAST LEG.

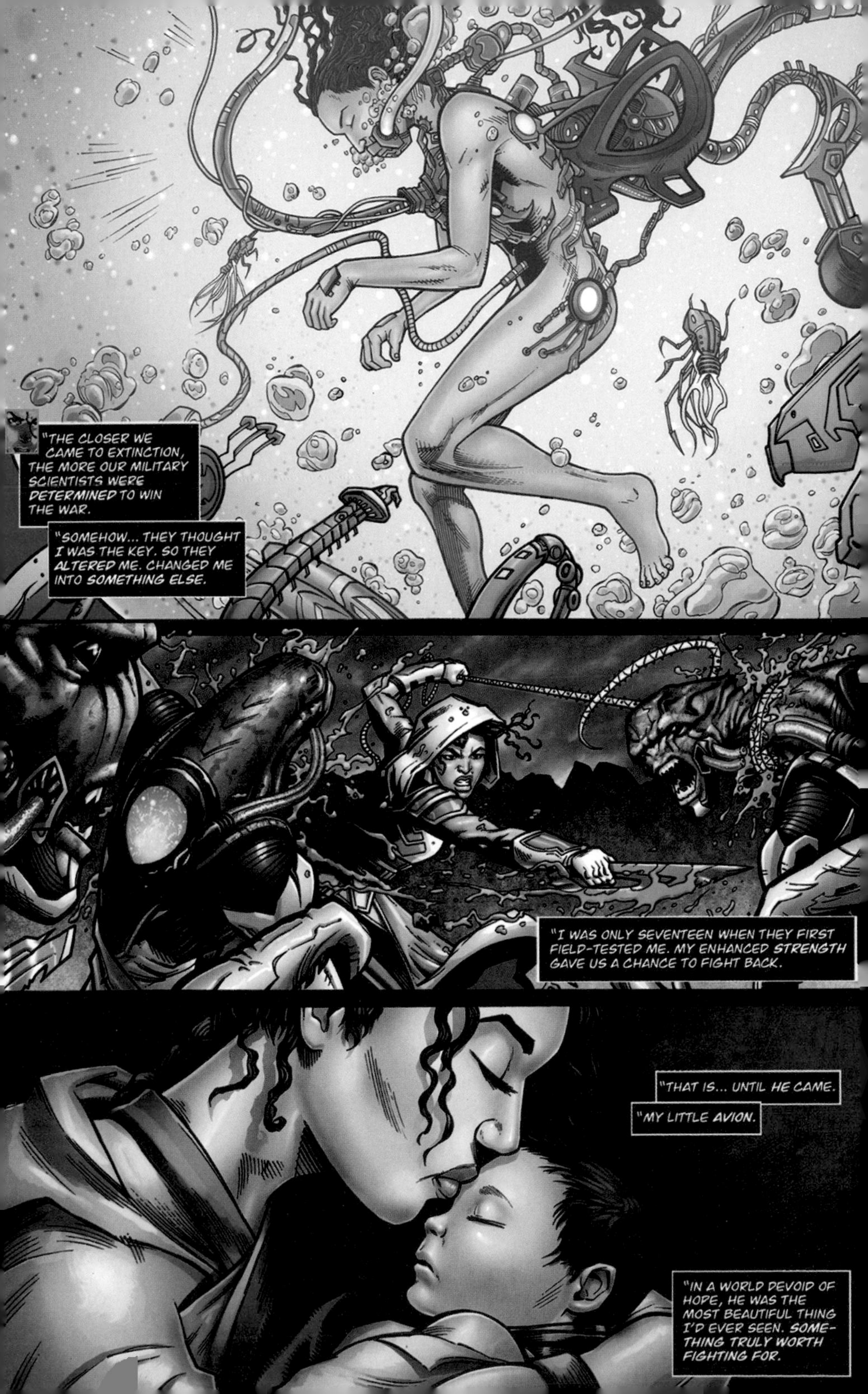
"THE CLOSER WE CAME TO EXTINCTION, THE MORE OUR MILITARY SCIENTISTS WERE DETERMINED TO WIN THE WAR.
"SOMEHOW... THEY THOUGHT I WAS THE KEY. SO THEY ALTERED ME. CHANGED ME INTO SOMETHING ELSE.
"I WAS ONLY SEVENTEEN WHEN THEY FIRST FIELD-TESTED ME. MY ENHANCED STRENGTH GAVE US A CHANCE TO FIGHT BACK.
"THAT IS... UNTIL HE CAME.
"MY LITTLE AVION.
"IN A WORLD DEVOID OF HOPE, HE WAS THE MOST BEAUTIFUL THING I'D EVER SEEN. SOMETHING TRULY WORTH FIGHTING FOR.

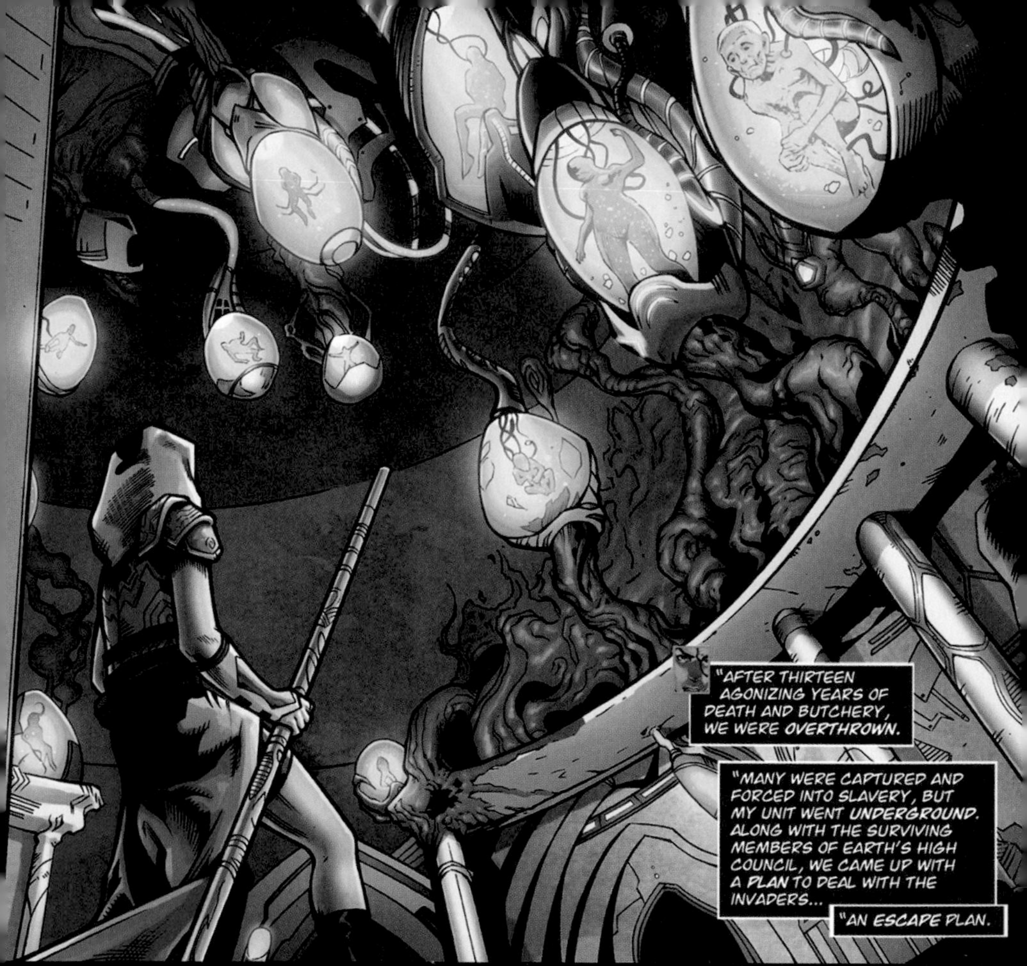
"AFTER THIRTEEN AGONIZING YEARS OF DEATH AND BUTCHERY, WE WERE *OVERTHROWN*.
"MANY WERE CAPTURED AND FORCED INTO SLAVERY, BUT MY UNIT WENT *UNDERGROUND*. ALONG WITH THE SURVIVING MEMBERS OF EARTH'S HIGH COUNCIL, WE CAME UP WITH A *PLAN* TO DEAL WITH THE INVADERS...
"AN *ESCAPE* PLAN.

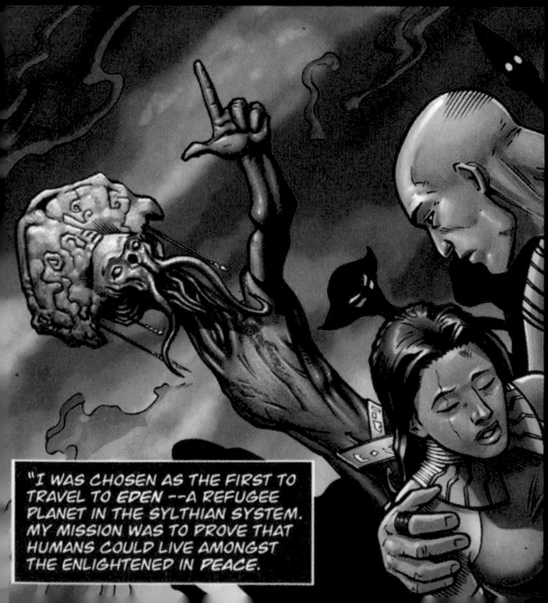
"I WAS CHOSEN AS THE FIRST TO TRAVEL TO *EDEN* --A REFUGEE PLANET IN THE SYLTHIAN SYSTEM. MY MISSION WAS TO PROVE THAT HUMANS COULD LIVE AMONGST THE ENLIGHTENED IN *PEACE*.

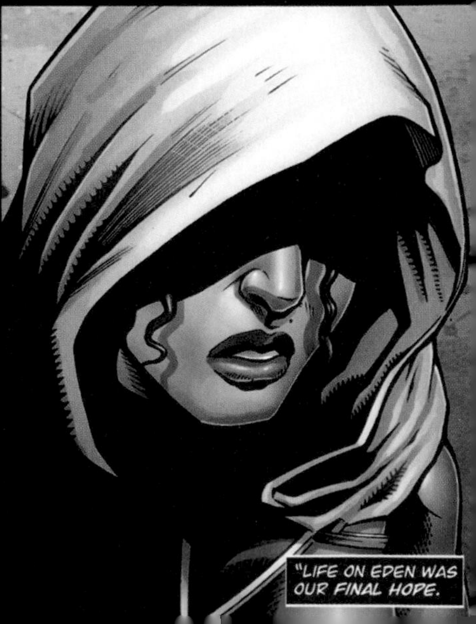
"LIFE ON EDEN WAS OUR *FINAL HOPE*.

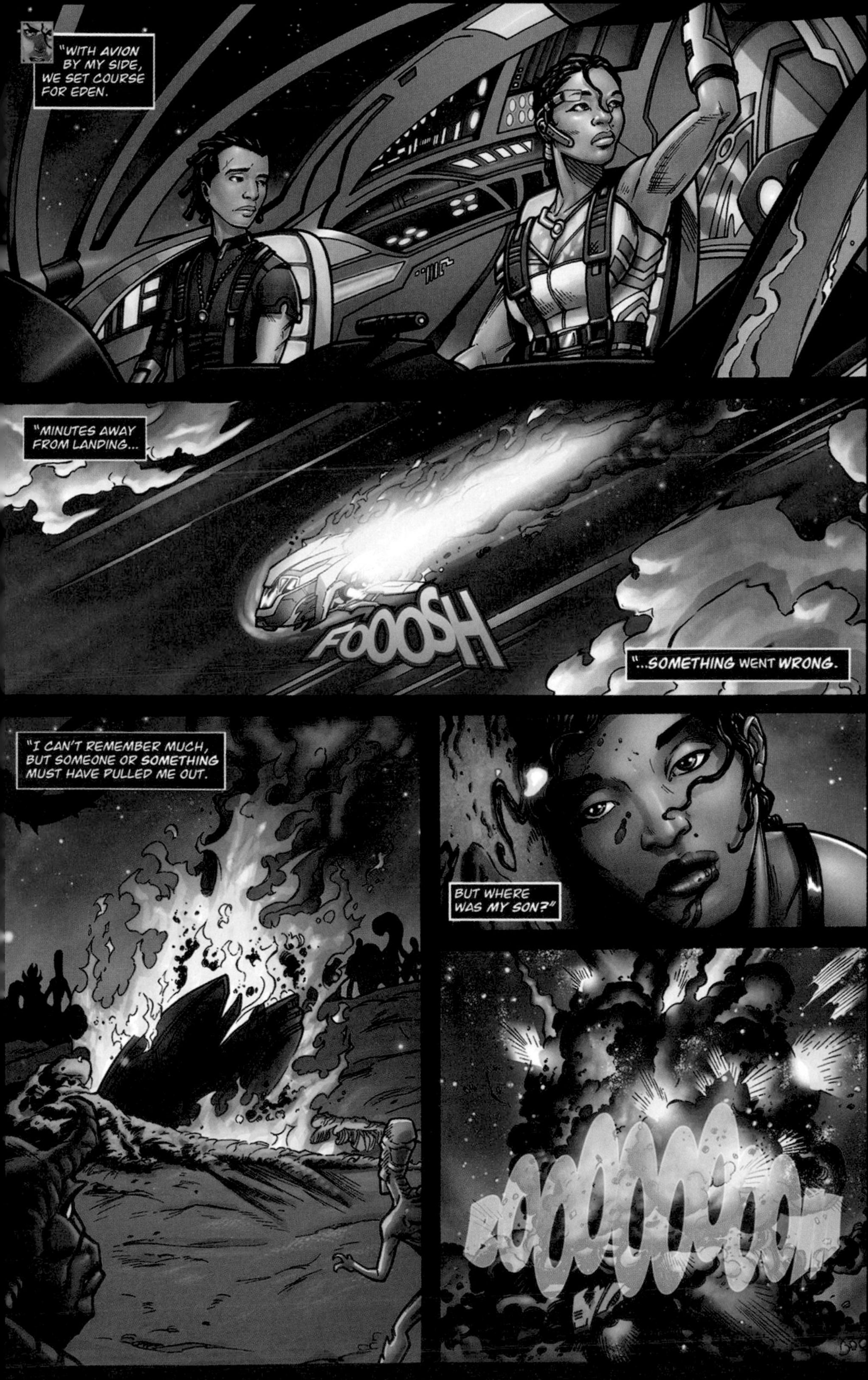
"WITH AVION BY MY SIDE, WE SET COURSE FOR EDEN.
"MINUTES AWAY FROM LANDING...
FOOOSH
"...SOMETHING WENT WRONG.
"I CAN'T REMEMBER MUCH, BUT SOMEONE OR SOMETHING MUST HAVE PULLED ME OUT.
BUT WHERE WAS MY SON?"

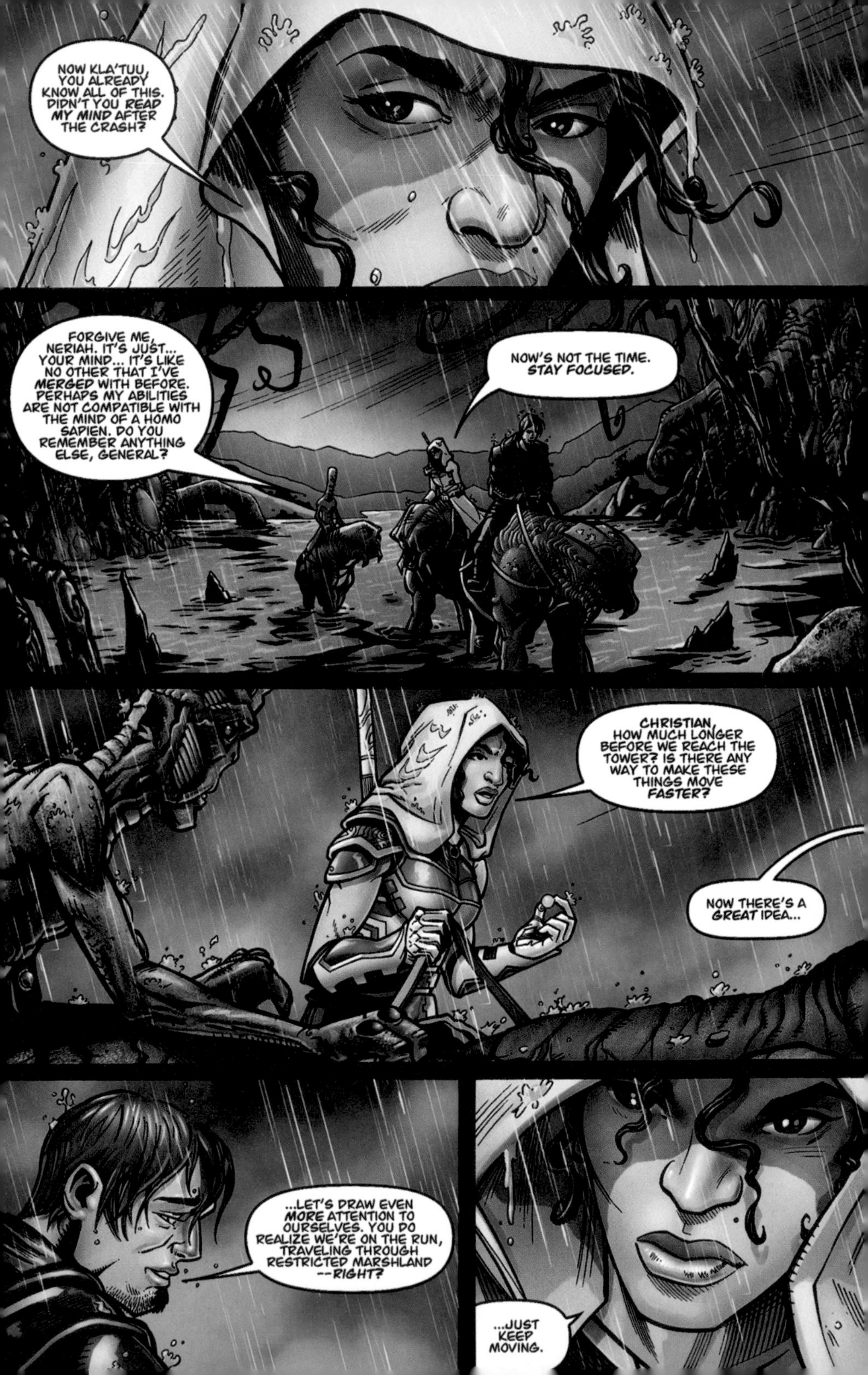
NOW KLA'TUU, YOU ALREADY KNOW ALL OF THIS. DIDN'T YOU READ MY MIND AFTER THE CRASH?
FORGIVE ME, NERIAH. IT'S JUST... YOUR MIND... IT'S LIKE NO OTHER THAT I'VE MERGED WITH BEFORE. PERHAPS MY ABILITIES ARE NOT COMPATIBLE WITH THE MIND OF A HOMO SAPIEN. DO YOU REMEMBER ANYTHING ELSE, GENERAL?
NOW'S NOT THE TIME. STAY FOCUSED.
CHRISTIAN, HOW MUCH LONGER BEFORE WE REACH THE TOWER? IS THERE ANY WAY TO MAKE THESE THINGS MOVE FASTER?
NOW THERE'S A GREAT IDEA...
...LET'S DRAW EVEN MORE ATTENTION TO OURSELVES. YOU DO REALIZE WE'RE ON THE RUN, TRAVELING THROUGH RESTRICTED MARSHLAND --RIGHT?
...JUST KEEP MOVING.

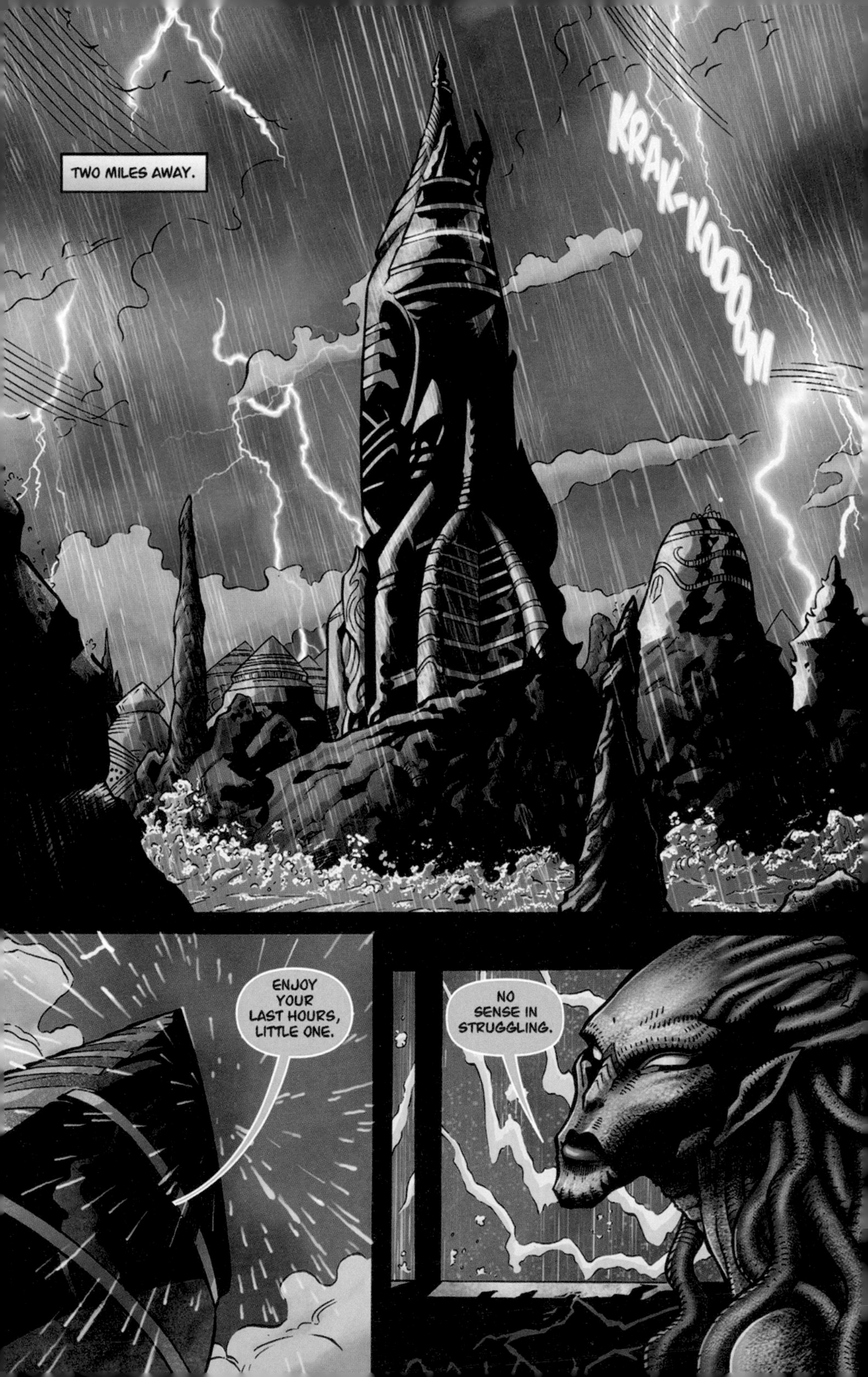
TWO MILES AWAY.
KRAK-KOOOOM
ENJOY YOUR LAST HOURS, LITTLE ONE.
NO SENSE IN STRUGGLING.

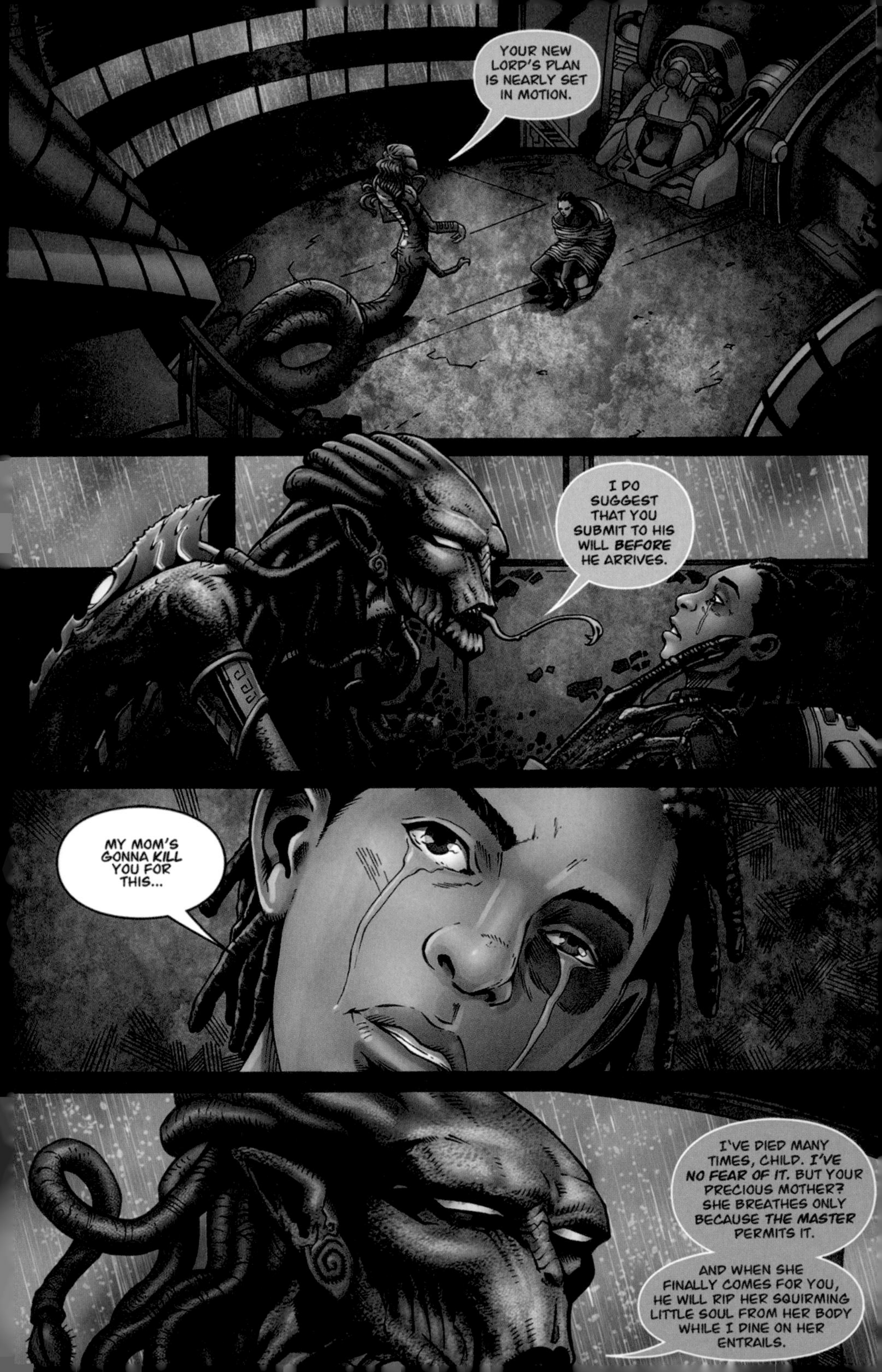
YOUR NEW LORD'S PLAN IS NEARLY SET IN MOTION.
I DO SUGGEST THAT YOU SUBMIT TO HIS WILL BEFORE HE ARRIVES.
MY MOM'S GONNA KILL YOU FOR THIS...
I'VE DIED MANY TIMES, CHILD. I'VE NO FEAR OF IT. BUT YOUR PRECIOUS MOTHER? SHE BREATHES ONLY BECAUSE THE MASTER PERMITS IT.
AND WHEN SHE FINALLY COMES FOR YOU, HE WILL RIP HER SQUIRMING LITTLE SOUL FROM HER BODY WHILE I DINE ON HER ENTRAILS.

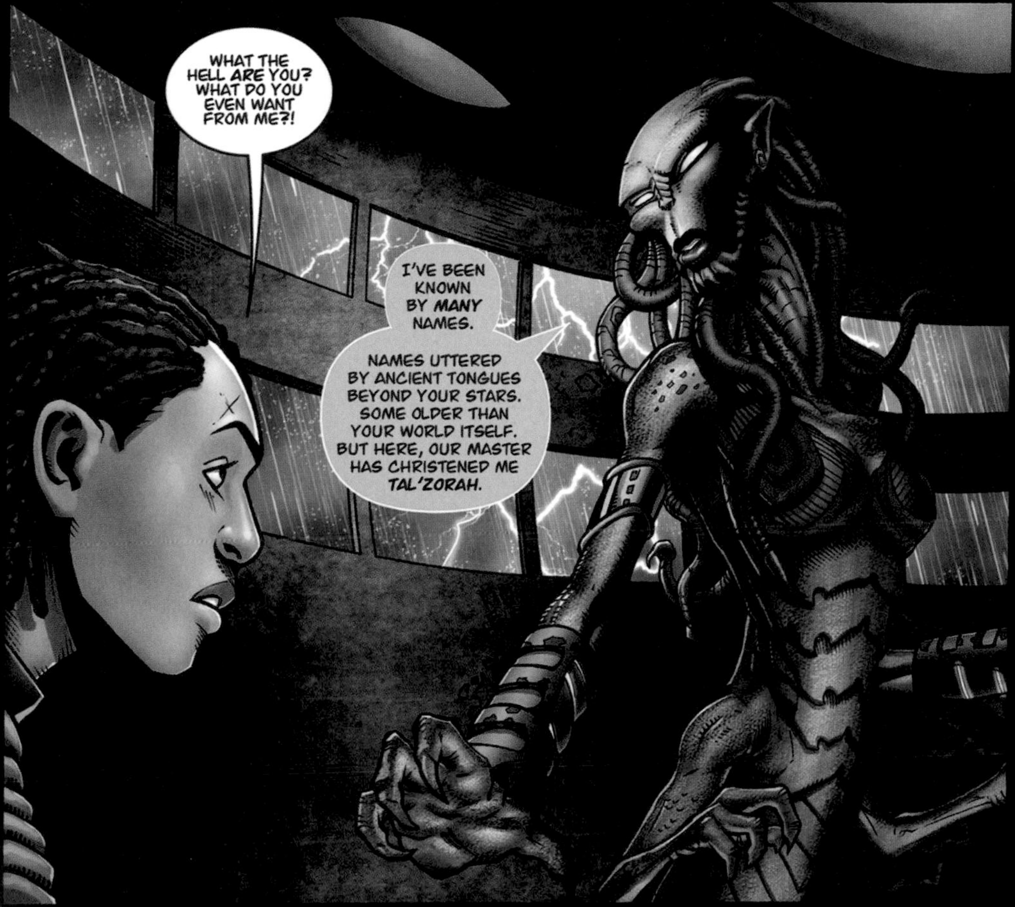
WHAT THE HELL ARE YOU? WHAT DO YOU EVEN WANT FROM ME?!
I'VE BEEN KNOWN BY MANY NAMES.
NAMES UTTERED BY ANCIENT TONGUES BEYOND YOUR STARS. SOME OLDER THAN YOUR WORLD ITSELF. BUT HERE, OUR MASTER HAS CHRISTENED ME TAL'ZORAH.

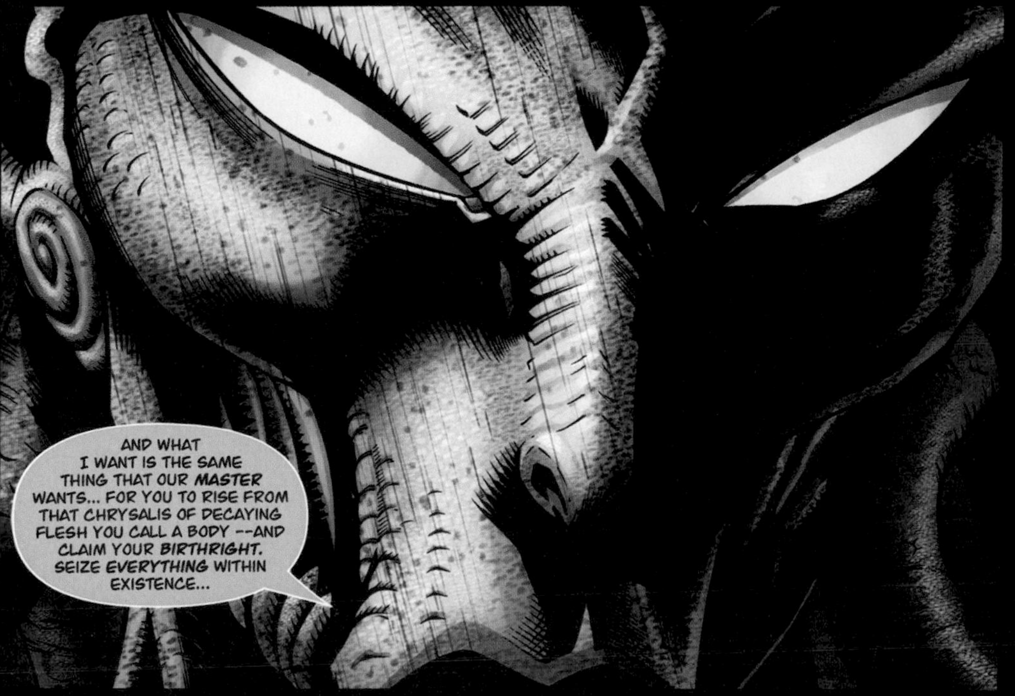
AND WHAT I WANT IS THE SAME THING THAT OUR MASTER WANTS... FOR YOU TO RISE FROM THAT CHRYSALIS OF DECAYING FLESH YOU CALL A BODY --AND CLAIM YOUR BIRTHRIGHT. SEIZE EVERYTHING WITHIN EXISTENCE...

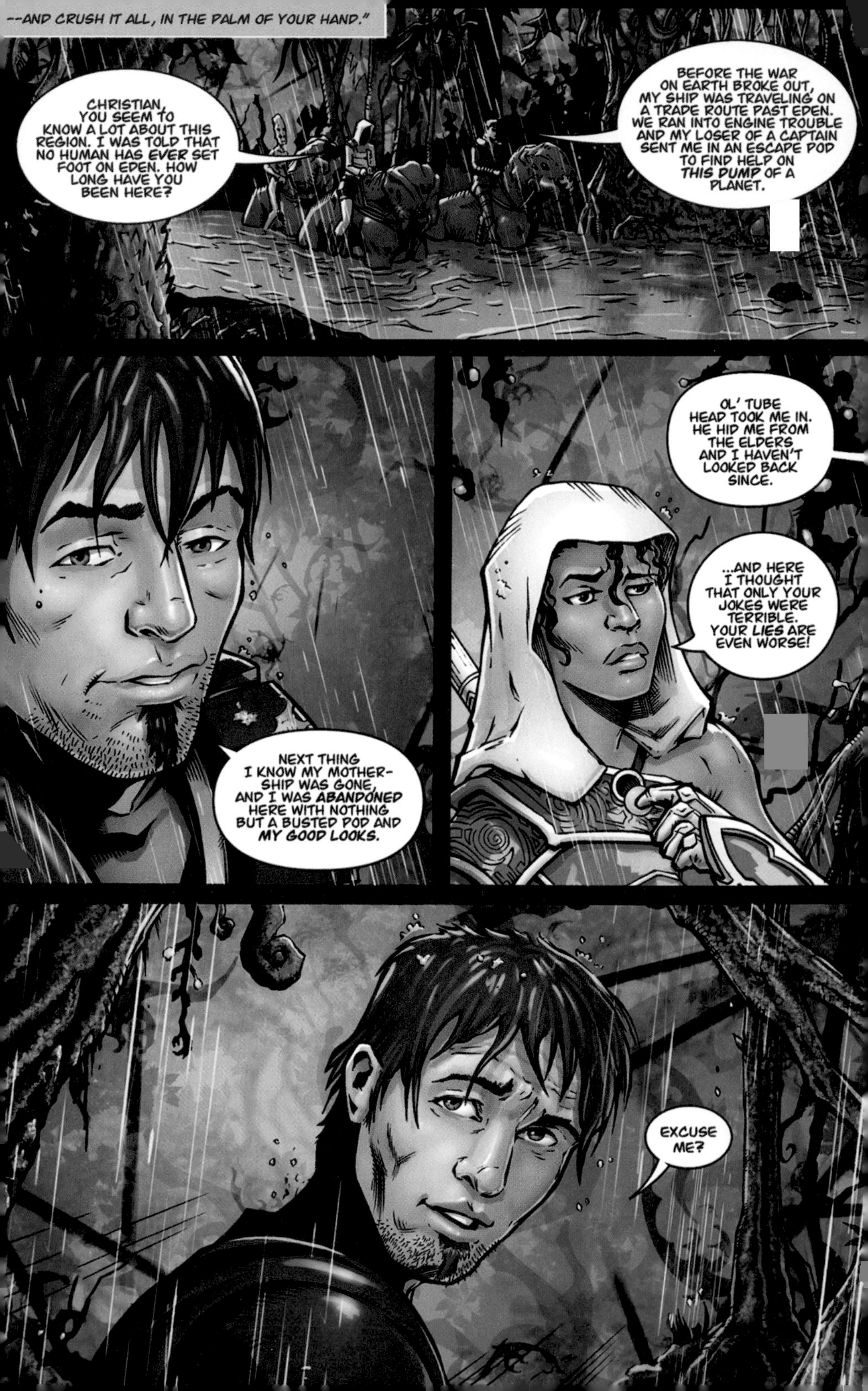
--AND CRUSH IT ALL, IN THE PALM OF YOUR HAND."
CHRISTIAN, YOU SEEM TO KNOW A LOT ABOUT THIS REGION. I WAS TOLD THAT NO HUMAN HAS EVER SET FOOT ON EDEN. HOW LONG HAVE YOU BEEN HERE?
BEFORE THE WAR ON EARTH BROKE OUT, MY SHIP WAS TRAVELING ON A TRADE ROUTE PAST EDEN. WE RAN INTO ENGINE TROUBLE AND MY LOSER OF A CAPTAIN SENT ME IN AN ESCAPE POD TO FIND HELP ON THIS DUMP OF A PLANET.
NEXT THING I KNOW MY MOTHER-SHIP WAS GONE, AND I WAS ABANDONED HERE WITH NOTHING BUT A BUSTED POD AND MY GOOD LOOKS.
OL' TUBE HEAD TOOK ME IN. HE HID ME FROM THE ELDERS AND I HAVEN'T LOOKED BACK SINCE.
...AND HERE I THOUGHT THAT ONLY YOUR JOKES WERE TERRIBLE. YOUR LIES ARE EVEN WORSE!
EXCUSE ME?

KLA'TUU'S MIND-SCAN. IT WORKS BOTH WAYS, YOU KNOW. WHEN HE TAPPED INTO MY MEMORIES, I COULD SEE SOME OF HIS TOO. YOU'RE NOT WHAT YOU CLAIM TO BE. YOU'RE NOT SOME STRANDED MERCHANT...
YOU'RE A TRAITOR.
YOU DESERTED EARTH AS SOON AS THE WAR STARTED. YOU WENT AWOL FROM THE CORPS, STOLE THE FIRST SHIP YOU COULD GET YOUR GREEDY LITTLE HANDS ON AND HID HERE OUTSIDE THE GATES! WHILE THE REST OF HUMANITY WAS FIGHTING AND DYING FOR OUR HOME, YOU WERE HERE ...TREMBLING UNDER A ROCK LIKE A COWARD!
WHAT THE HELL DO YOU EVEN CARE, GENERAL?! I'VE DONE NOTHING BUT SAVE YOUR SORRY SKIN SINCE YOU GOT HERE! YOU THINK YOU'RE A HERO? I DID WHAT I HAD TO DO TO SURVIVE. YOU THINK YOU'RE SO MUCH BETTER THAN ME BECAUSE YOU STAYED BEHIND AND FOUGHT?!
WELL, I HATE TO BREAK IT TO YOU, BUT EARTH AND YOUR KID ARE PROBABLY BOTH AS GOOD AS DEAD!
YOU SON OF A--
PARDON ME HUMANS...

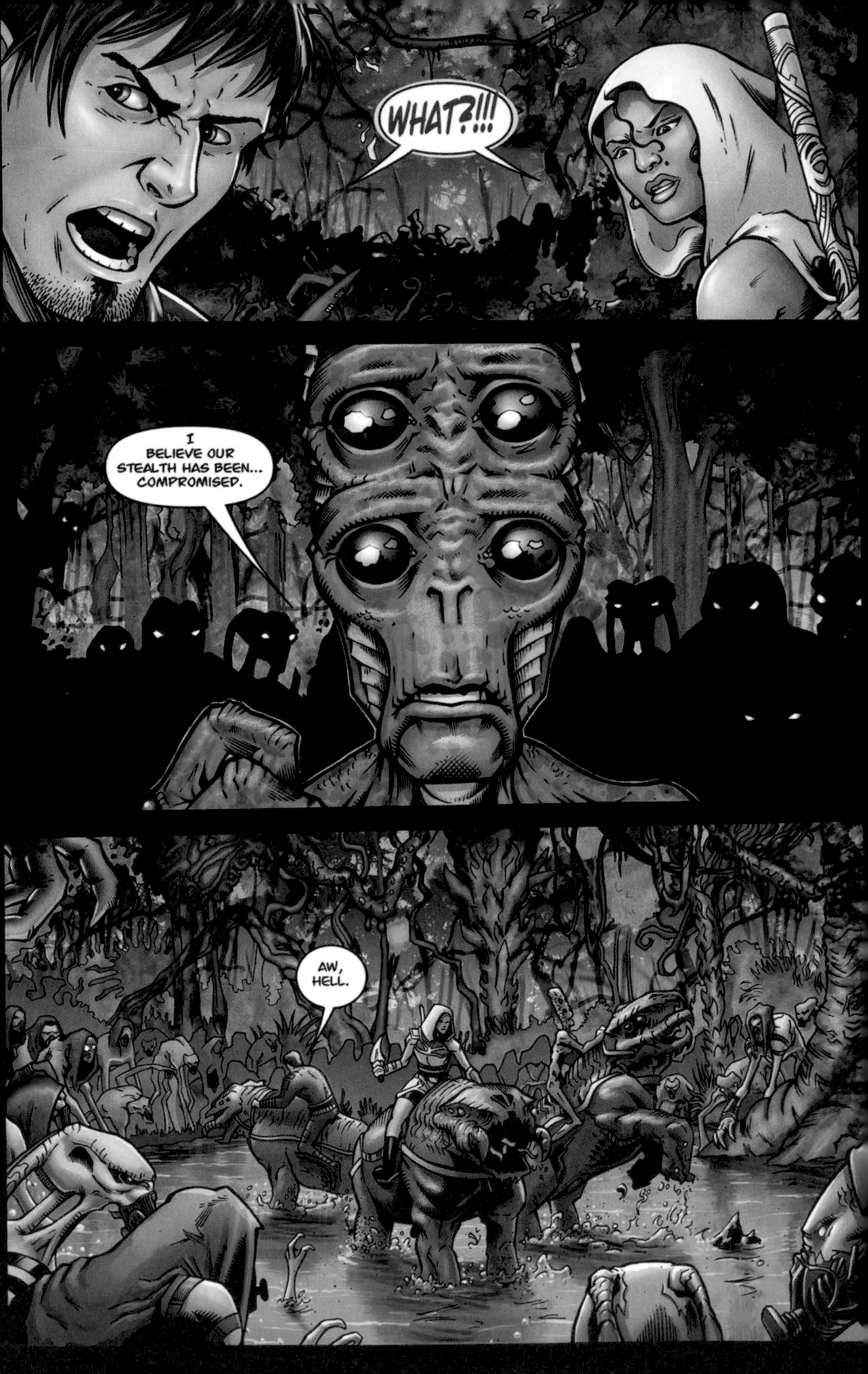
WHAT?!!!
I BELIEVE OUR STEALTH HAS BEEN... COMPROMISED.
AW, HELL.

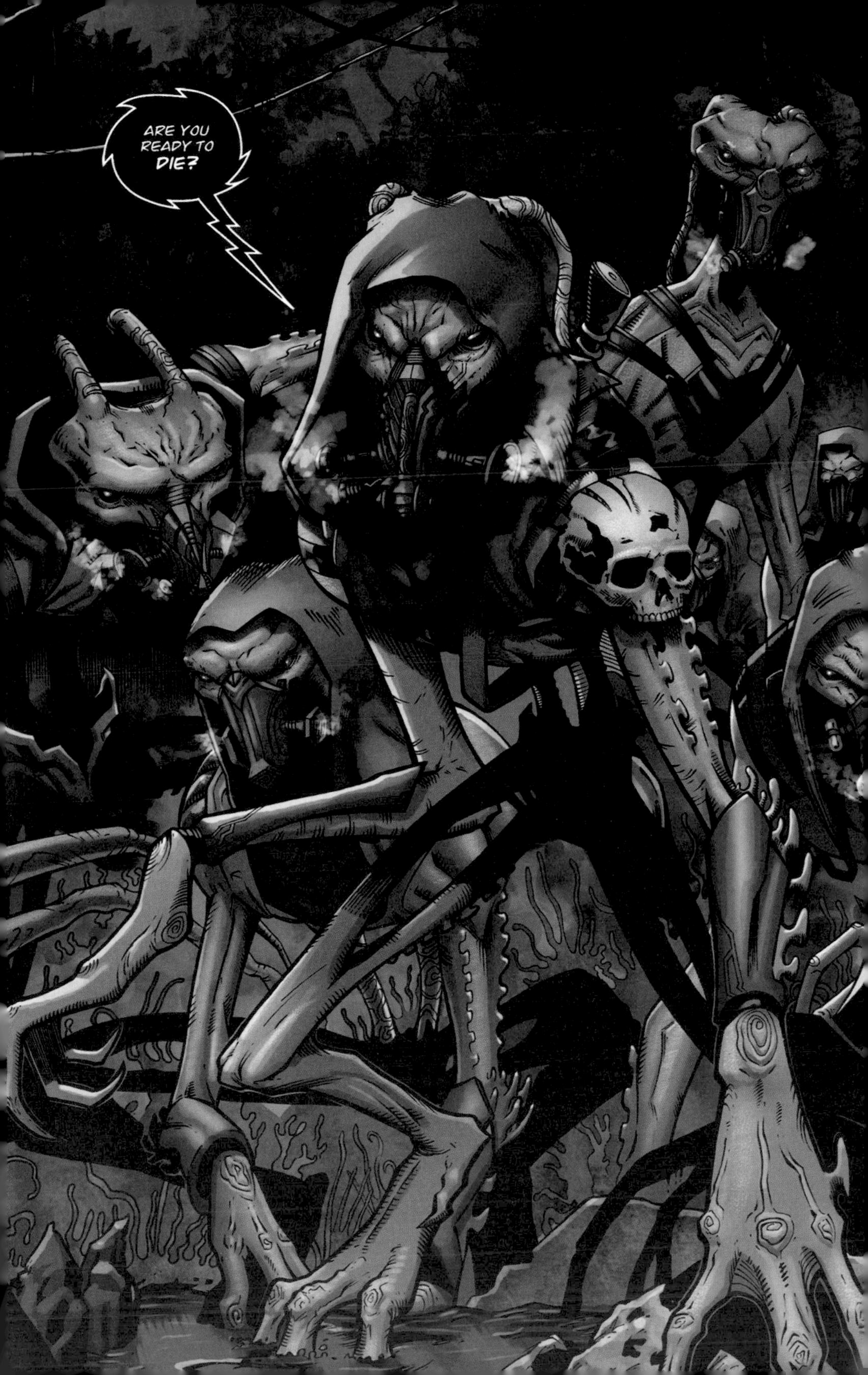
ARE YOU READY TO DIE?

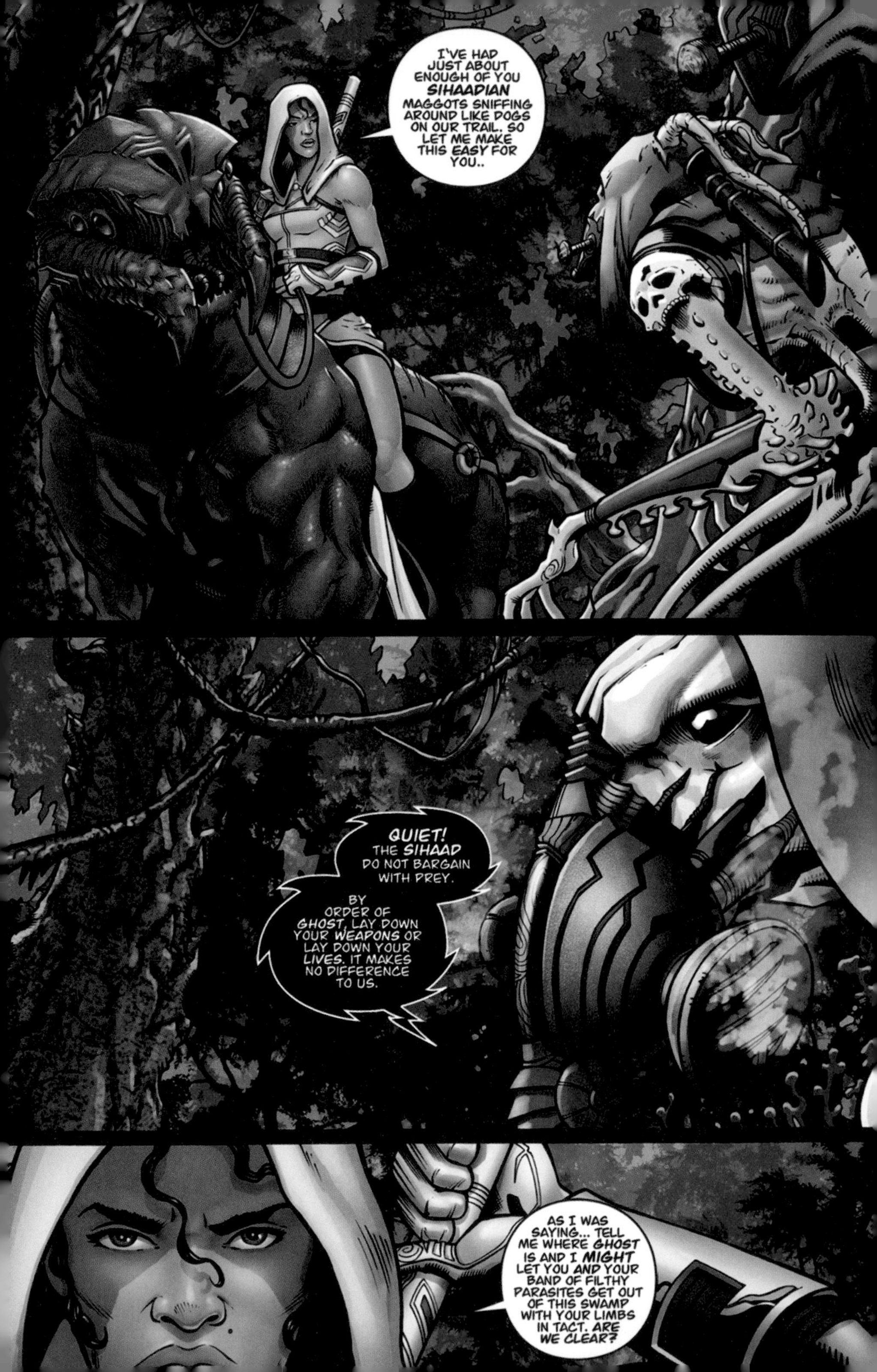
I'VE HAD JUST ABOUT ENOUGH OF YOU SIHAADIAN MAGGOTS SNIFFING AROUND LIKE DOGS ON OUR TRAIL. SO LET ME MAKE THIS EASY FOR YOU..
QUIET! THE SIHAAD DO NOT BARGAIN WITH PREY.
BY ORDER OF GHOST, LAY DOWN YOUR WEAPONS OR LAY DOWN YOUR LIVES. IT MAKES NO DIFFERENCE TO US.
AS I WAS SAYING... TELL ME WHERE GHOST IS AND I MIGHT LET YOU AND YOUR BAND OF FILTHY PARASITES GET OUT OF THIS SWAMP WITH YOUR LIMBS IN TACT. ARE WE CLEAR?

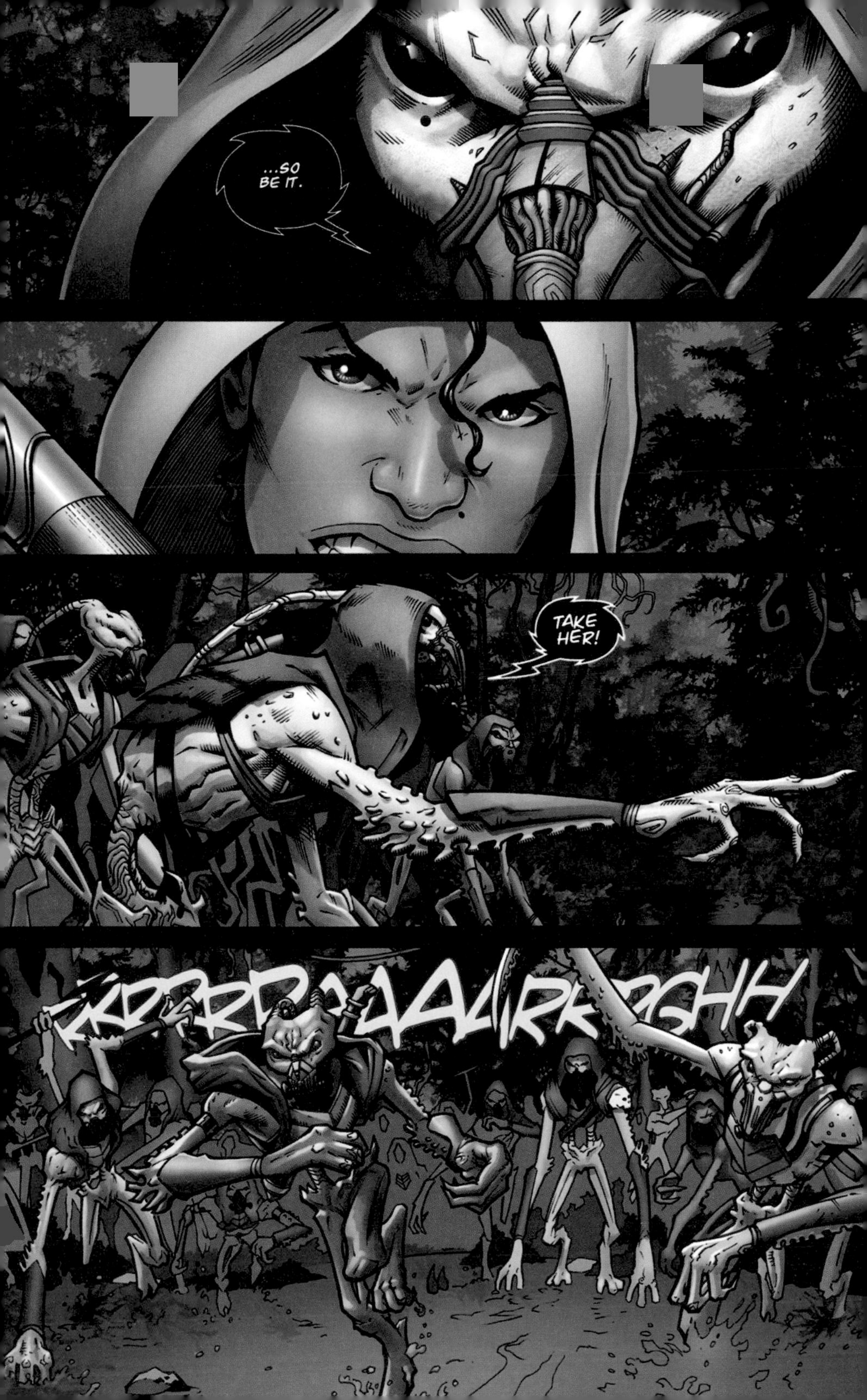
...SO BE IT.
TAKE HER!

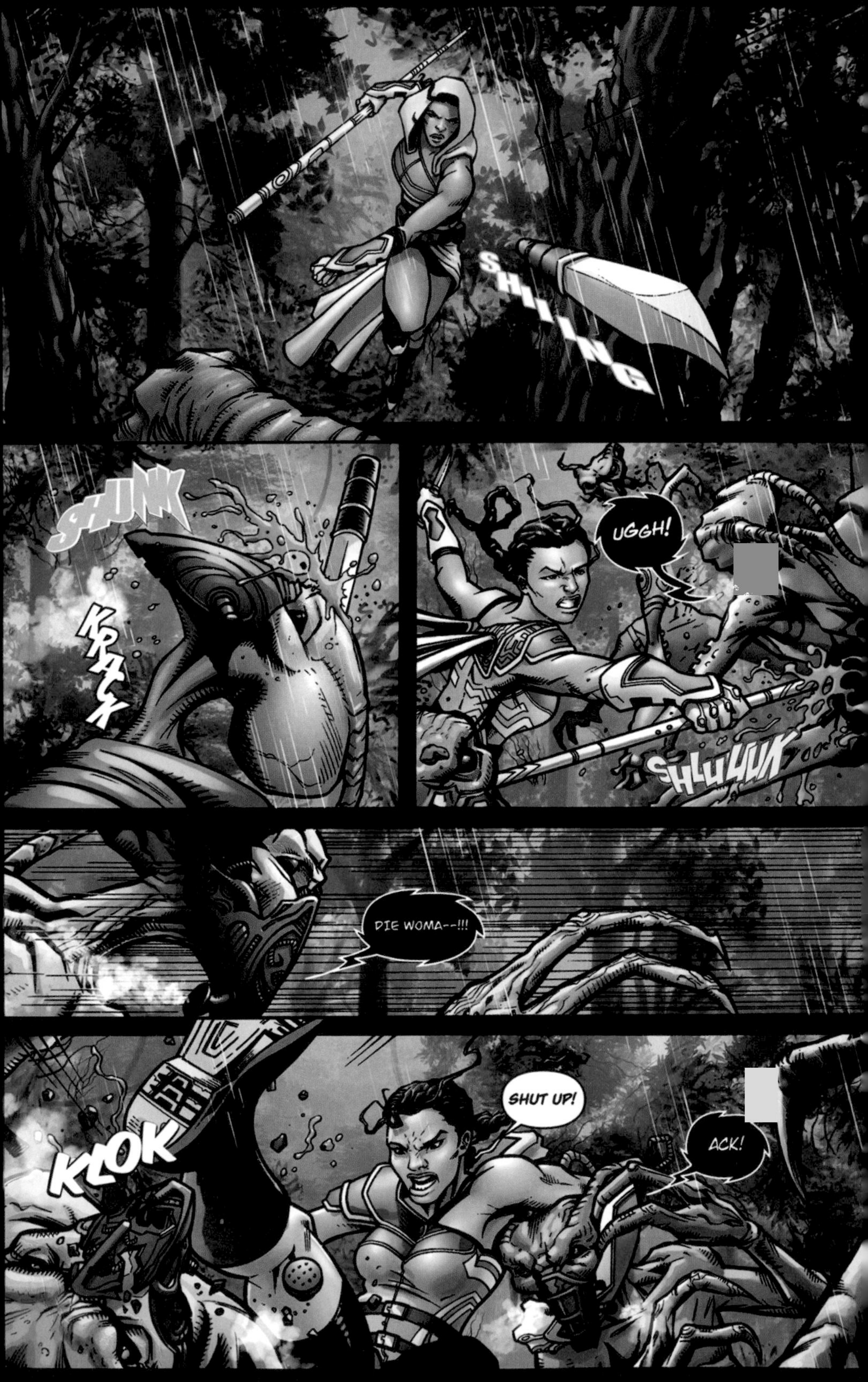
SHIIING
SHUNK
KRACK
UGGH!
SHLUUUK
DIE WOMA--!!!
KLOK
SHUT UP!
ACK!

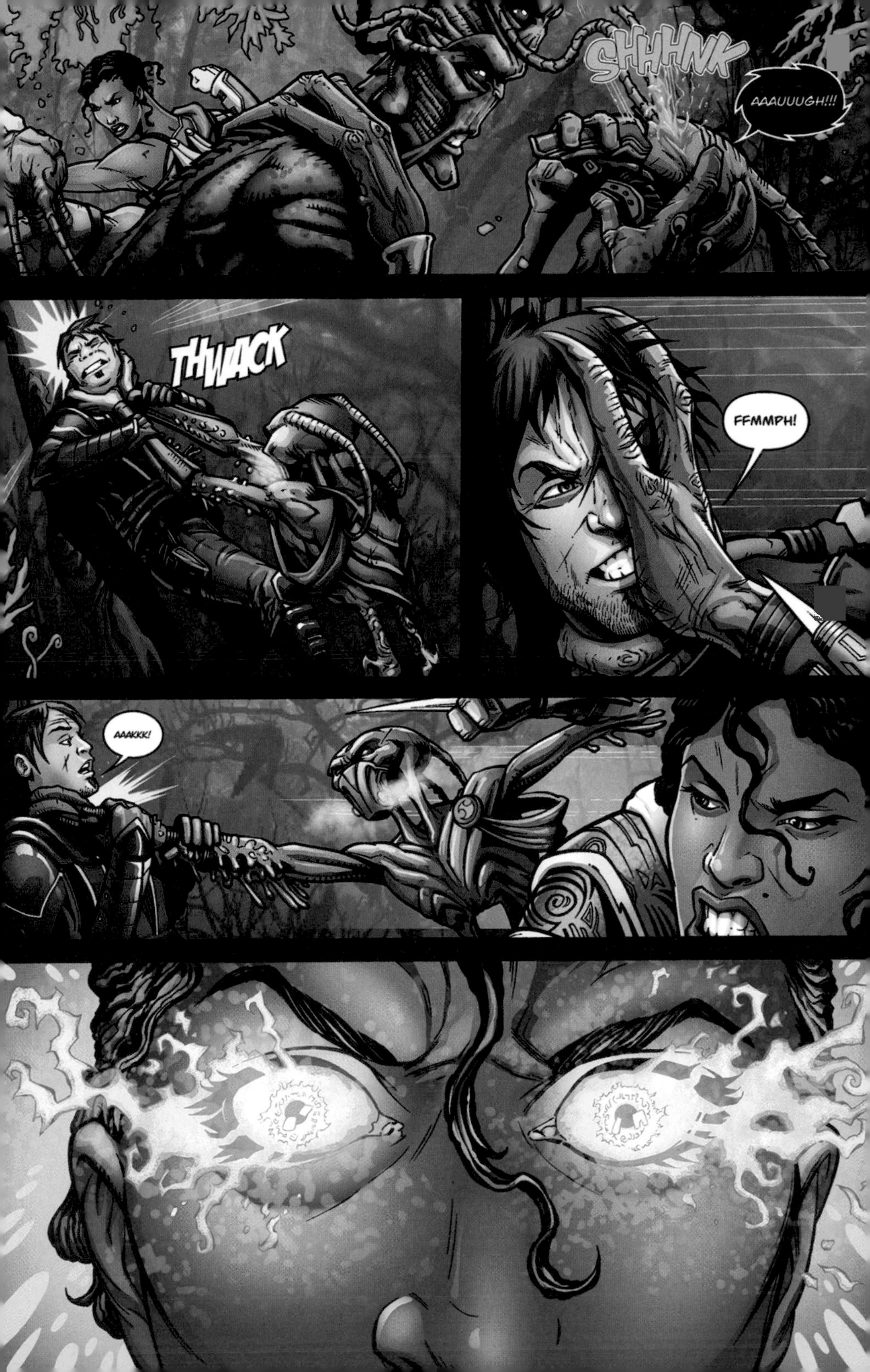
SHHHNK
AAAUUUGH!!!
THWACK
FFMMPH!
AAAKKK!

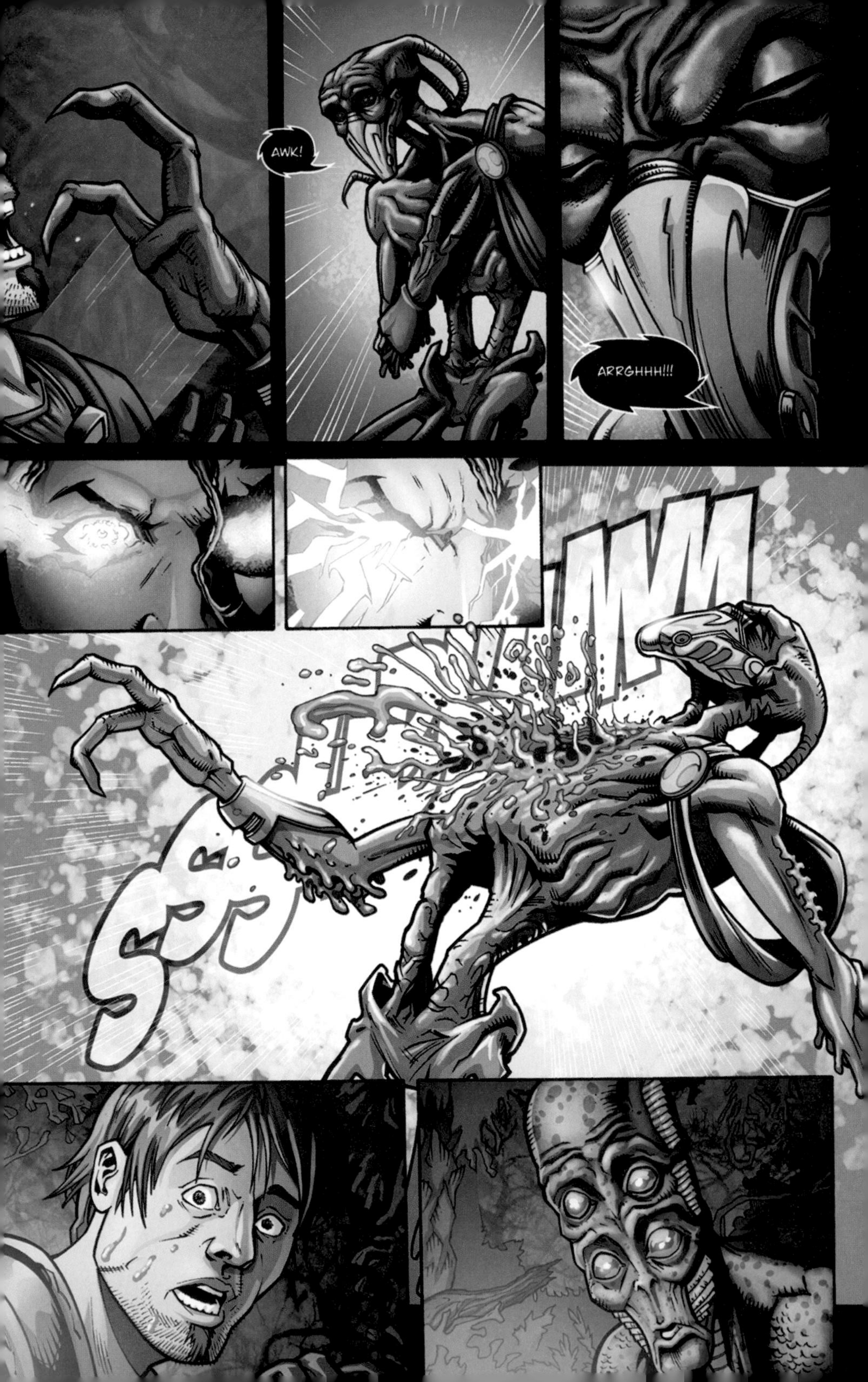
AWK!
ARRGHHH!!!

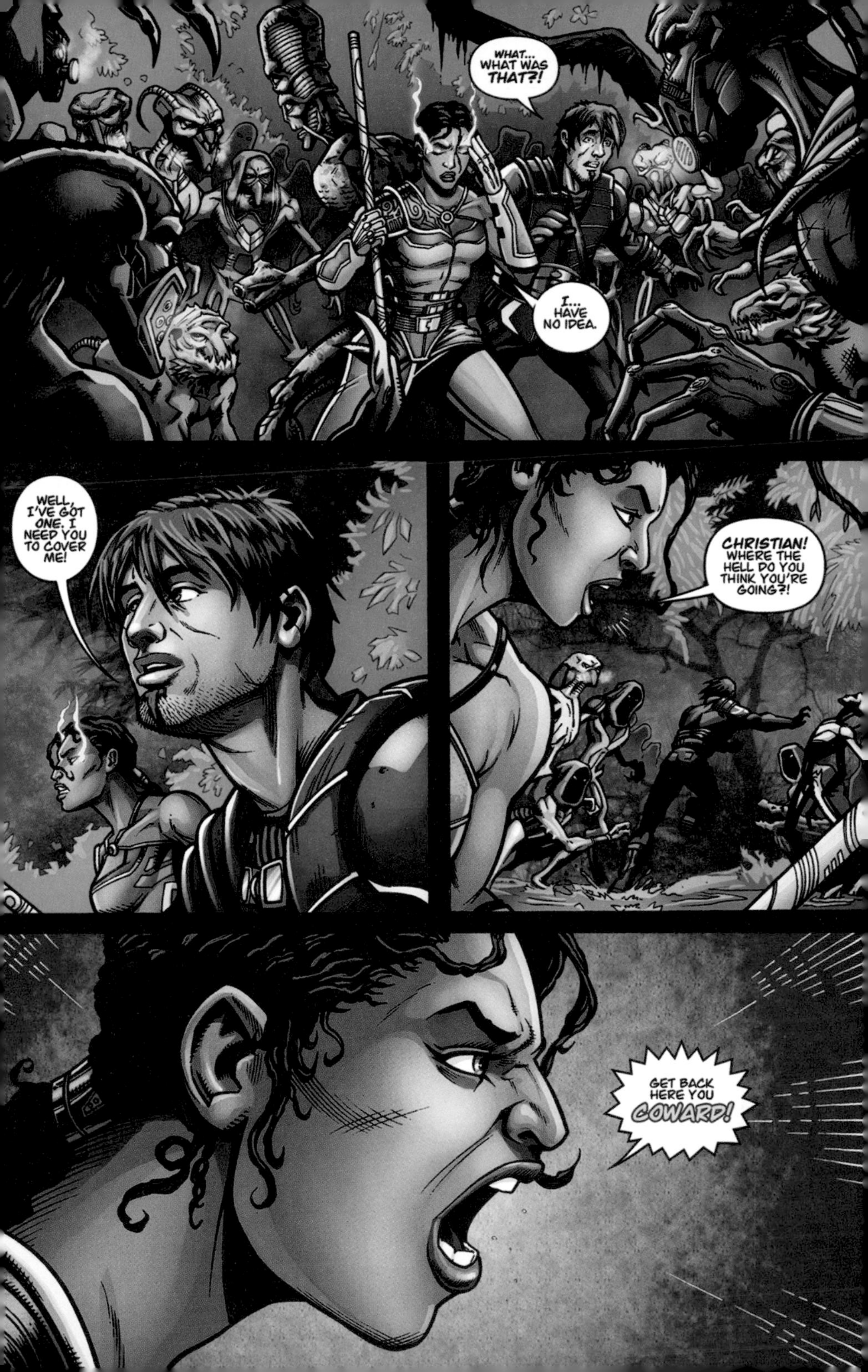
WHAT... WHAT WAS THAT?!
I... HAVE NO IDEA.
WELL, I'VE GOT ONE. I NEED YOU TO COVER ME!
CHRISTIAN! WHERE THE HELL DO YOU THINK YOU'RE GOING?!
GET BACK HERE YOU COWARD!

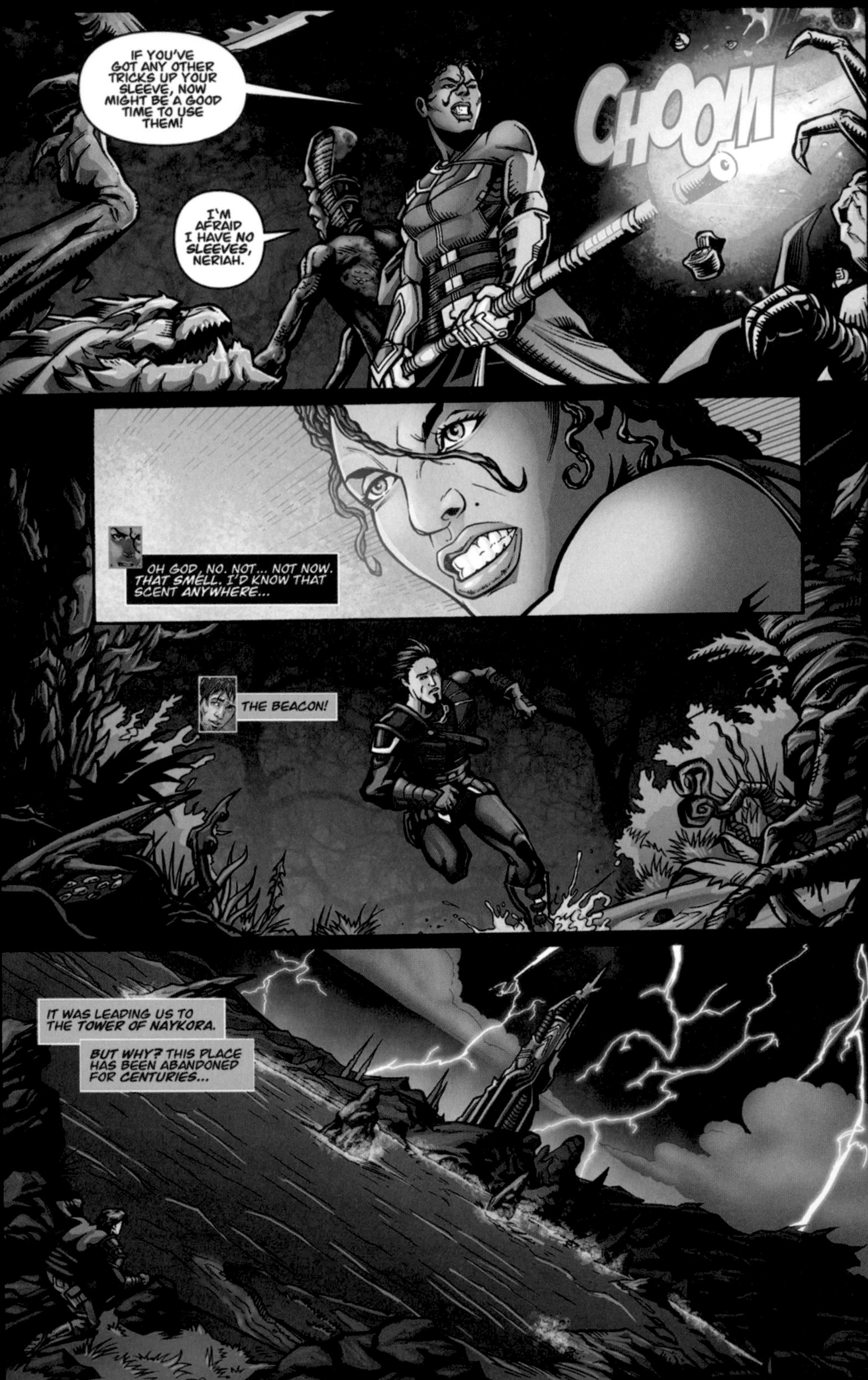
IF YOU'VE GOT ANY OTHER TRICKS UP YOUR SLEEVE, NOW MIGHT BE A GOOD TIME TO USE THEM!
CHOOM
I'M AFRAID I HAVE NO SLEEVES, NERIAH.
OH GOD, NO. NOT... NOT NOW. THAT SMELL. I'D KNOW THAT SCENT ANYWHERE...
THE BEACON!
IT WAS LEADING US TO THE TOWER OF NAYKORA.
BUT WHY? THIS PLACE HAS BEEN ABANDONED FOR CENTURIES...

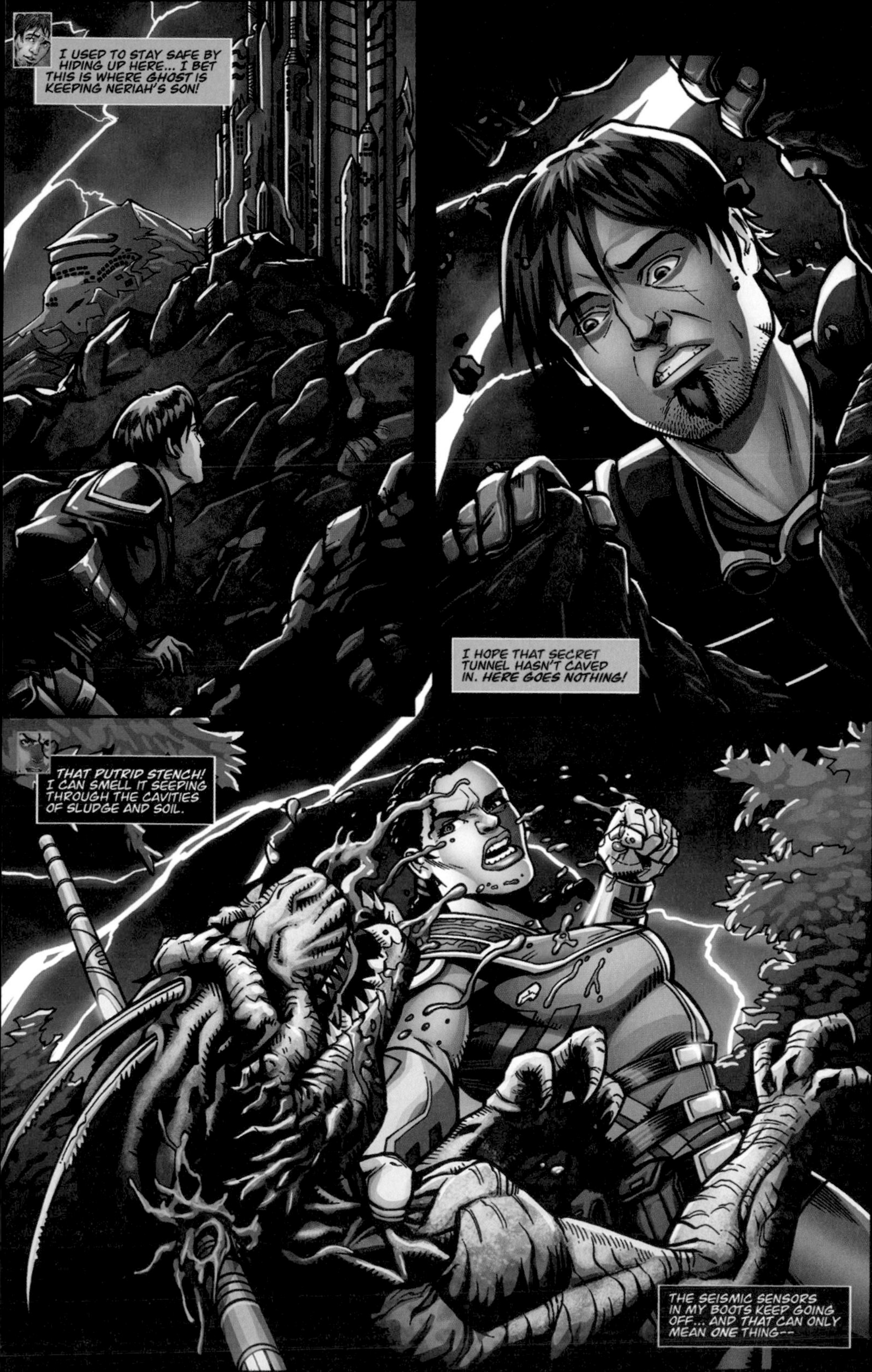
I USED TO STAY SAFE BY HIDING UP HERE... I BET THIS IS WHERE GHOST IS KEEPING NERIAH'S SON!
I HOPE THAT SECRET TUNNEL HASN'T CAVED IN. HERE GOES NOTHING!
THAT PUTRID STENCH! I CAN SMELL IT SEEPING THROUGH THE CAVITIES OF SLUDGE AND SOIL.
THE SEISMIC SENSORS IN MY BOOTS KEEP GOING OFF... AND THAT CAN ONLY MEAN ONE THING--

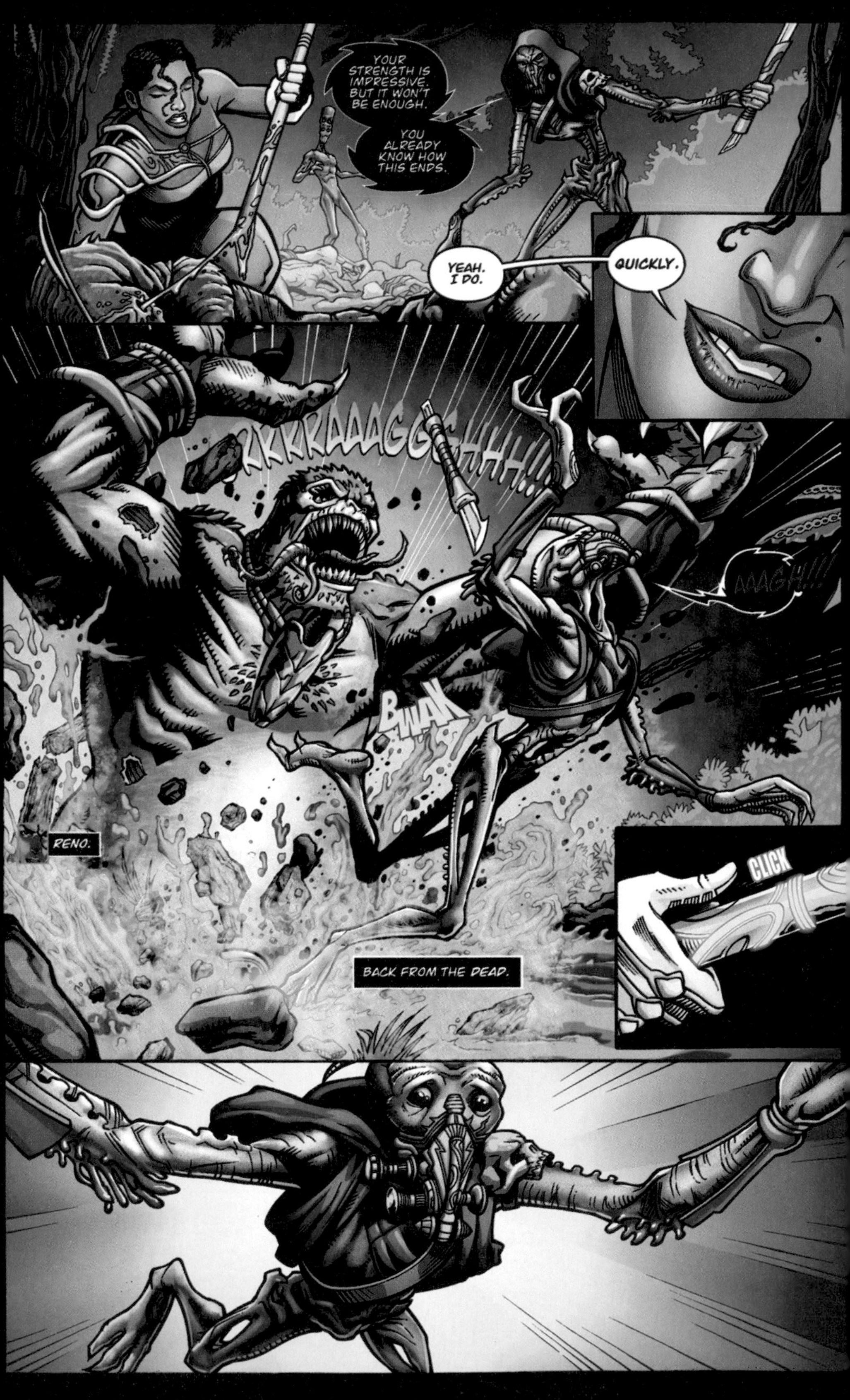

YOUR STRENGTH IS IMPRESSIVE. BUT IT WON'T BE ENOUGH.
YOU ALREADY KNOW HOW THIS ENDS.
YEAH. I DO.
QUICKLY.
KKKRRAAAGGGHHH!!!
AAAGH!!!
BWAK
RENO.
CLICK
BACK FROM THE DEAD.

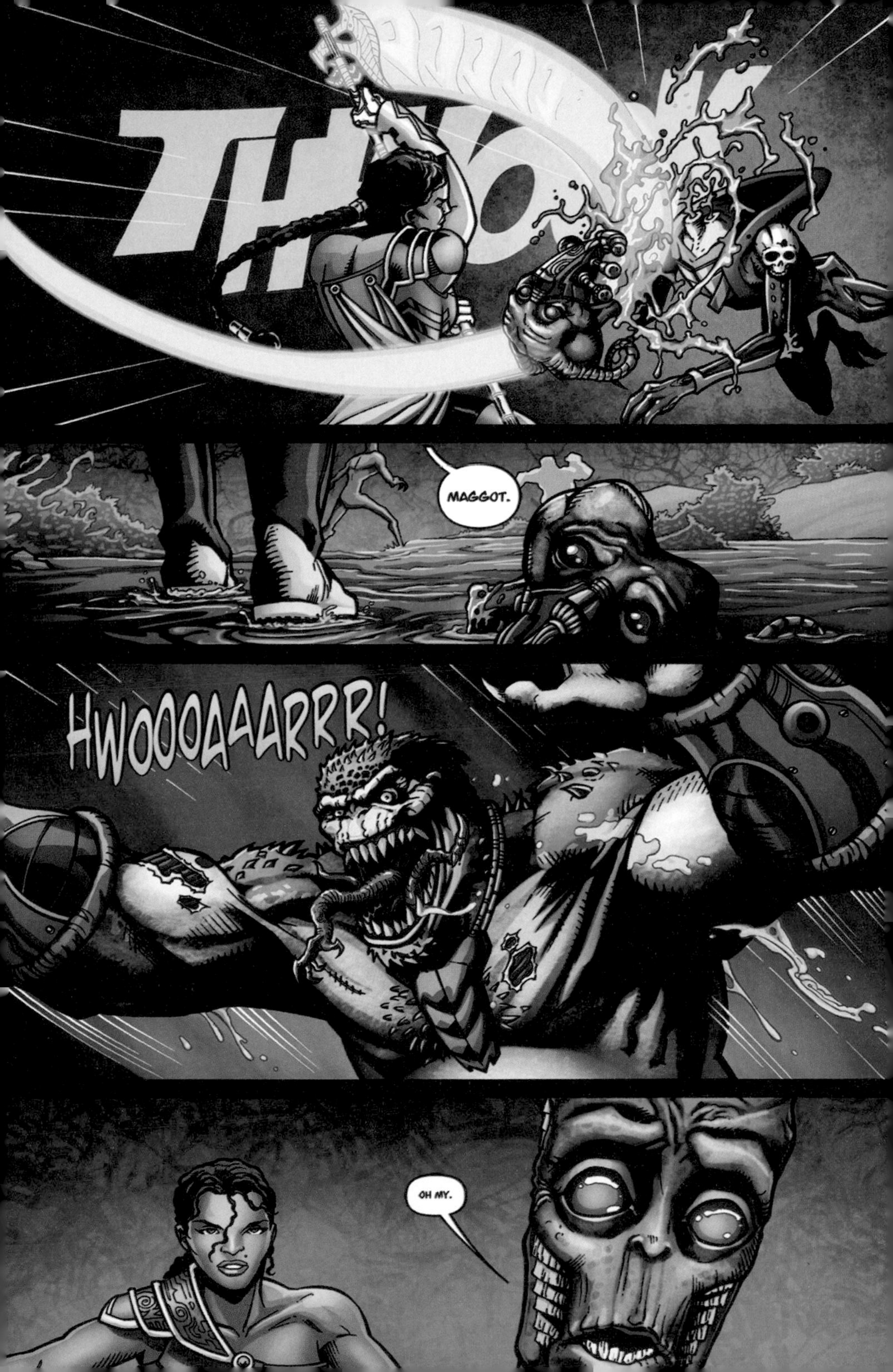
THWOK
MAGGOT.
HWOOOAAARRR!
OH MY.

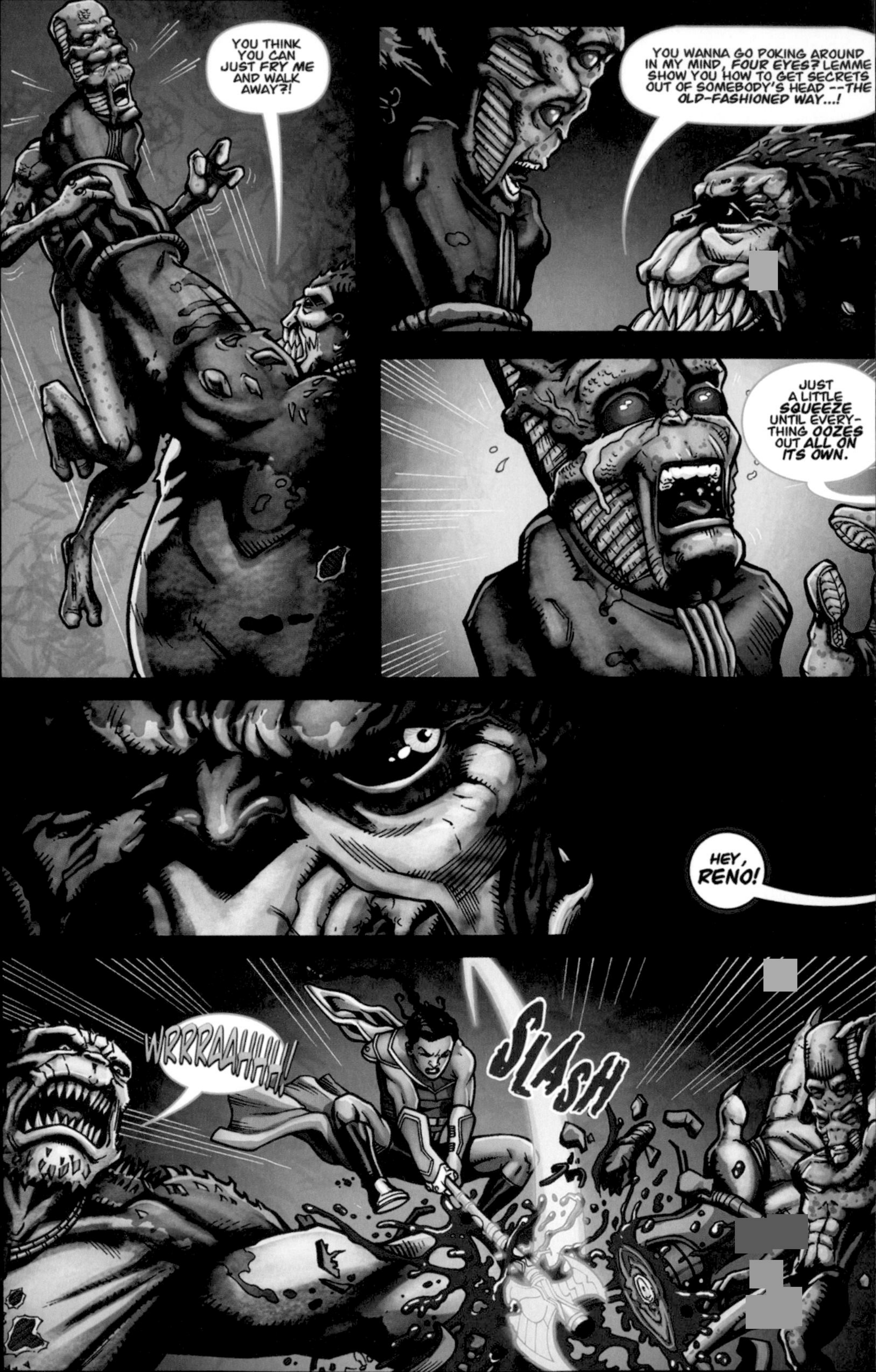
YOU THINK YOU CAN JUST FRY ME AND WALK AWAY?!
YOU WANNA GO POKING AROUND IN MY MIND, FOUR EYES? LEMME SHOW YOU HOW TO GET SECRETS OUT OF SOMEBODY'S HEAD --THE OLD-FASHIONED WAY...!
JUST A LITTLE SQUEEZE UNTIL EVERY-THING OOZES OUT ALL ON ITS OWN.
HEY, RENO!
WRRRAAHHHH!
SLASH

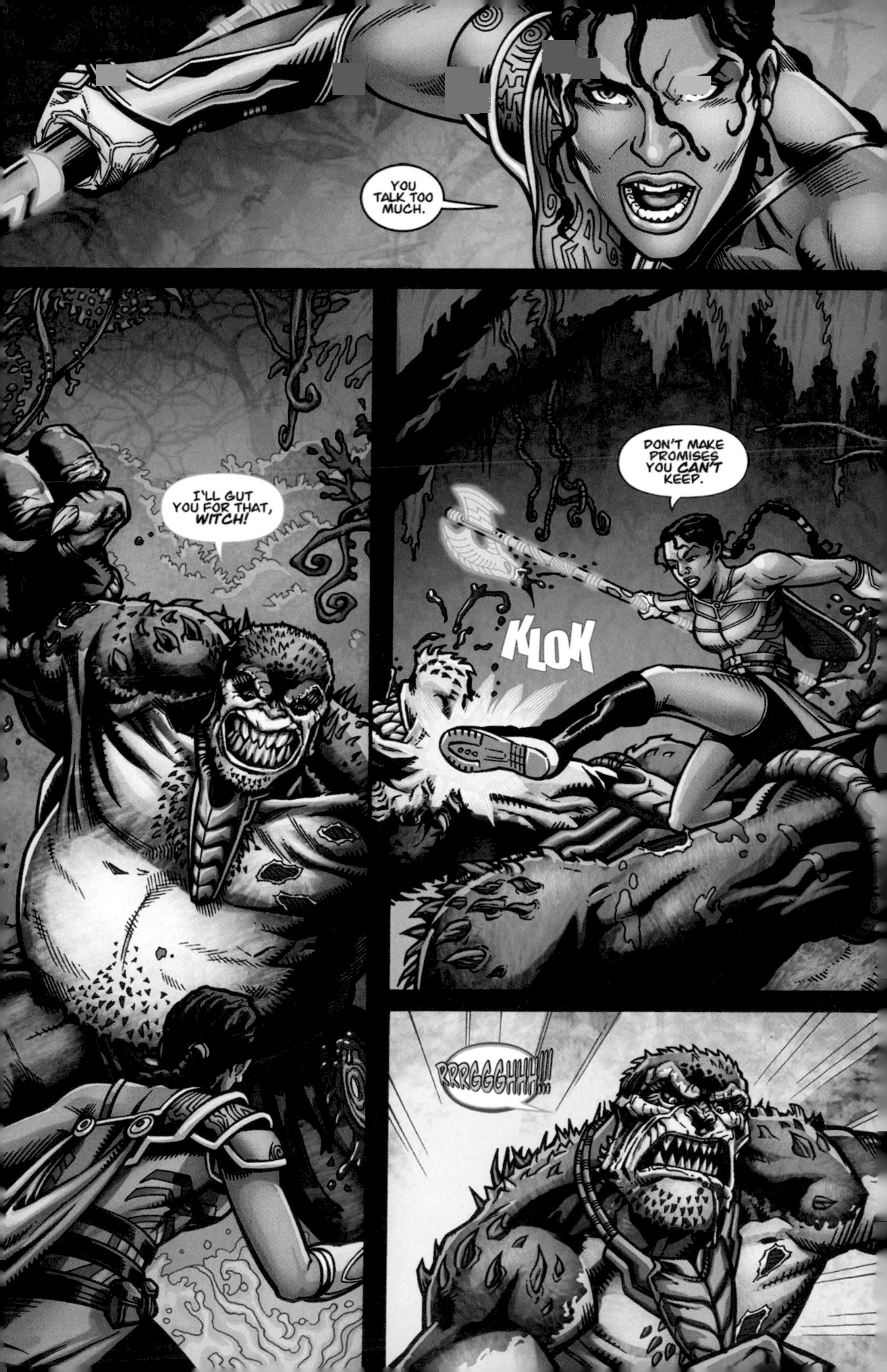
YOU TALK TOO MUCH.
I'LL GUT YOU FOR THAT, *WITCH!*
DON'T MAKE PROMISES YOU *CAN'T* KEEP.
KLOK
RRRGGGHHH!!!

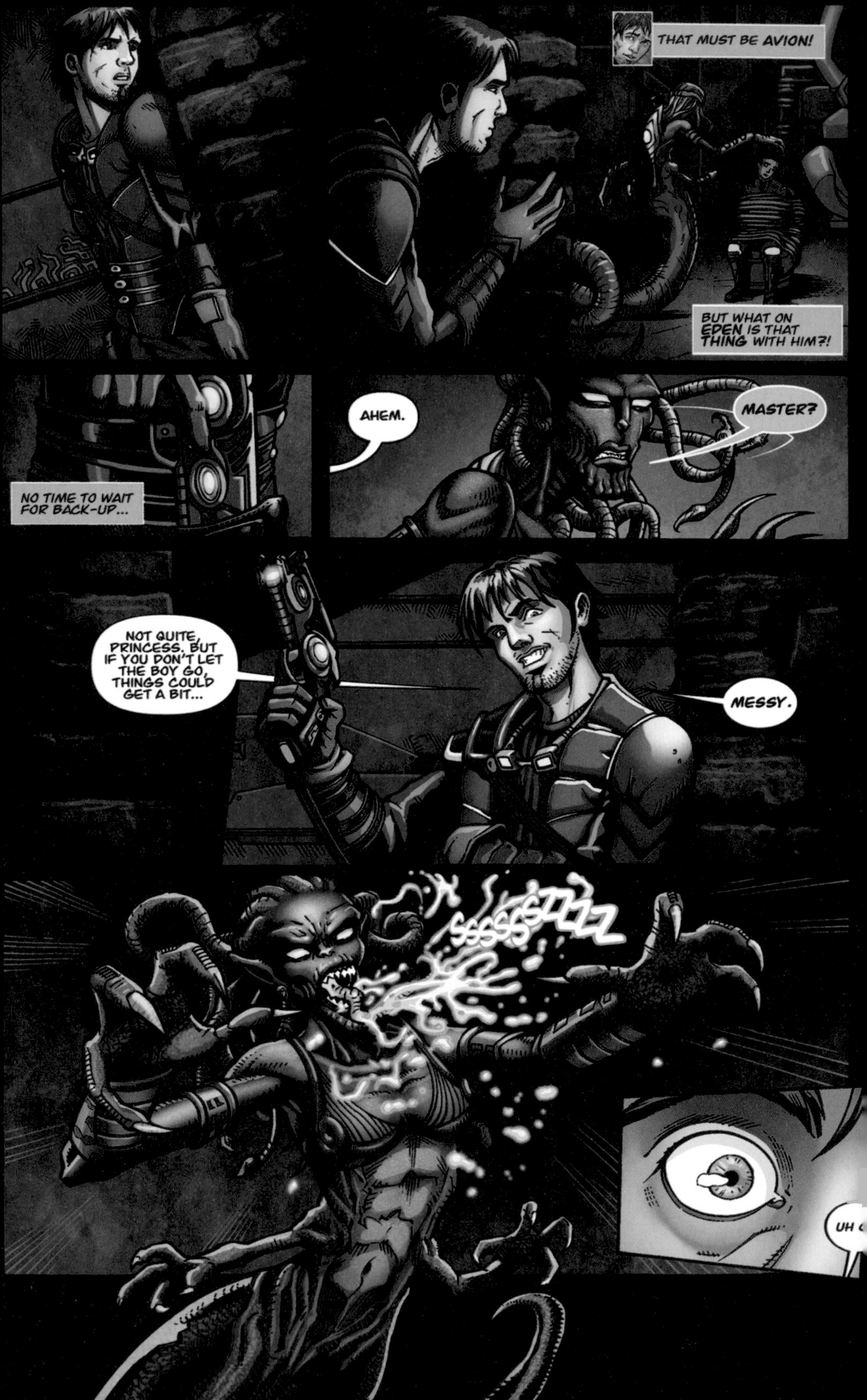
THAT MUST BE AVION!
BUT WHAT ON EDEN IS THAT THING WITH HIM?!
NO TIME TO WAIT FOR BACK-UP...
AHEM.
MASTER?
NOT QUITE, PRINCESS. BUT IF YOU DON'T LET THE BOY GO, THINGS COULD GET A BIT...
MESSY.
SSSSSGZZZZ

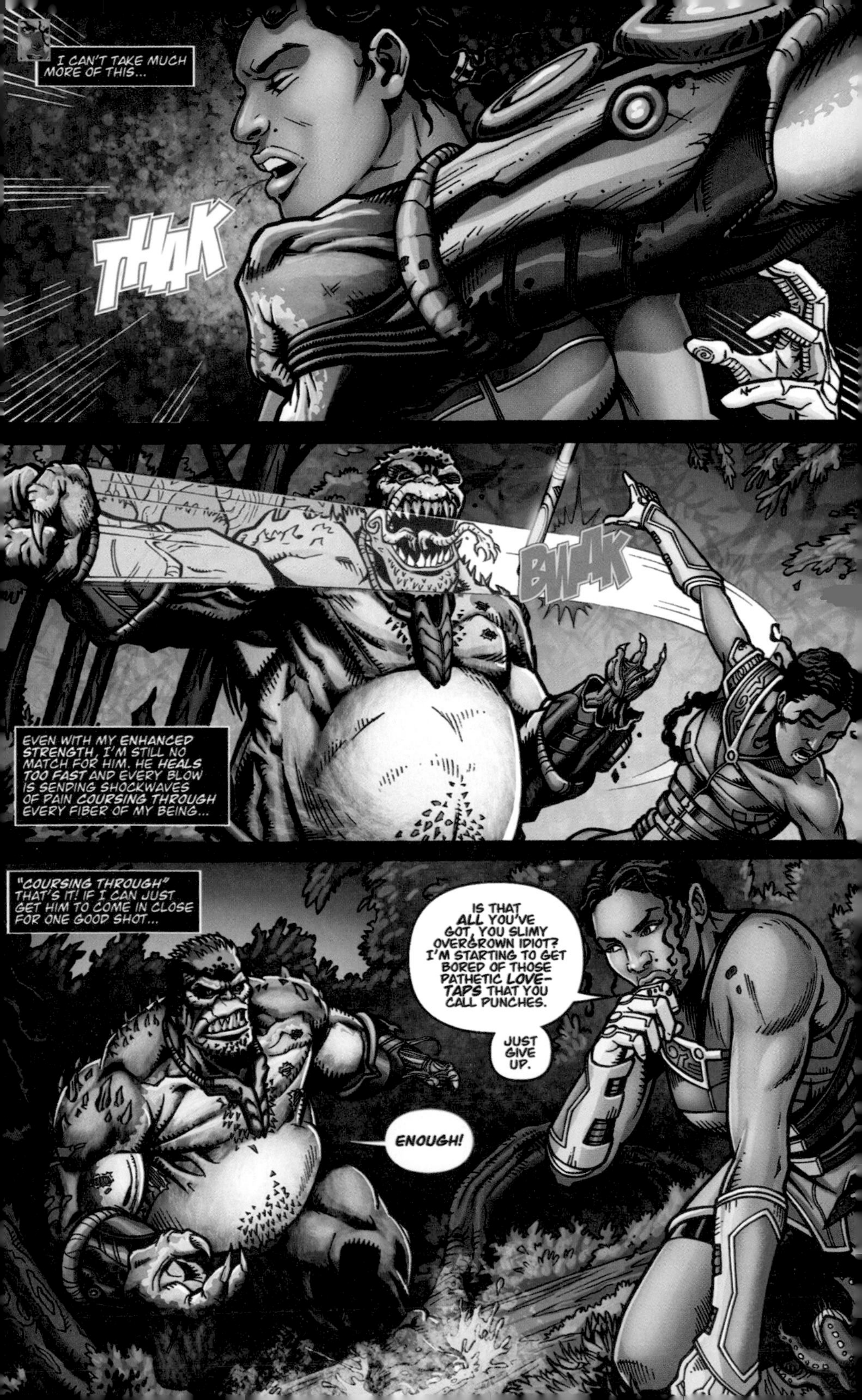
I CAN'T TAKE MUCH MORE OF THIS...
THAK
BWAK
EVEN WITH MY ENHANCED STRENGTH, I'M STILL NO MATCH FOR HIM. HE HEALS TOO FAST AND EVERY BLOW IS SENDING SHOCKWAVES OF PAIN COURSING THROUGH EVERY FIBER OF MY BEING...
"COURSING THROUGH" THAT'S IT! IF I CAN JUST GET HIM TO COME IN CLOSE FOR ONE GOOD SHOT...
IS THAT ALL YOU'VE GOT, YOU SLIMY OVERGROWN IDIOT? I'M STARTING TO GET BORED OF THOSE PATHETIC LOVE-TAPS THAT YOU CALL PUNCHES.
JUST GIVE UP.
ENOUGH!

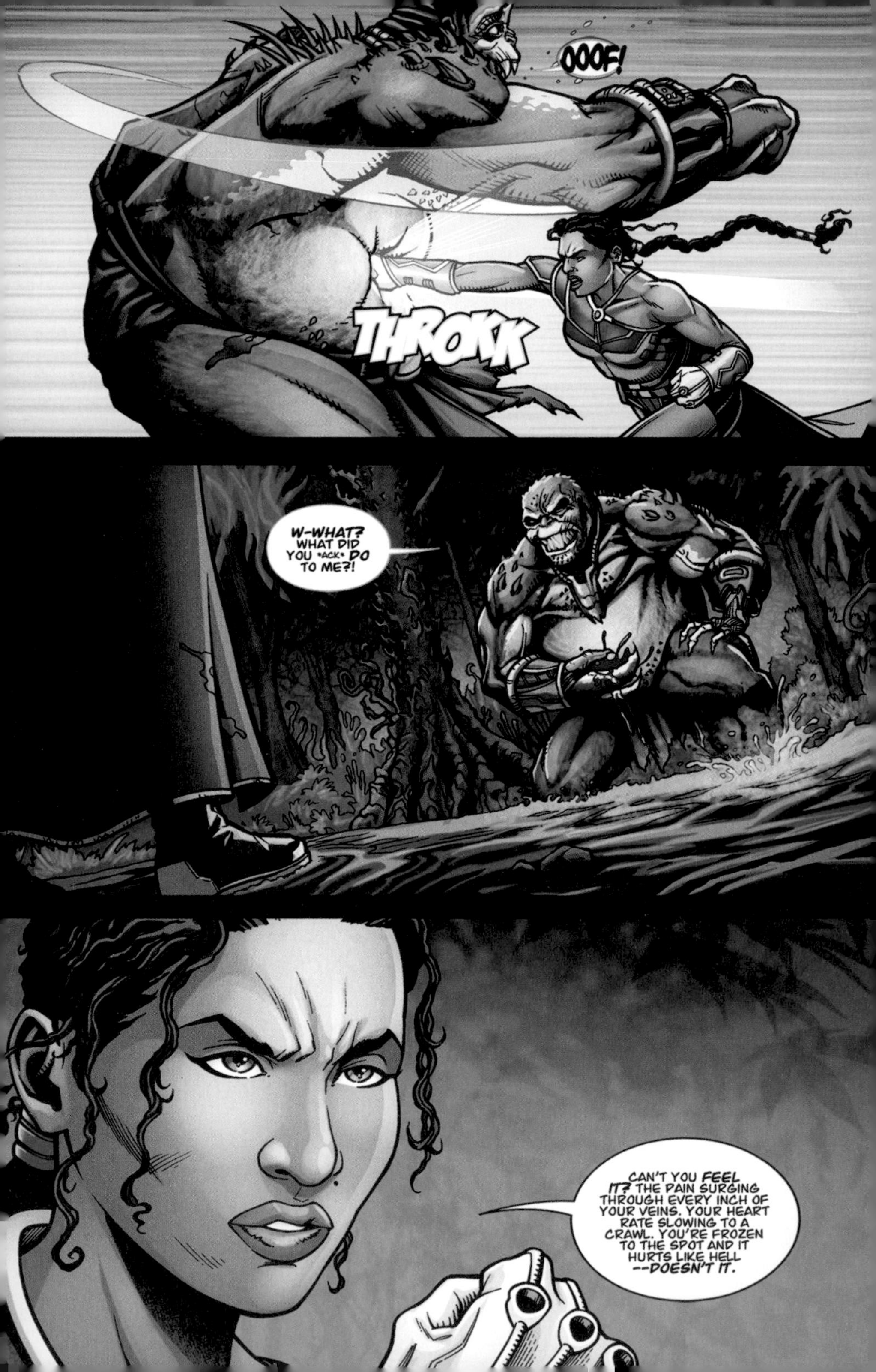
OOOF!
THROKK
W-WHAT? WHAT DID YOU *ACK* DO TO ME?!
CAN'T YOU FEEL IT? THE PAIN SURGING THROUGH EVERY INCH OF YOUR VEINS. YOUR HEART RATE SLOWING TO A CRAWL. YOU'RE FROZEN TO THE SPOT AND IT HURTS LIKE HELL --DOESN'T IT.

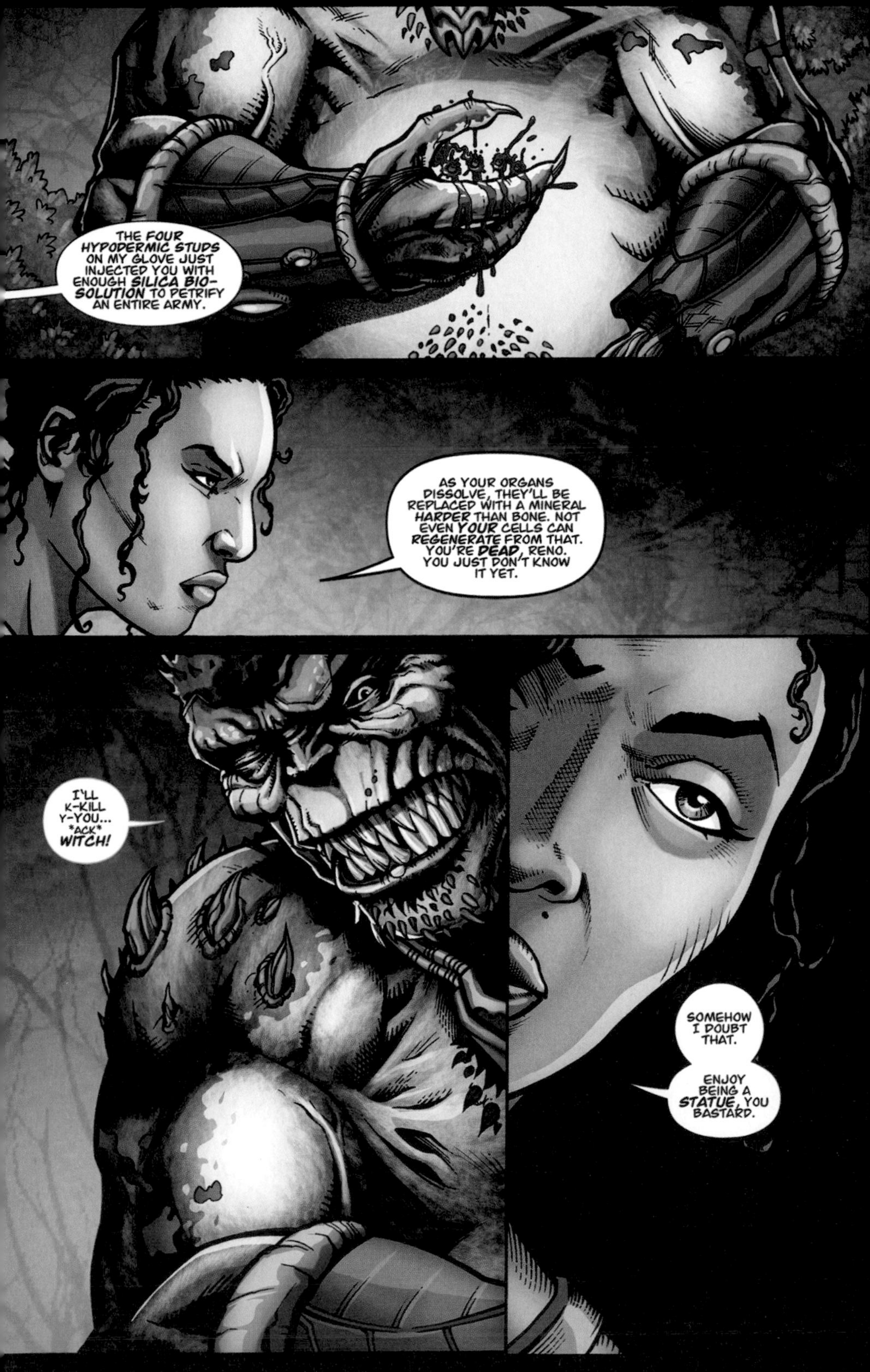
THE FOUR HYPODERMIC STUDS ON MY GLOVE JUST INJECTED YOU WITH ENOUGH SILICA BIO-SOLUTION TO PETRIFY AN ENTIRE ARMY.
AS YOUR ORGANS DISSOLVE, THEY'LL BE REPLACED WITH A MINERAL HARDER THAN BONE. NOT EVEN YOUR CELLS CAN REGENERATE FROM THAT. YOU'RE DEAD, RENO. YOU JUST DON'T KNOW IT YET.
I'LL K-KILL Y-YOU... *ACK* WITCH!
SOMEHOW I DOUBT THAT.
ENJOY BEING A STATUE, YOU BASTARD.

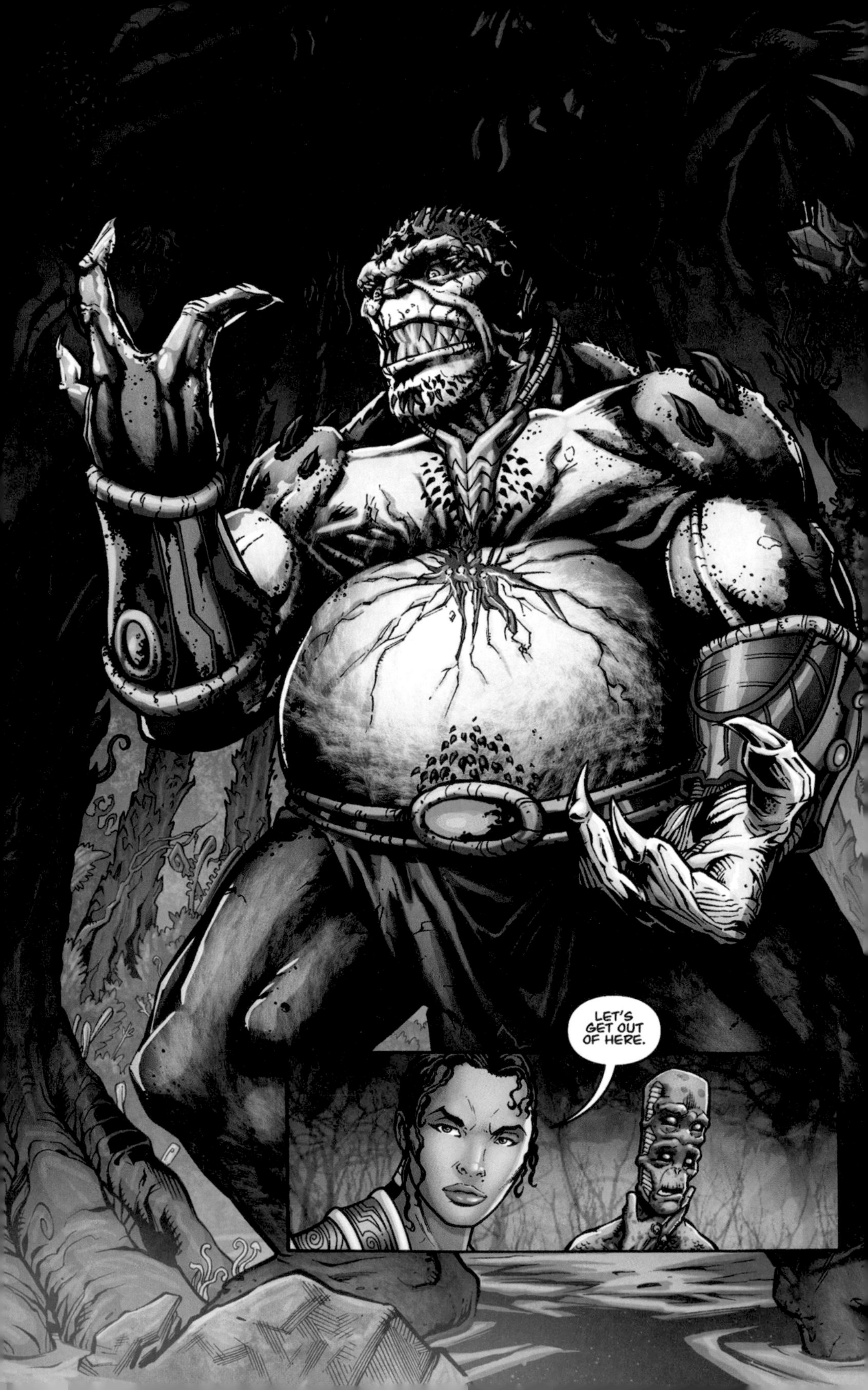
LET'S GET OUT OF HERE.

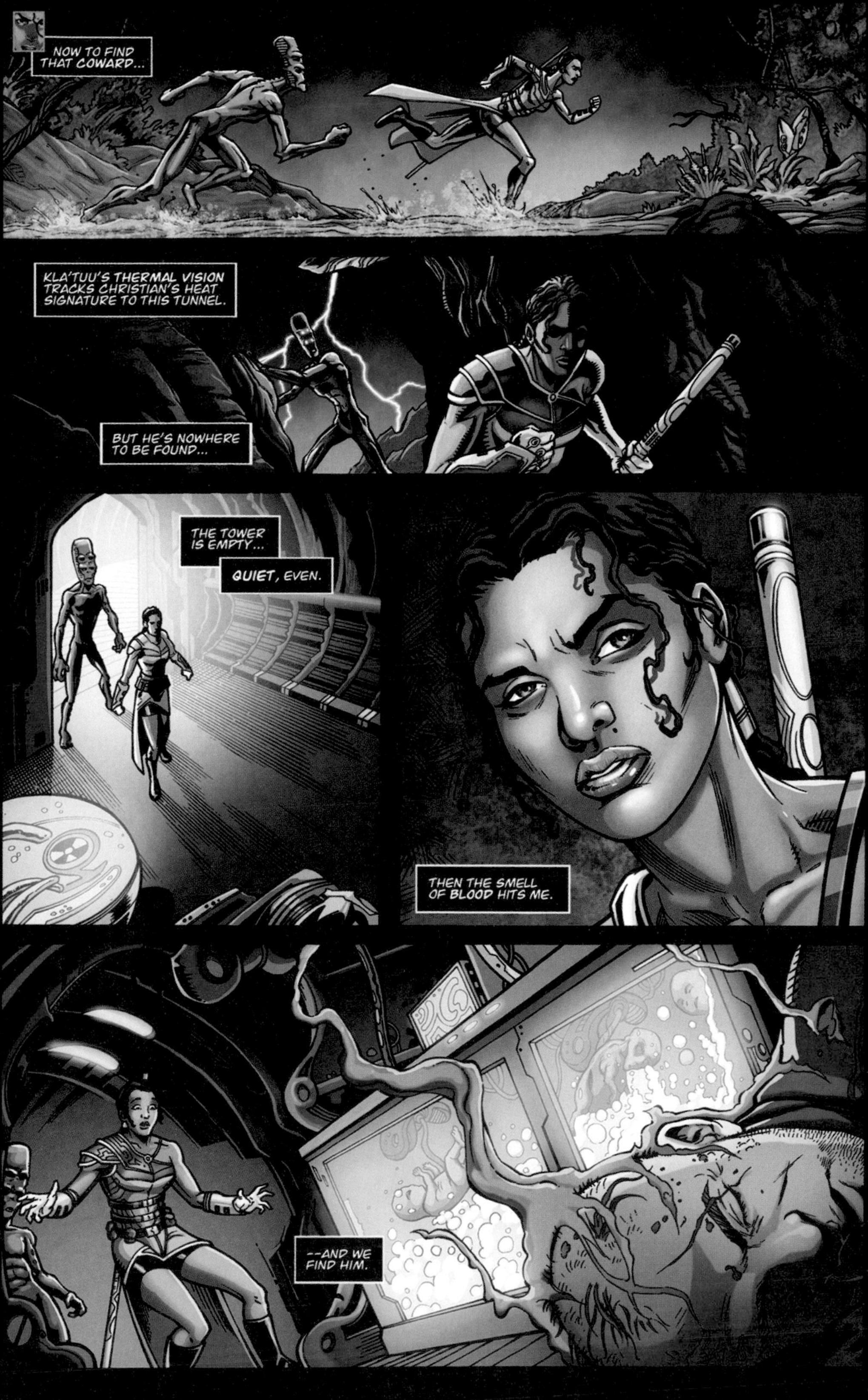
NOW TO FIND THAT COWARD...
KLA'TUU'S THERMAL VISION TRACKS CHRISTIAN'S HEAT SIGNATURE TO THIS TUNNEL.
BUT HE'S NOWHERE TO BE FOUND...
THE TOWER IS EMPTY...
QUIET, EVEN.
THEN THE SMELL OF BLOOD HITS ME.
--AND WE FIND HIM.

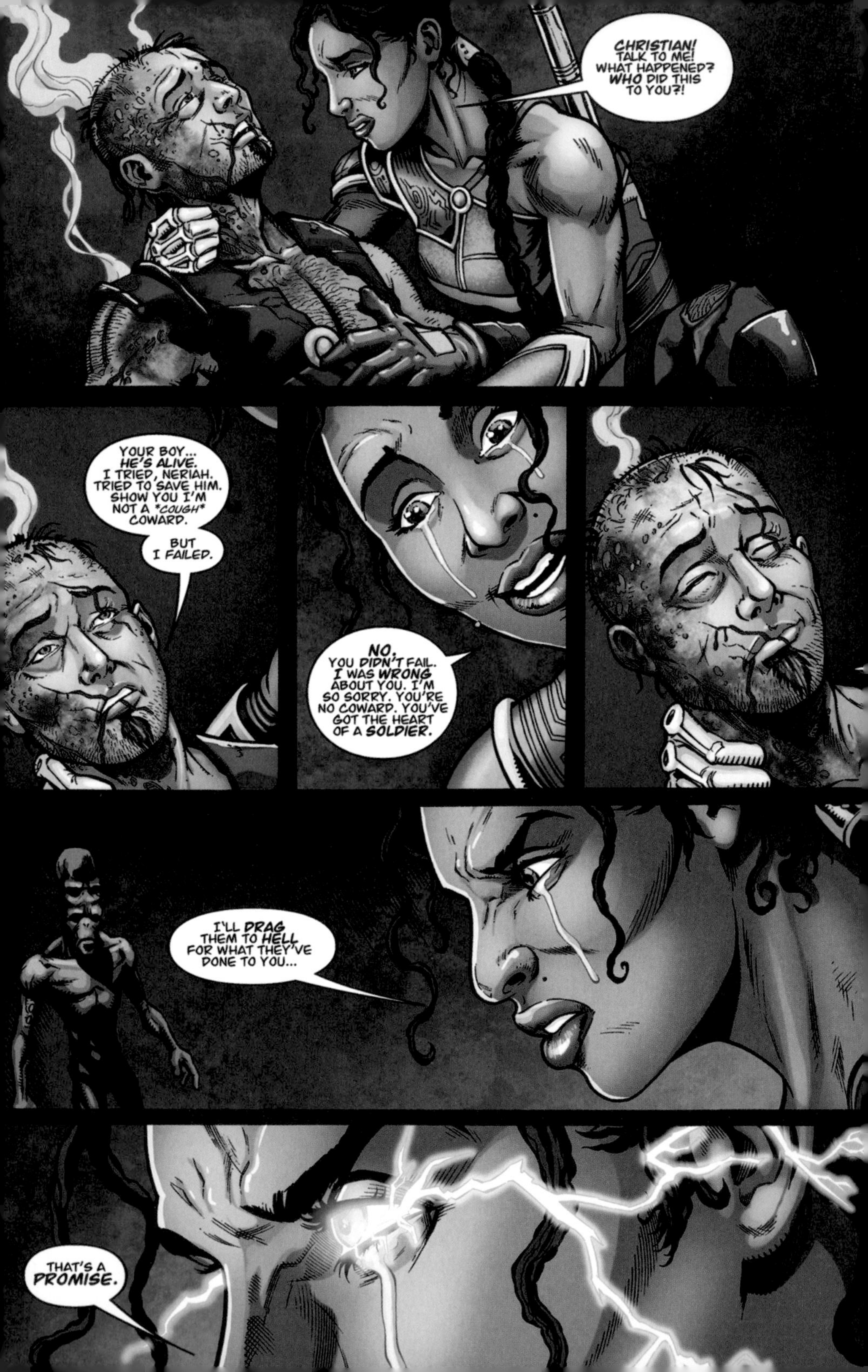
CHRISTIAN! TALK TO ME! WHAT HAPPENED? WHO DID THIS TO YOU?!
YOUR BOY... HE'S ALIVE. I TRIED, NERIAH. TRIED TO SAVE HIM. SHOW YOU I'M NOT A *COUGH* COWARD.
BUT I FAILED.
NO. YOU DIDN'T FAIL. I WAS WRONG ABOUT YOU. I'M SO SORRY. YOU'RE NO COWARD. YOU'VE GOT THE HEART OF A SOLDIER.
I'LL DRAG THEM TO HELL FOR WHAT THEY'VE DONE TO YOU...
THAT'S A PROMISE.

CHAPTER THREE

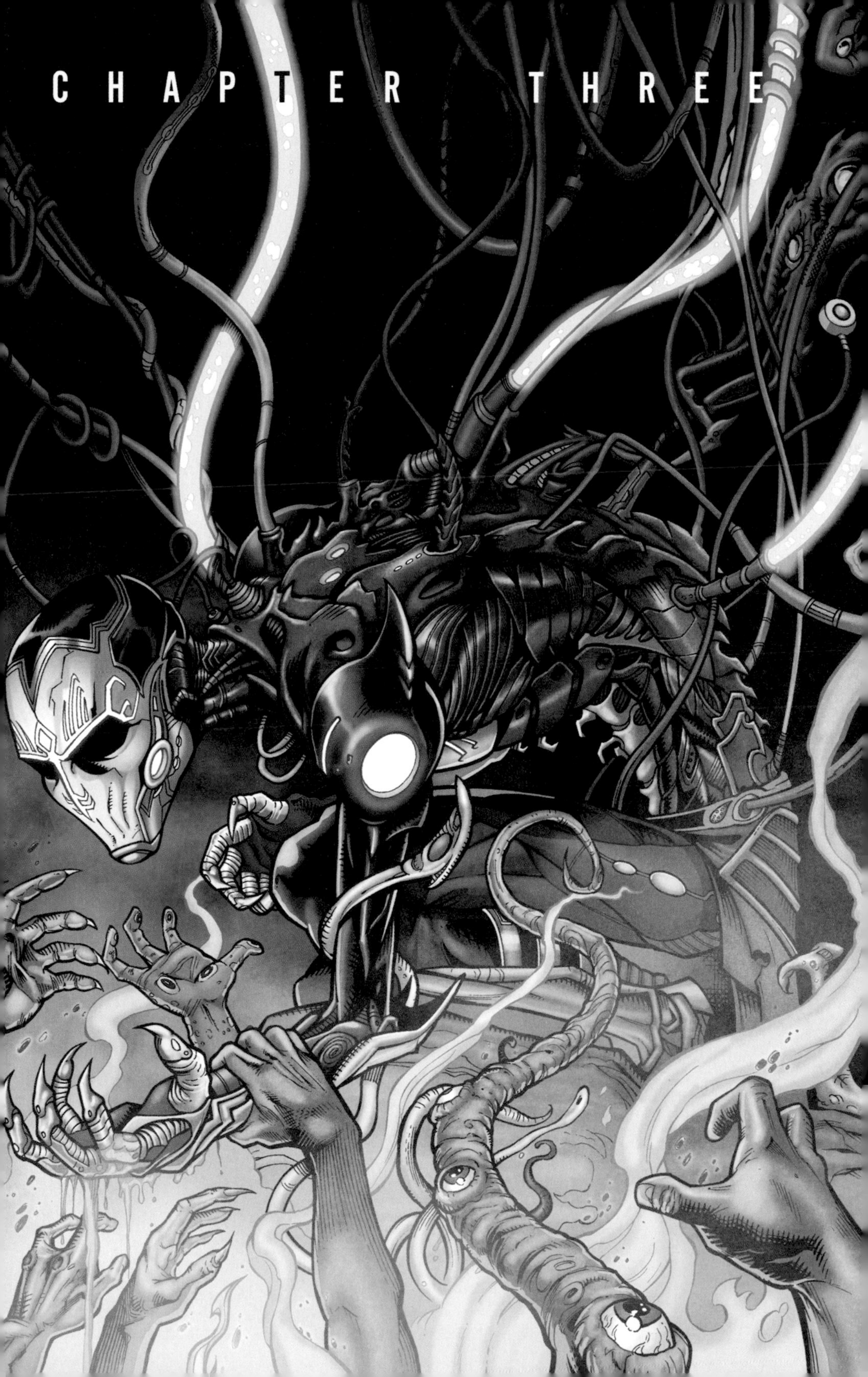

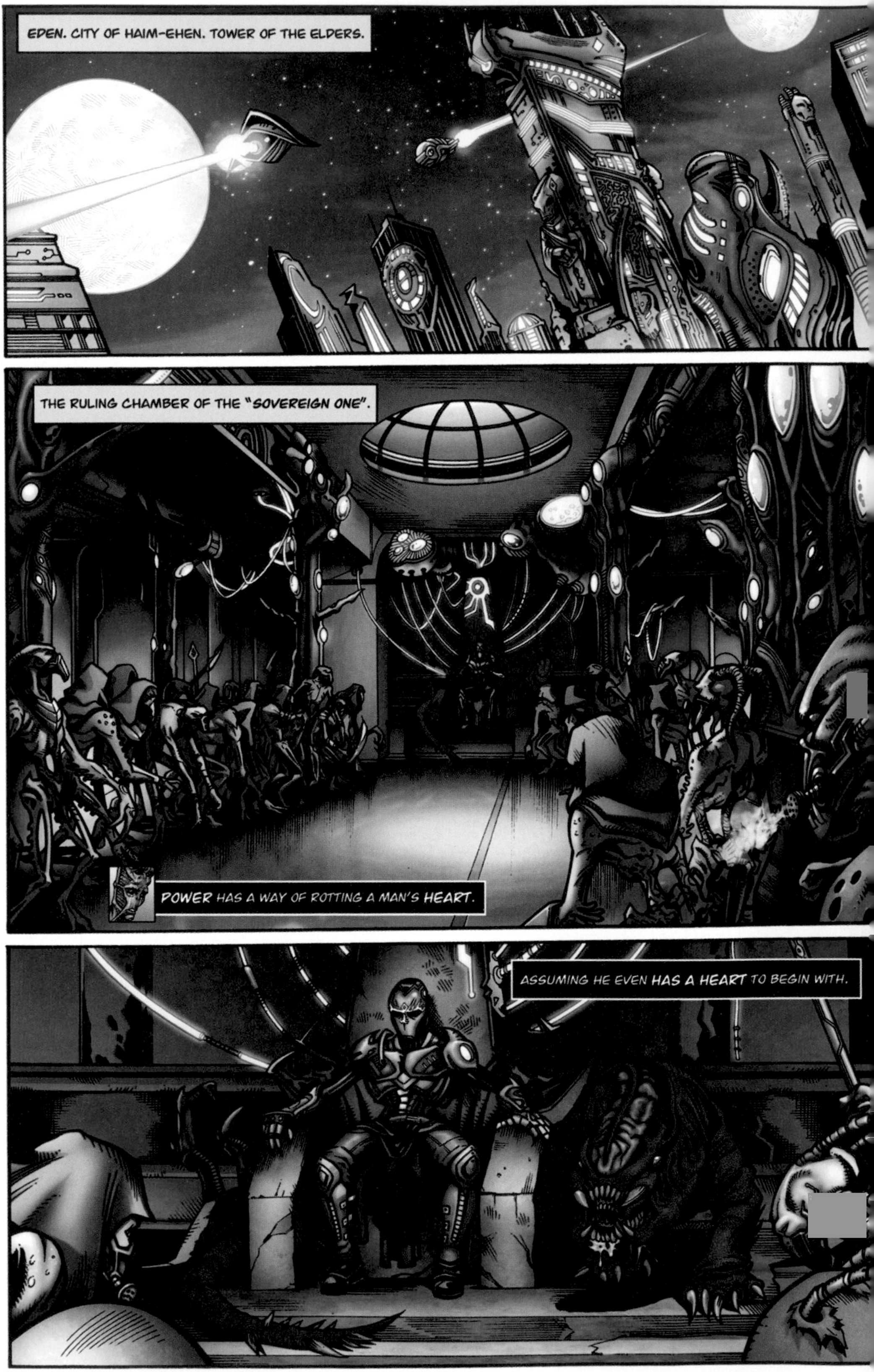
EDEN. CITY OF HAIM-EHEN. TOWER OF THE ELDERS.
THE RULING CHAMBER OF THE "SOVEREIGN ONE".
POWER HAS A WAY OF ROTTING A MAN'S HEART.
ASSUMING HE EVEN HAS A HEART TO BEGIN WITH.

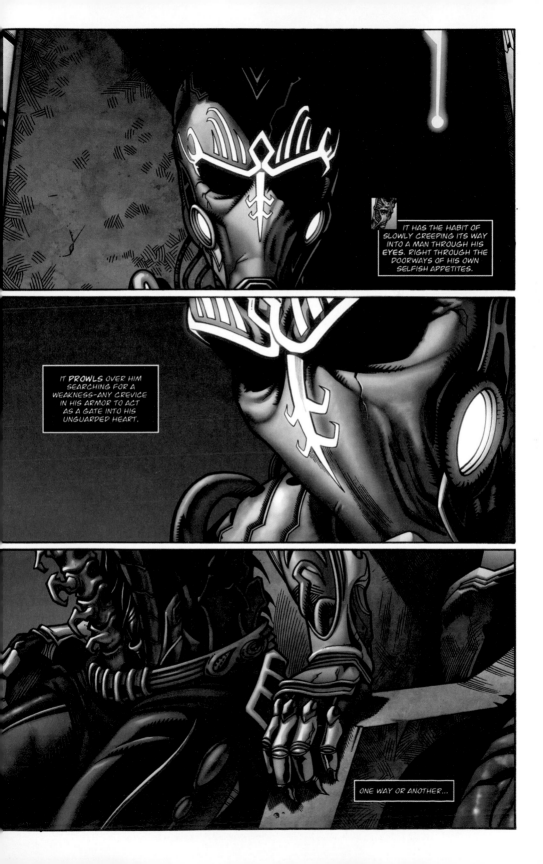

IT HAS THE HABIT OF SLOWLY CREEPING ITS WAY INTO A MAN THROUGH HIS EYES. RIGHT THROUGH THE DOORWAYS OF HIS OWN SELFISH APPETITES.

IT **PROWLS** OVER HIM SEARCHING FOR A WEAKNESS-ANY CREVICE IN HIS ARMOR TO ACT AS A GATE INTO HIS UNGUARDED HEART.

ONE WAY OR ANOTHER...

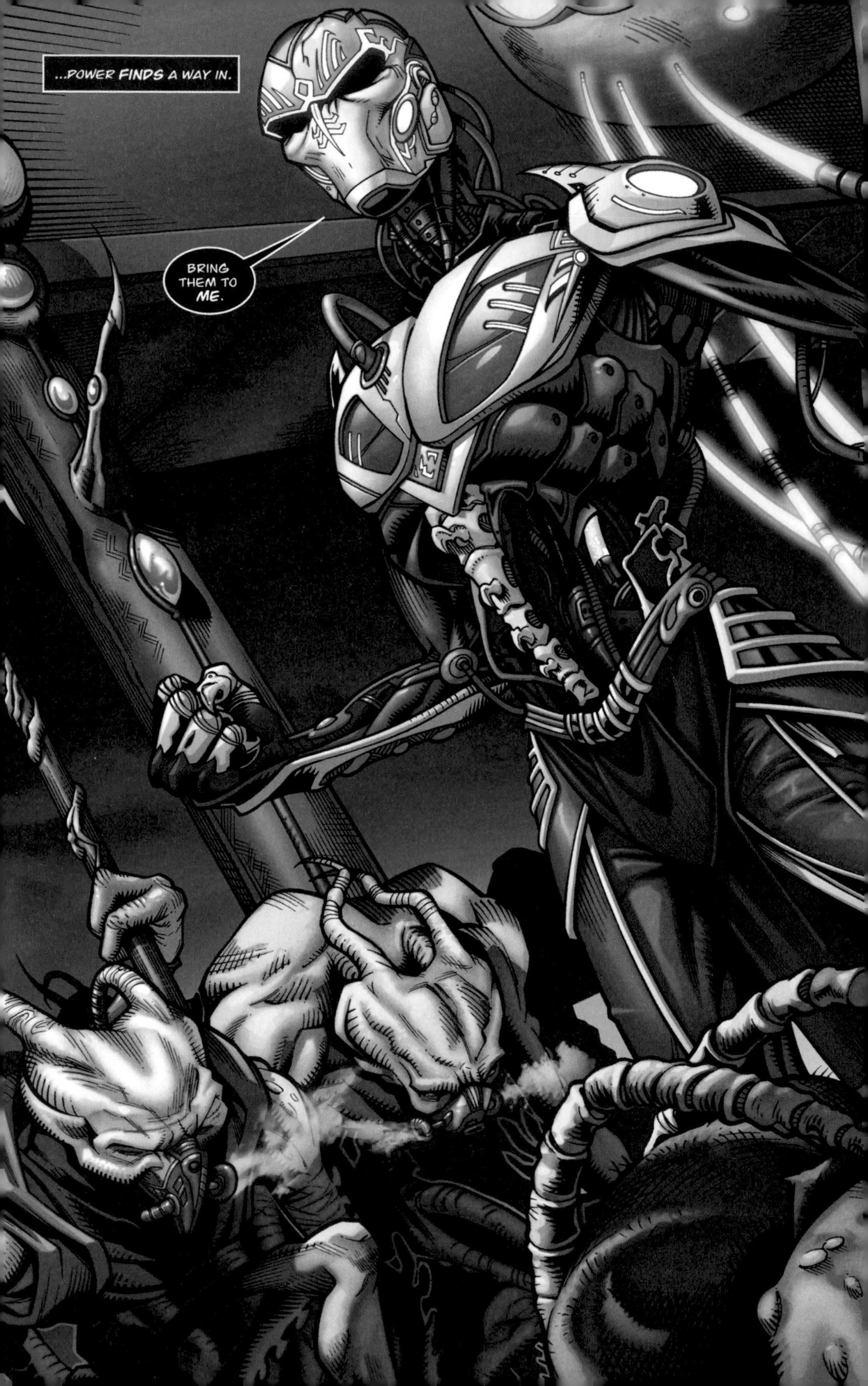
...POWER FINDS A WAY IN.
BRING THEM TO ME.

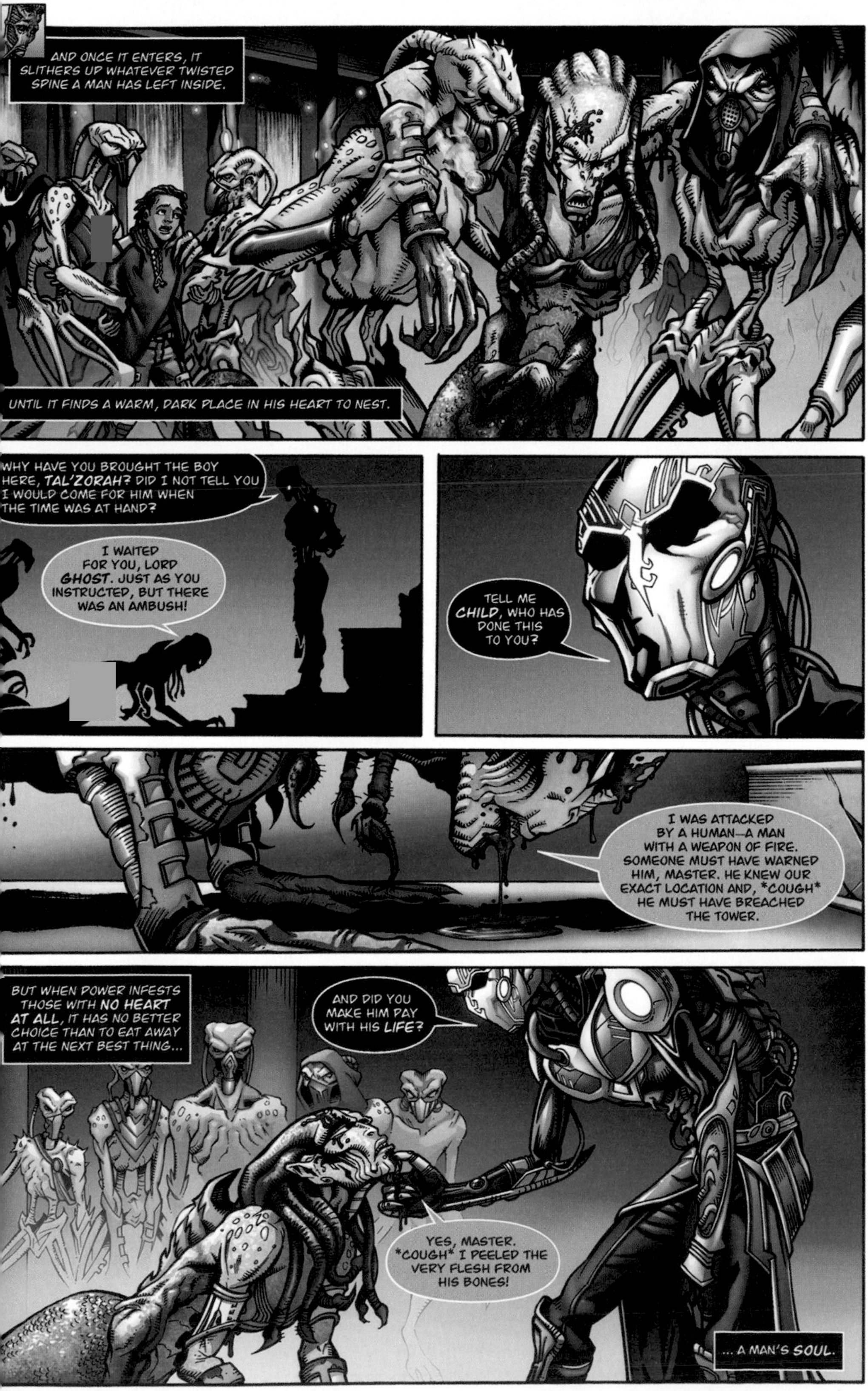
AND ONCE IT ENTERS, IT SLITHERS UP WHATEVER TWISTED SPINE A MAN HAS LEFT INSIDE.
UNTIL IT FINDS A WARM, DARK PLACE IN HIS HEART TO NEST.
WHY HAVE YOU BROUGHT THE BOY HERE, TAL'ZORAH? DID I NOT TELL YOU I WOULD COME FOR HIM WHEN THE TIME WAS AT HAND?
I WAITED FOR YOU, LORD GHOST. JUST AS YOU INSTRUCTED, BUT THERE WAS AN AMBUSH!
TELL ME CHILD, WHO HAS DONE THIS TO YOU?
I WAS ATTACKED BY A HUMAN—A MAN WITH A WEAPON OF FIRE. SOMEONE MUST HAVE WARNED HIM, MASTER. HE KNEW OUR EXACT LOCATION AND, *COUGH* HE MUST HAVE BREACHED THE TOWER.
BUT WHEN POWER INFESTS THOSE WITH NO HEART AT ALL, IT HAS NO BETTER CHOICE THAN TO EAT AWAY AT THE NEXT BEST THING...
AND DID YOU MAKE HIM PAY WITH HIS LIFE?
YES, MASTER. *COUGH* I PEELED THE VERY FLESH FROM HIS BONES!
... A MAN'S SOUL.

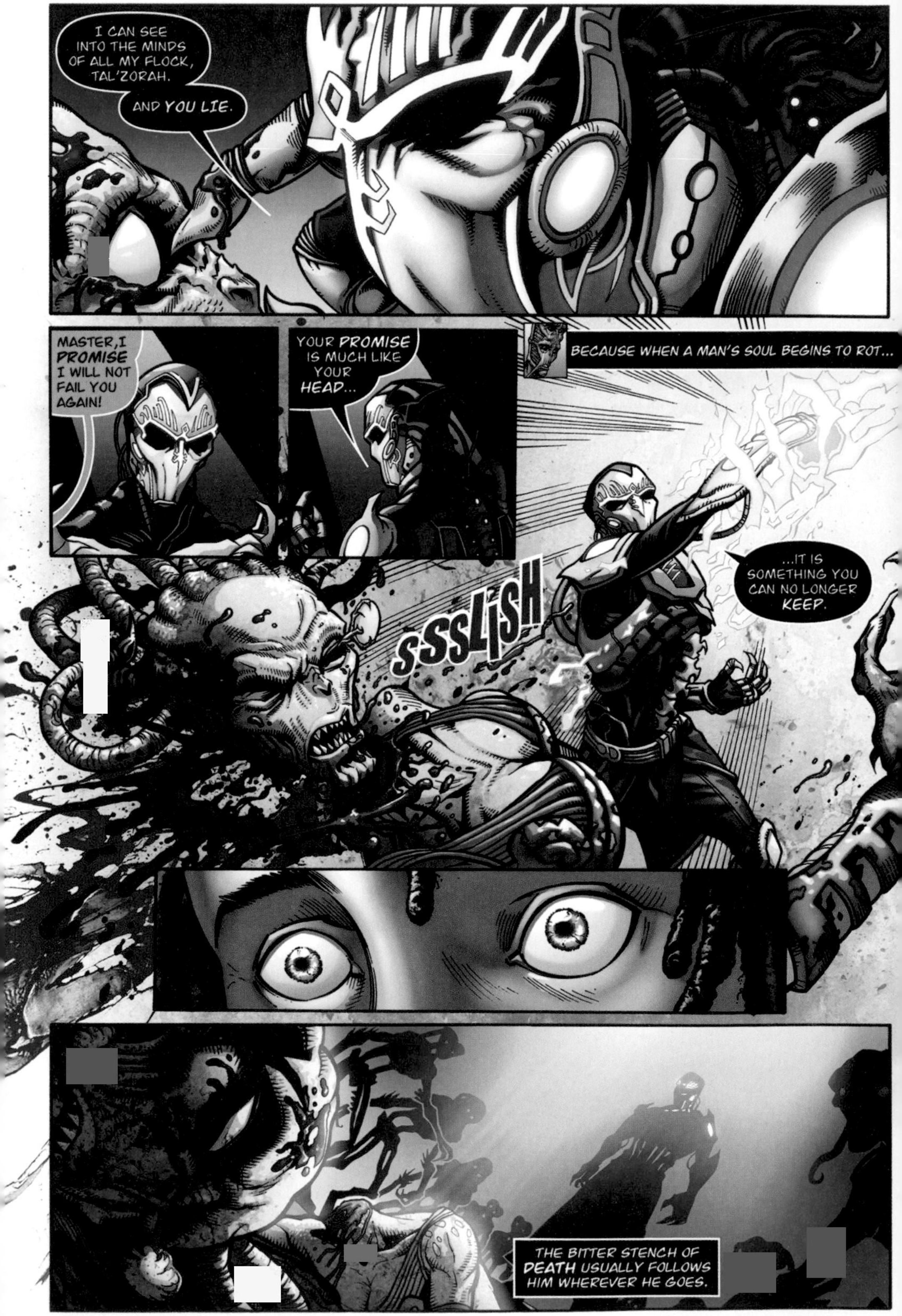
I CAN SEE INTO THE MINDS OF ALL MY FLOCK, TAL'ZORAH.
AND YOU LIE.
MASTER, I PROMISE I WILL NOT FAIL YOU AGAIN!
YOUR PROMISE IS MUCH LIKE YOUR HEAD...
BECAUSE WHEN A MAN'S SOUL BEGINS TO ROT...
SSSLISH
...IT IS SOMETHING YOU CAN NO LONGER KEEP.
THE BITTER STENCH OF DEATH USUALLY FOLLOWS HIM WHEREVER HE GOES.

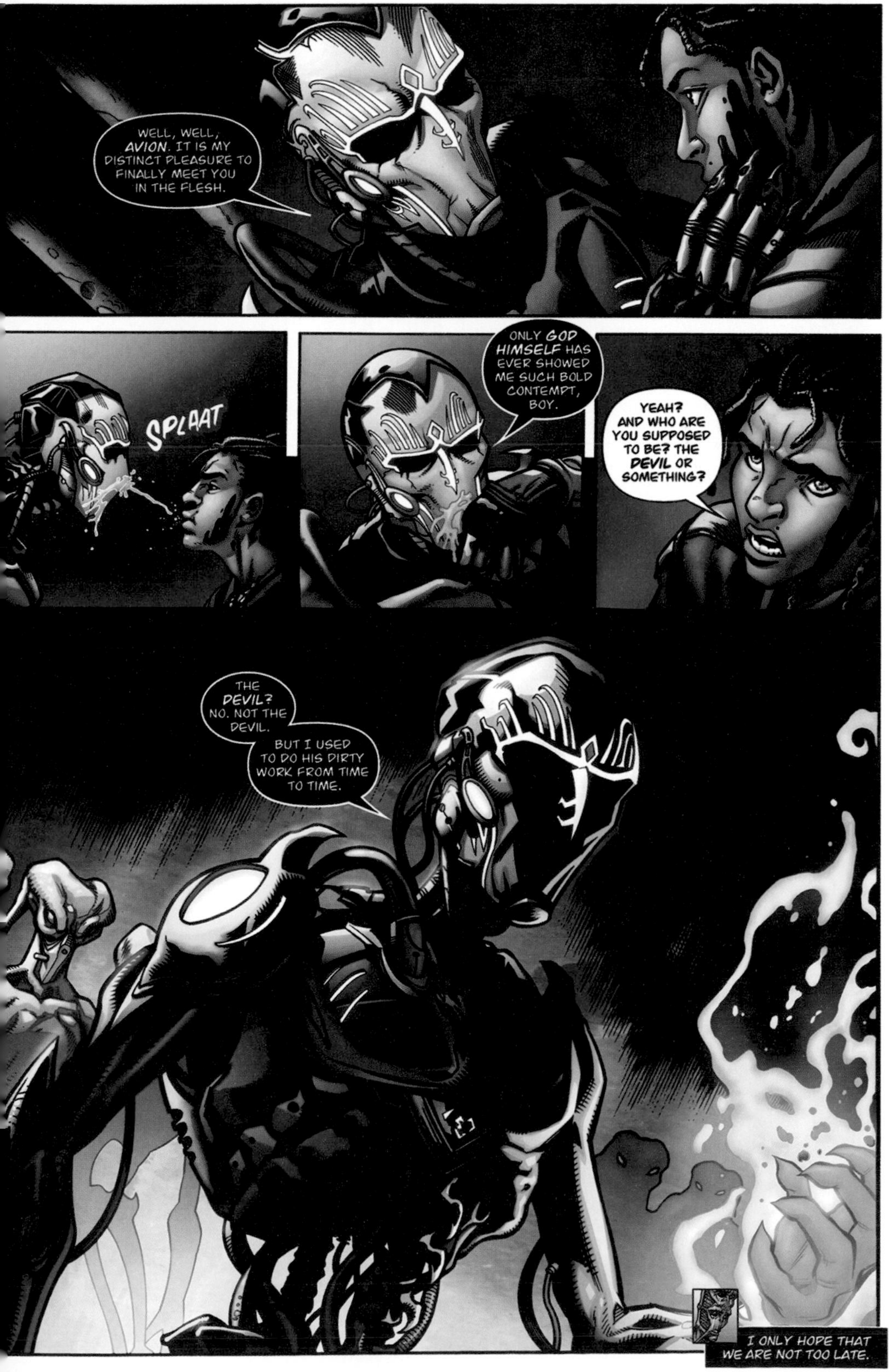
WELL, WELL, AVION. IT IS MY DISTINCT PLEASURE TO FINALLY MEET YOU IN THE FLESH.
SPLAAT
ONLY GOD HIMSELF HAS EVER SHOWED ME SUCH BOLD CONTEMPT, BOY.
YEAH? AND WHO ARE YOU SUPPOSED TO BE? THE DEVIL OR SOMETHING?
THE DEVIL? NO. NOT THE DEVIL.
BUT I USED TO DO HIS DIRTY WORK FROM TIME TO TIME.
I ONLY HOPE THAT WE ARE NOT TOO LATE.

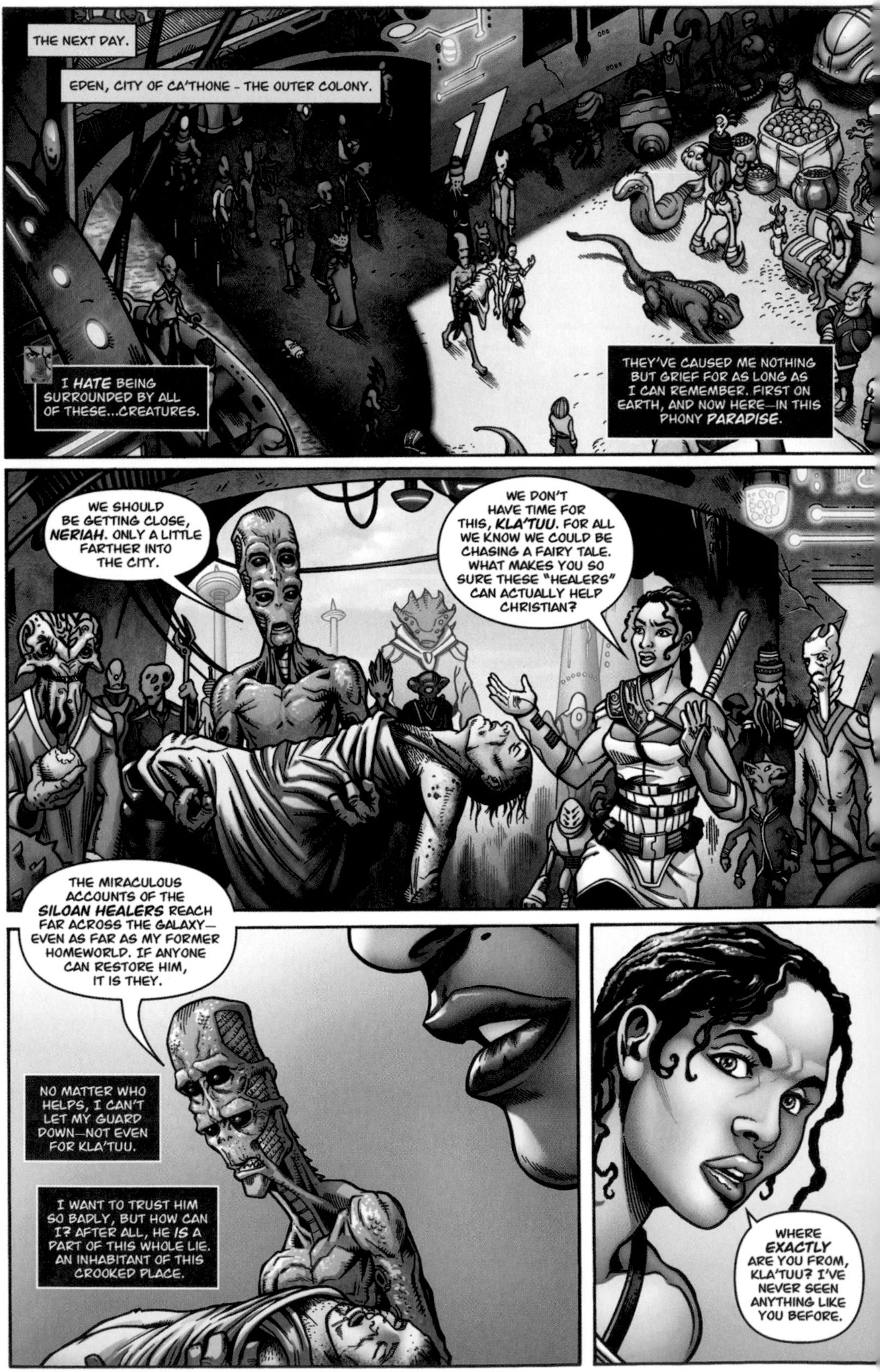
THE NEXT DAY.
EDEN, CITY OF CA'THONE - THE OUTER COLONY.
I HATE BEING SURROUNDED BY ALL OF THESE...CREATURES.
THEY'VE CAUSED ME NOTHING BUT GRIEF FOR AS LONG AS I CAN REMEMBER. FIRST ON EARTH, AND NOW HERE—IN THIS PHONY PARADISE.
WE SHOULD BE GETTING CLOSE, NERIAH. ONLY A LITTLE FARTHER INTO THE CITY.
WE DON'T HAVE TIME FOR THIS, KLA'TUU. FOR ALL WE KNOW WE COULD BE CHASING A FAIRY TALE. WHAT MAKES YOU SO SURE THESE "HEALERS" CAN ACTUALLY HELP CHRISTIAN?
THE MIRACULOUS ACCOUNTS OF THE SILOAN HEALERS REACH FAR ACROSS THE GALAXY—EVEN AS FAR AS MY FORMER HOMEWORLD. IF ANYONE CAN RESTORE HIM, IT IS THEY.
NO MATTER WHO HELPS, I CAN'T LET MY GUARD DOWN—NOT EVEN FOR KLA'TUU.
I WANT TO TRUST HIM SO BADLY, BUT HOW CAN I? AFTER ALL, HE IS A PART OF THIS WHOLE LIE. AN INHABITANT OF THIS CROOKED PLACE.
WHERE EXACTLY ARE YOU FROM, KLA'TUU? I'VE NEVER SEEN ANYTHING LIKE YOU BEFORE.

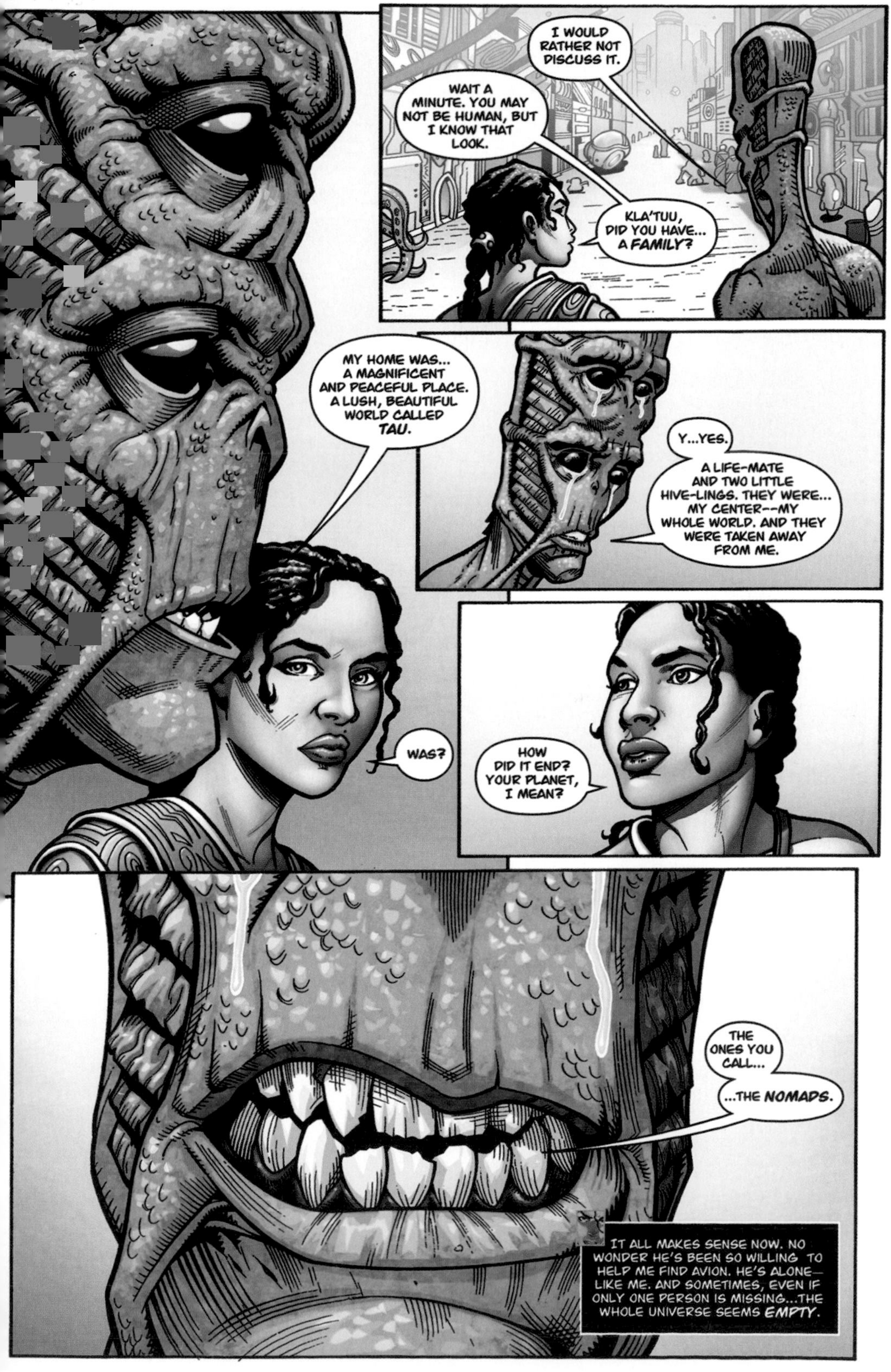
WAIT A MINUTE. YOU MAY NOT BE HUMAN, BUT I KNOW THAT LOOK.
I WOULD RATHER NOT DISCUSS IT.
KLA'TUU, DID YOU HAVE... A *FAMILY*?
Y...YES.
A LIFE-MATE AND TWO LITTLE HIVE-LINGS. THEY WERE... MY CENTER--MY WHOLE WORLD. AND THEY WERE TAKEN AWAY FROM ME.
MY HOME WAS... A MAGNIFICENT AND PEACEFUL PLACE. A LUSH, BEAUTIFUL WORLD CALLED *TAU*.
WAS?
HOW DID IT END? YOUR PLANET, I MEAN?
THE ONES YOU CALL...
...THE *NOMADS*.
IT ALL MAKES SENSE NOW. NO WONDER HE'S BEEN SO WILLING TO HELP ME FIND AVION. HE'S ALONE— LIKE ME. AND SOMETIMES, EVEN IF ONLY ONE PERSON IS MISSING...THE WHOLE UNIVERSE SEEMS *EMPTY*.

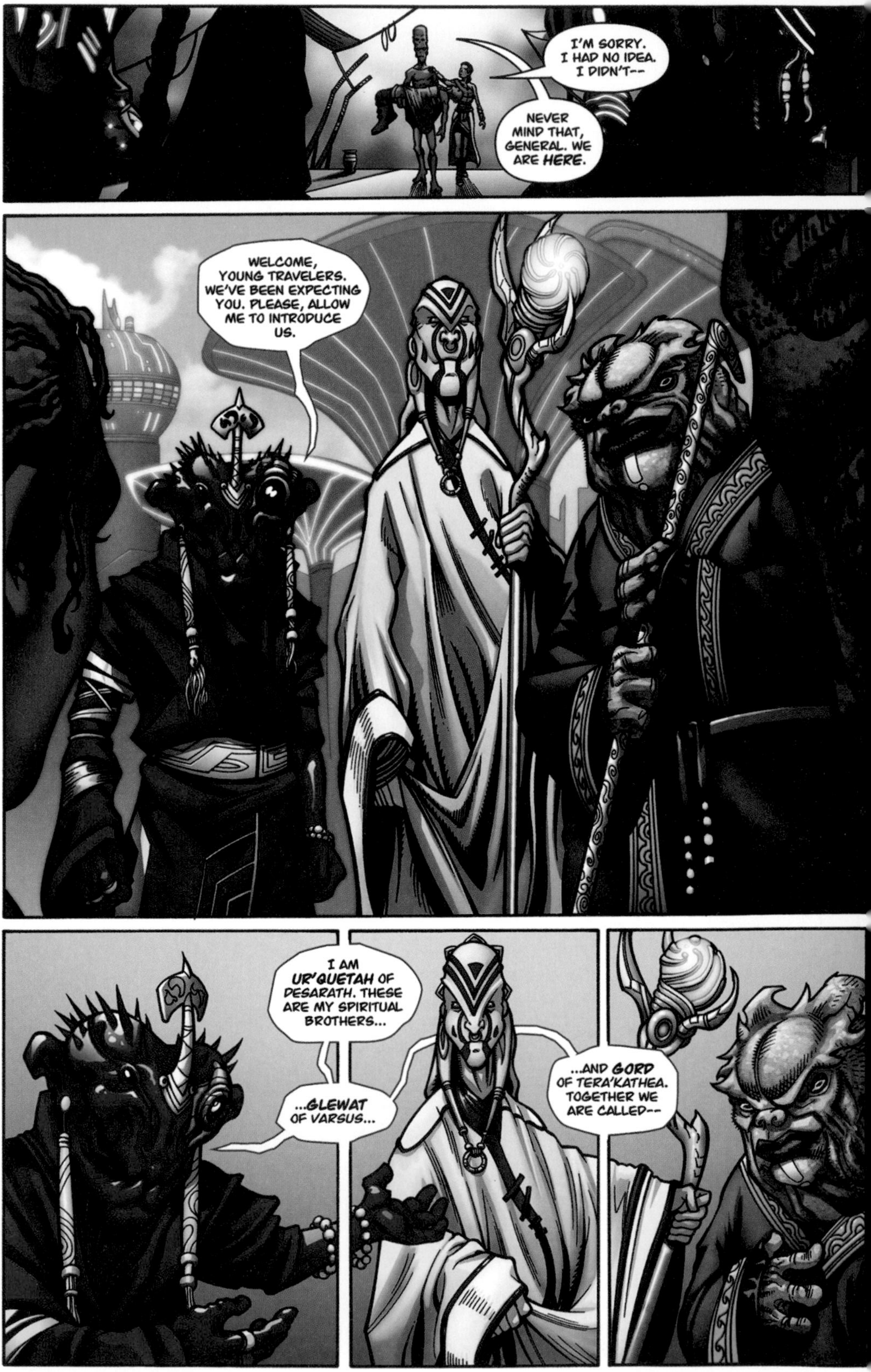
I'M SORRY. I HAD NO IDEA. I DIDN'T--
NEVER MIND THAT, GENERAL. WE ARE **HERE**.
WELCOME, YOUNG TRAVELERS. WE'VE BEEN EXPECTING YOU. PLEASE, ALLOW ME TO INTRODUCE US.
I AM **UR'QUETAH** OF DESARATH. THESE ARE MY SPIRITUAL BROTHERS...
...**GLEWAT** OF VARSUS...
...AND **GORD** OF TERA'KATHEA. TOGETHER WE ARE CALLED--

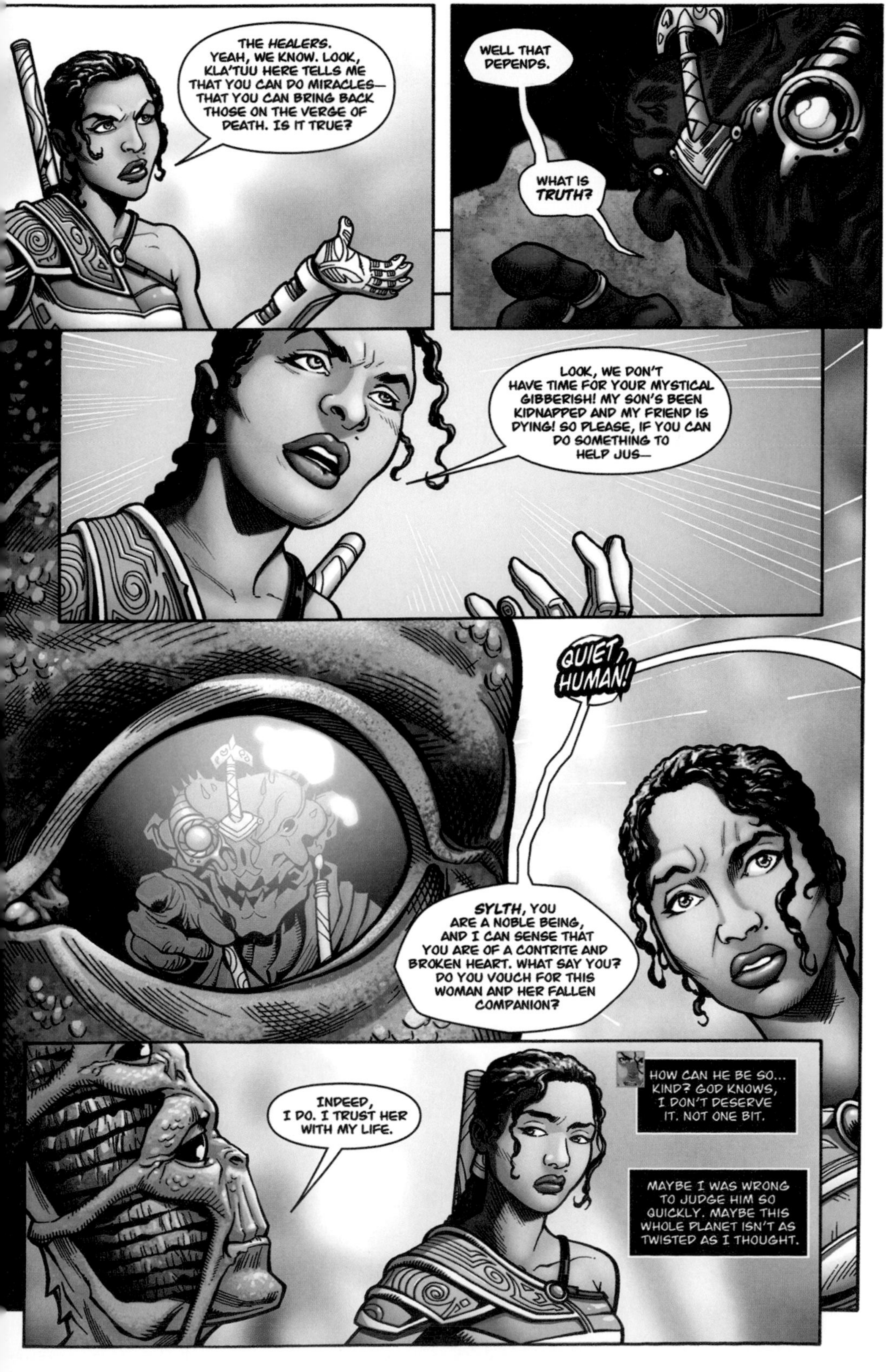
THE HEALERS. YEAH, WE KNOW. LOOK, KLA'TUU HERE TELLS ME THAT YOU CAN DO MIRACLES— THAT YOU CAN BRING BACK THOSE ON THE VERGE OF DEATH. IS IT TRUE?
WELL THAT DEPENDS.
WHAT IS *TRUTH?*
LOOK, WE DON'T HAVE TIME FOR YOUR MYSTICAL GIBBERISH! MY SON'S BEEN KIDNAPPED AND MY FRIEND IS DYING! SO PLEASE, IF YOU CAN DO SOMETHING TO HELP JUS—
QUIET, HUMAN!
SYLTH, YOU ARE A NOBLE BEING, AND I CAN SENSE THAT YOU ARE OF A CONTRITE AND BROKEN HEART. WHAT SAY YOU? DO YOU VOUCH FOR THIS WOMAN AND HER FALLEN COMPANION?
INDEED, I DO. I TRUST HER WITH MY LIFE.
HOW CAN HE BE SO... KIND? GOD KNOWS, I DON'T DESERVE IT. NOT ONE BIT.
MAYBE I WAS WRONG TO JUDGE HIM SO QUICKLY. MAYBE THIS WHOLE PLANET ISN'T AS TWISTED AS I THOUGHT.

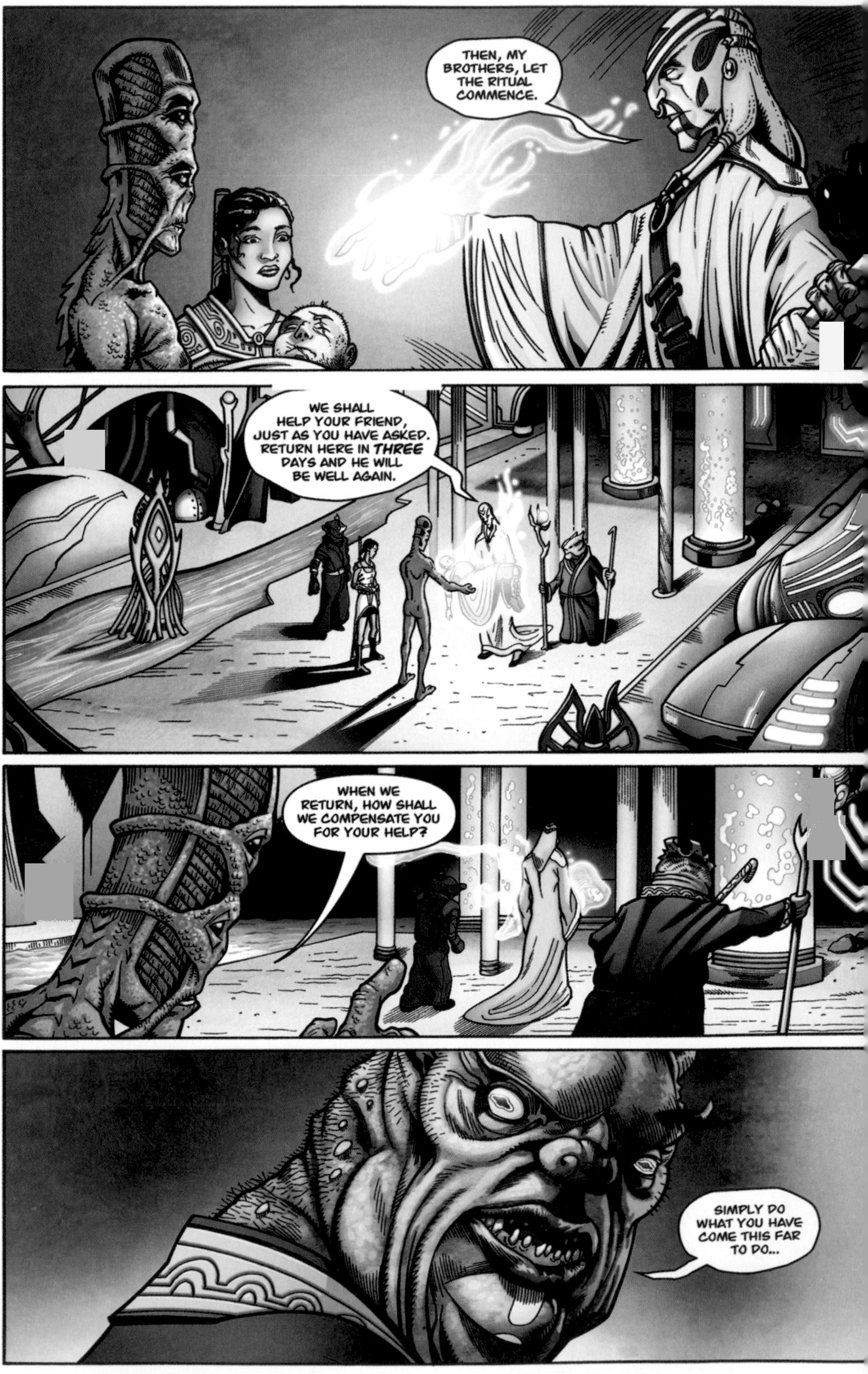
THEN, MY BROTHERS, LET THE RITUAL COMMENCE.
WE SHALL HELP YOUR FRIEND, JUST AS YOU HAVE ASKED. RETURN HERE IN THREE DAYS AND HE WILL BE WELL AGAIN.
WHEN WE RETURN, HOW SHALL WE COMPENSATE YOU FOR YOUR HELP?
SIMPLY DO WHAT YOU HAVE COME THIS FAR TO DO...

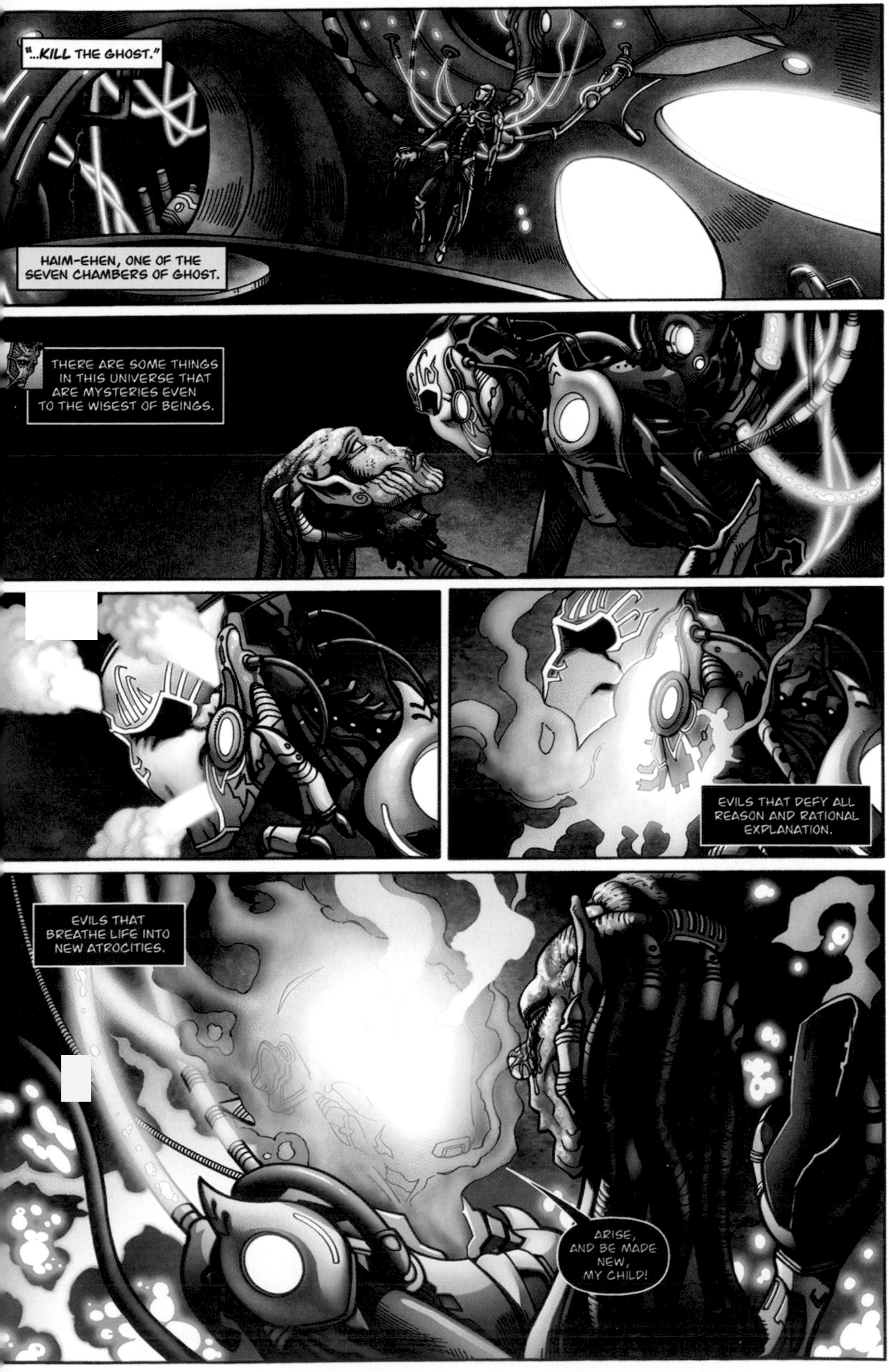
"...KILL THE GHOST."
HAIM-EHEN, ONE OF THE SEVEN CHAMBERS OF GHOST.
THERE ARE SOME THINGS IN THIS UNIVERSE THAT ARE MYSTERIES EVEN TO THE WISEST OF BEINGS.
EVILS THAT DEFY ALL REASON AND RATIONAL EXPLANATION.
EVILS THAT BREATHE LIFE INTO NEW ATROCITIES.
ARISE, AND BE MADE NEW, MY CHILD!

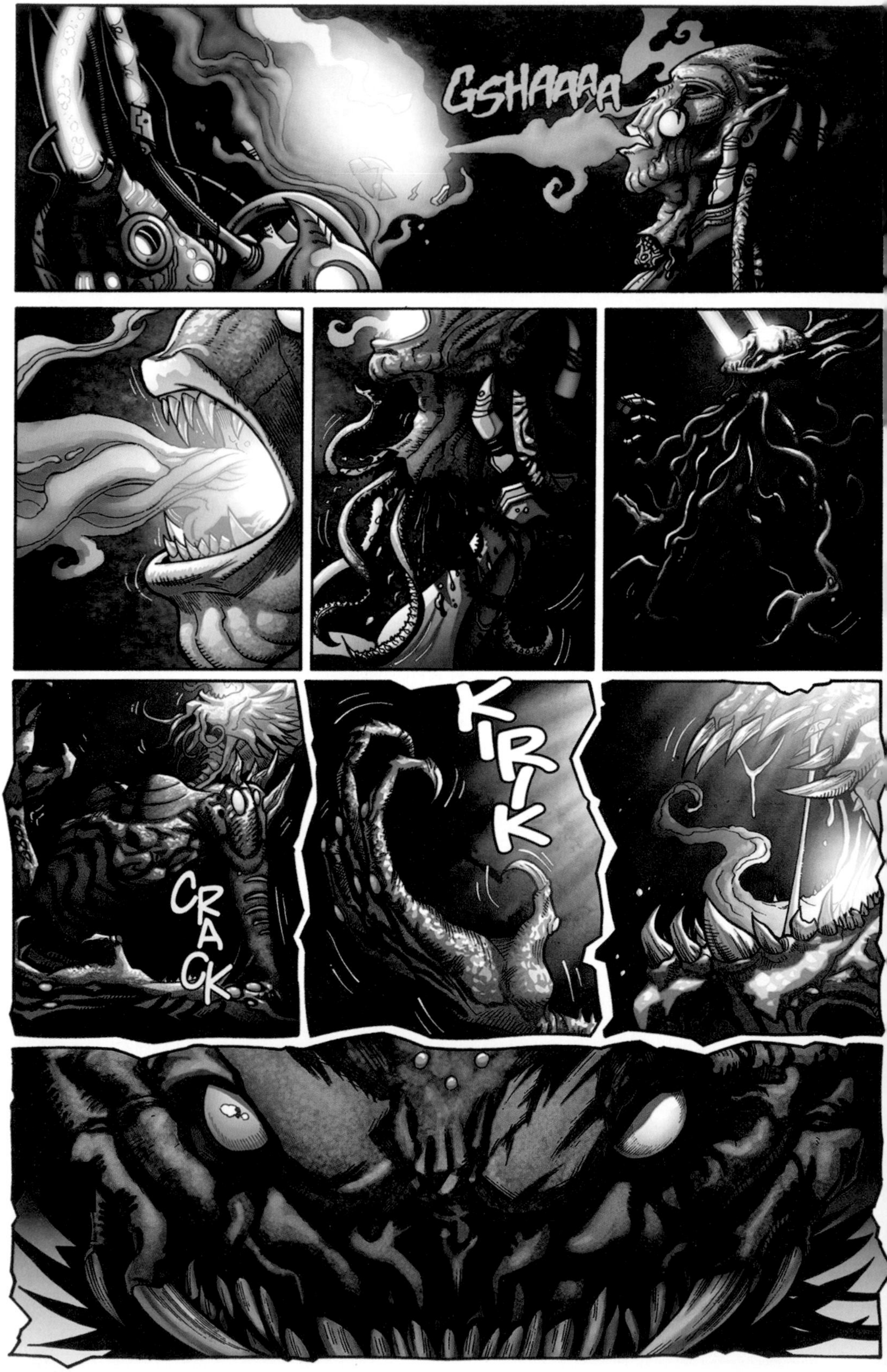
GSHAAAA
CRACK
KIRIK

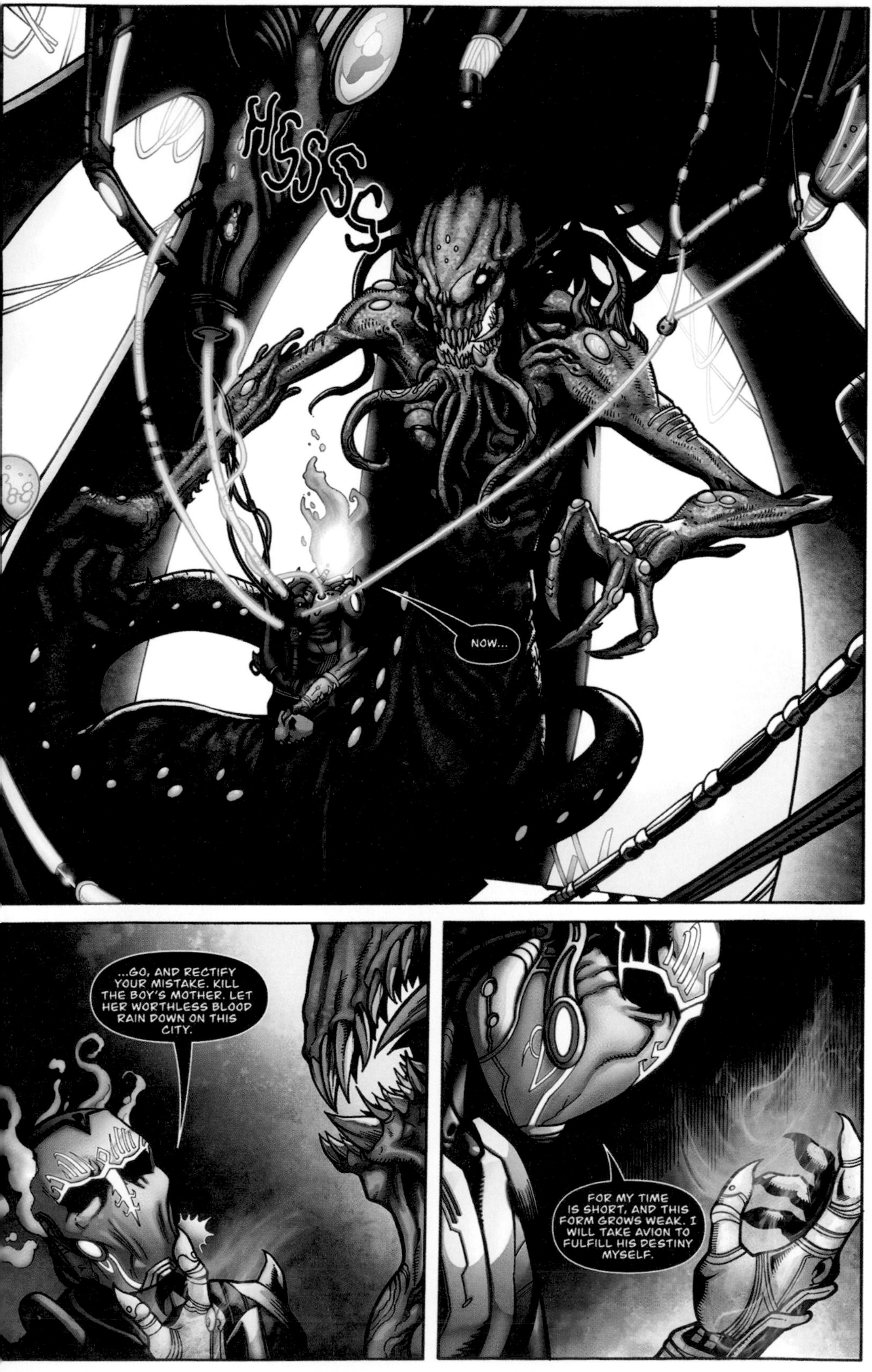
HSSSS
NOW...
...GO, AND RECTIFY YOUR MISTAKE. KILL THE BOY'S MOTHER. LET HER WORTHLESS BLOOD RAIN DOWN ON THIS CITY.
FOR MY TIME IS SHORT, AND THIS FORM GROWS WEAK. I WILL TAKE AVION TO FULFILL HIS DESTINY MYSELF.

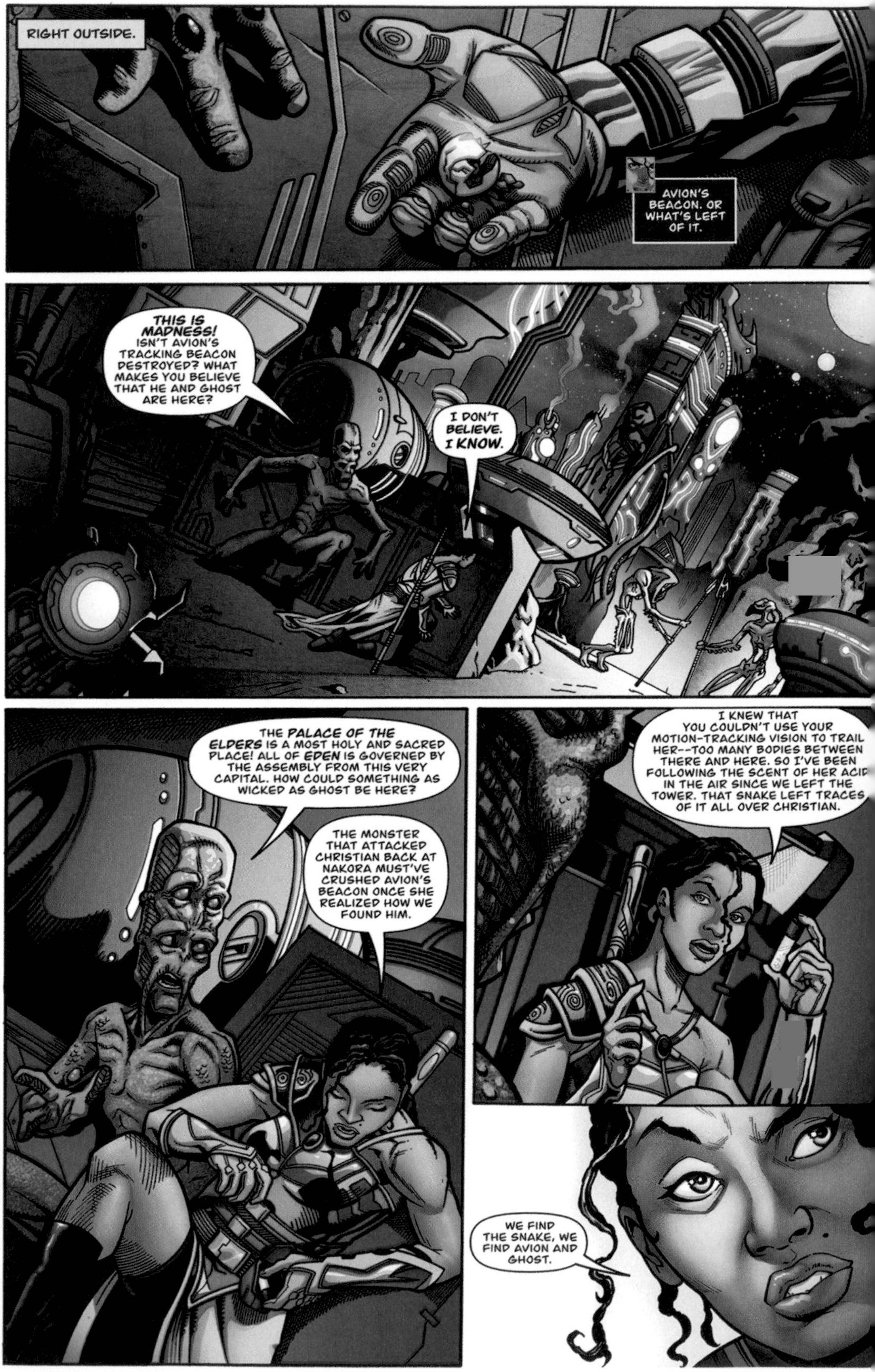
RIGHT OUTSIDE.
AVION'S BEACON. OR WHAT'S LEFT OF IT.
THIS IS MADNESS! ISN'T AVION'S TRACKING BEACON DESTROYED? WHAT MAKES YOU BELIEVE THAT HE AND GHOST ARE HERE?
I DON'T BELIEVE. I KNOW.
THE PALACE OF THE ELDERS IS A MOST HOLY AND SACRED PLACE! ALL OF EDEN IS GOVERNED BY THE ASSEMBLY FROM THIS VERY CAPITAL. HOW COULD SOMETHING AS WICKED AS GHOST BE HERE?
THE MONSTER THAT ATTACKED CHRISTIAN BACK AT NAKORA MUST'VE CRUSHED AVION'S BEACON ONCE SHE REALIZED HOW WE FOUND HIM.
I KNEW THAT YOU COULDN'T USE YOUR MOTION-TRACKING VISION TO TRAIL HER--TOO MANY BODIES BETWEEN THERE AND HERE. SO I'VE BEEN FOLLOWING THE SCENT OF HER ACID IN THE AIR SINCE WE LEFT THE TOWER. THAT SNAKE LEFT TRACES OF IT ALL OVER CHRISTIAN.
WE FIND THE SNAKE, WE FIND AVION AND GHOST.

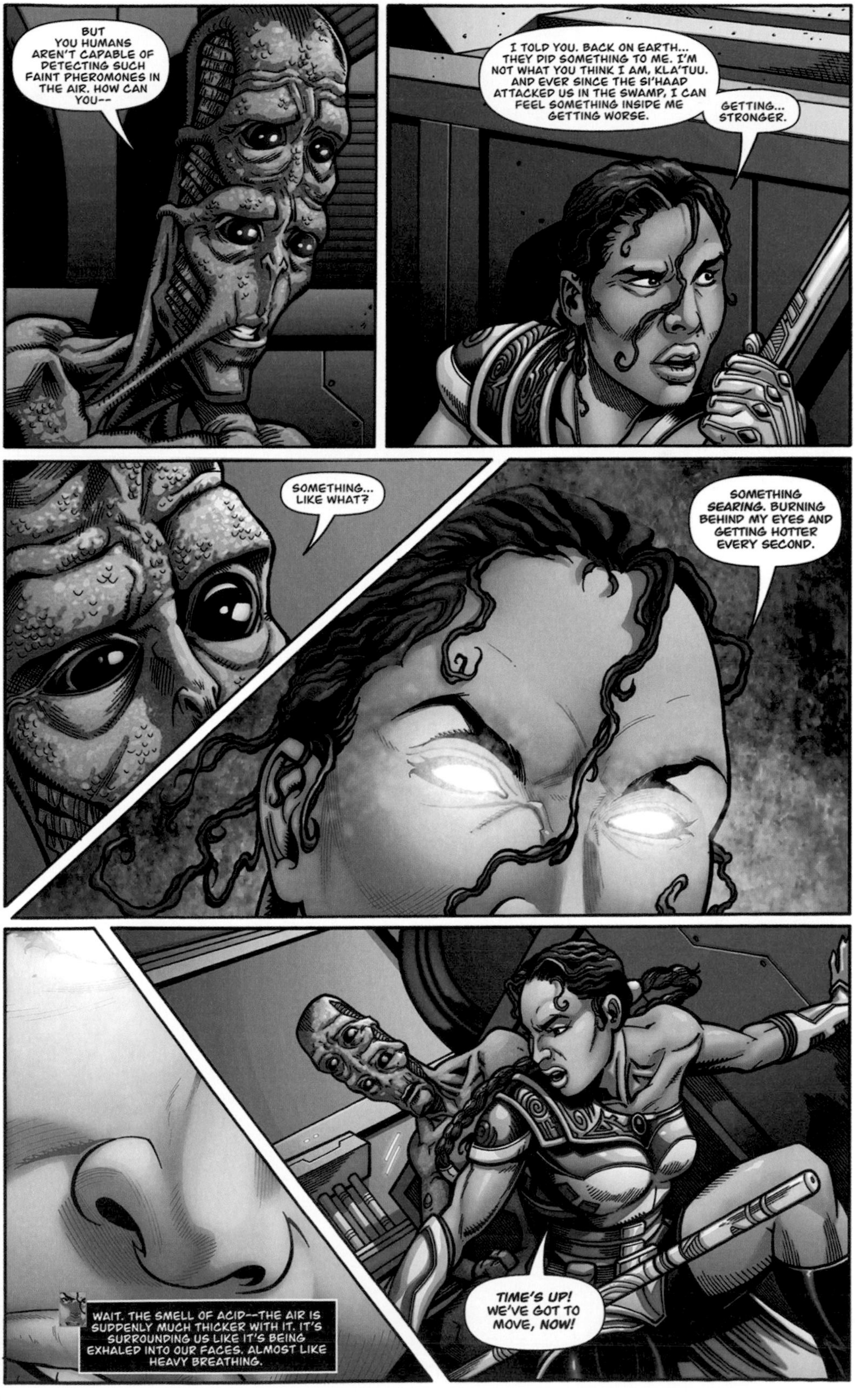

BUT YOU HUMANS AREN'T CAPABLE OF DETECTING SUCH FAINT PHEROMONES IN THE AIR. HOW CAN YOU--
I TOLD YOU. BACK ON EARTH... THEY DID SOMETHING TO ME. I'M NOT WHAT YOU THINK I AM, KLA'TUU. AND EVER SINCE THE SI'HAAD ATTACKED US IN THE SWAMP, I CAN FEEL SOMETHING INSIDE ME GETTING WORSE.
GETTING... STRONGER.
SOMETHING... LIKE WHAT?
SOMETHING SEARING. BURNING BEHIND MY EYES AND GETTING HOTTER EVERY SECOND.
WAIT. THE SMELL OF ACID--THE AIR IS SUDDENLY MUCH THICKER WITH IT. IT'S SURROUNDING US LIKE IT'S BEING EXHALED INTO OUR FACES. ALMOST LIKE HEAVY BREATHING.
TIME'S UP! WE'VE GOT TO MOVE, NOW!

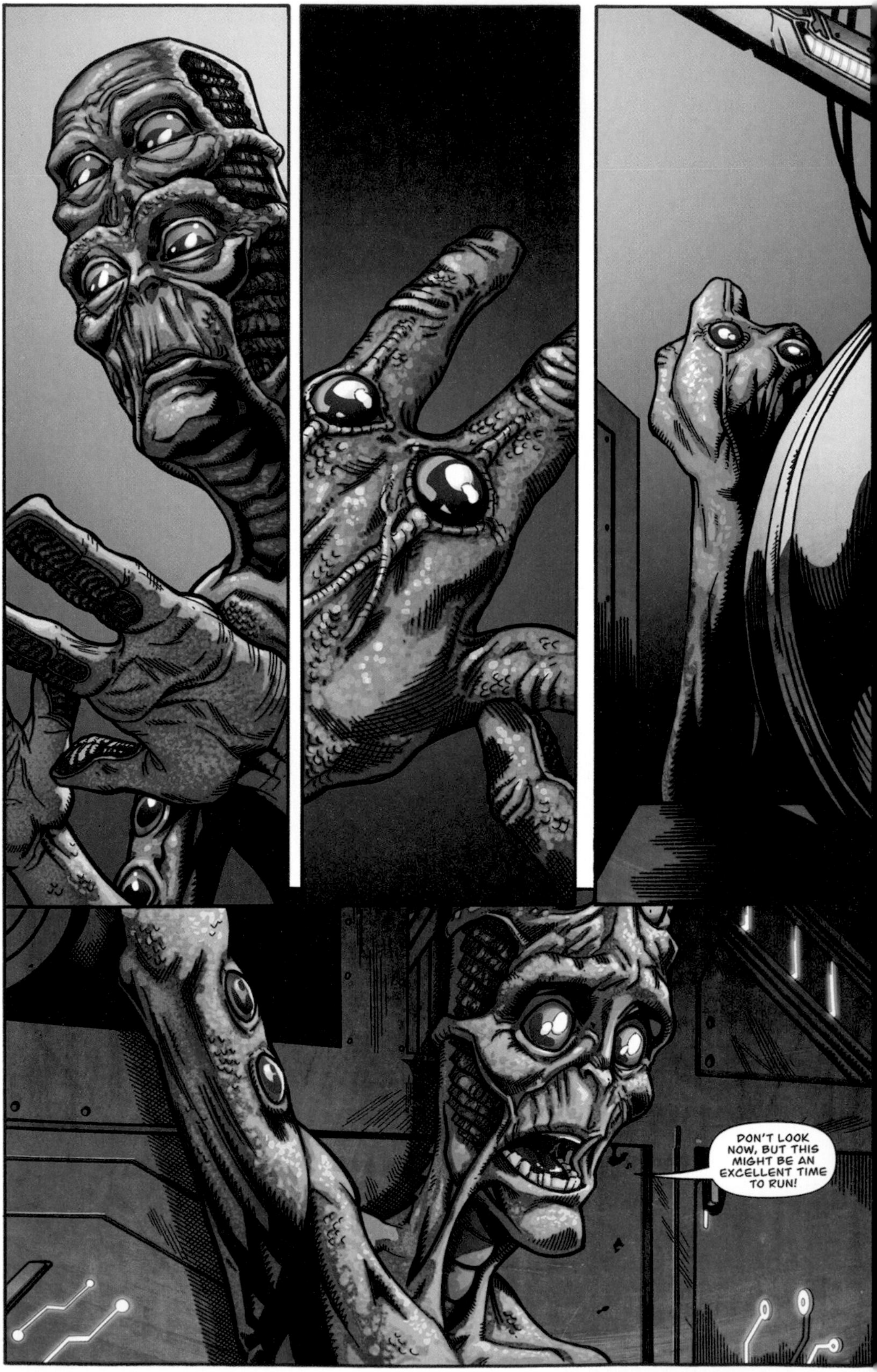
DON'T LOOK NOW, BUT THIS MIGHT BE AN EXCELLENT TIME TO RUN!

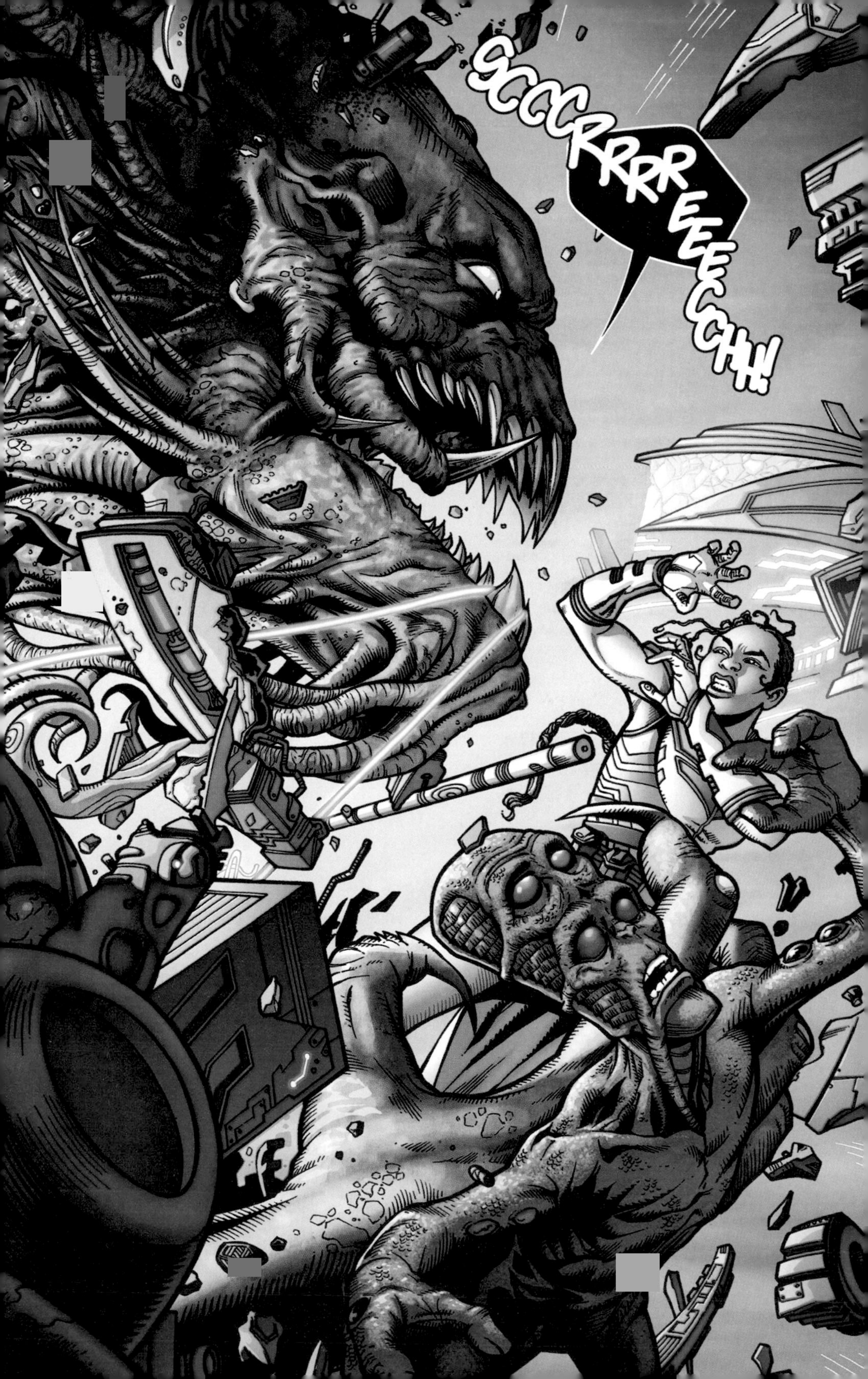
SCCCRRRREEECCHH!!

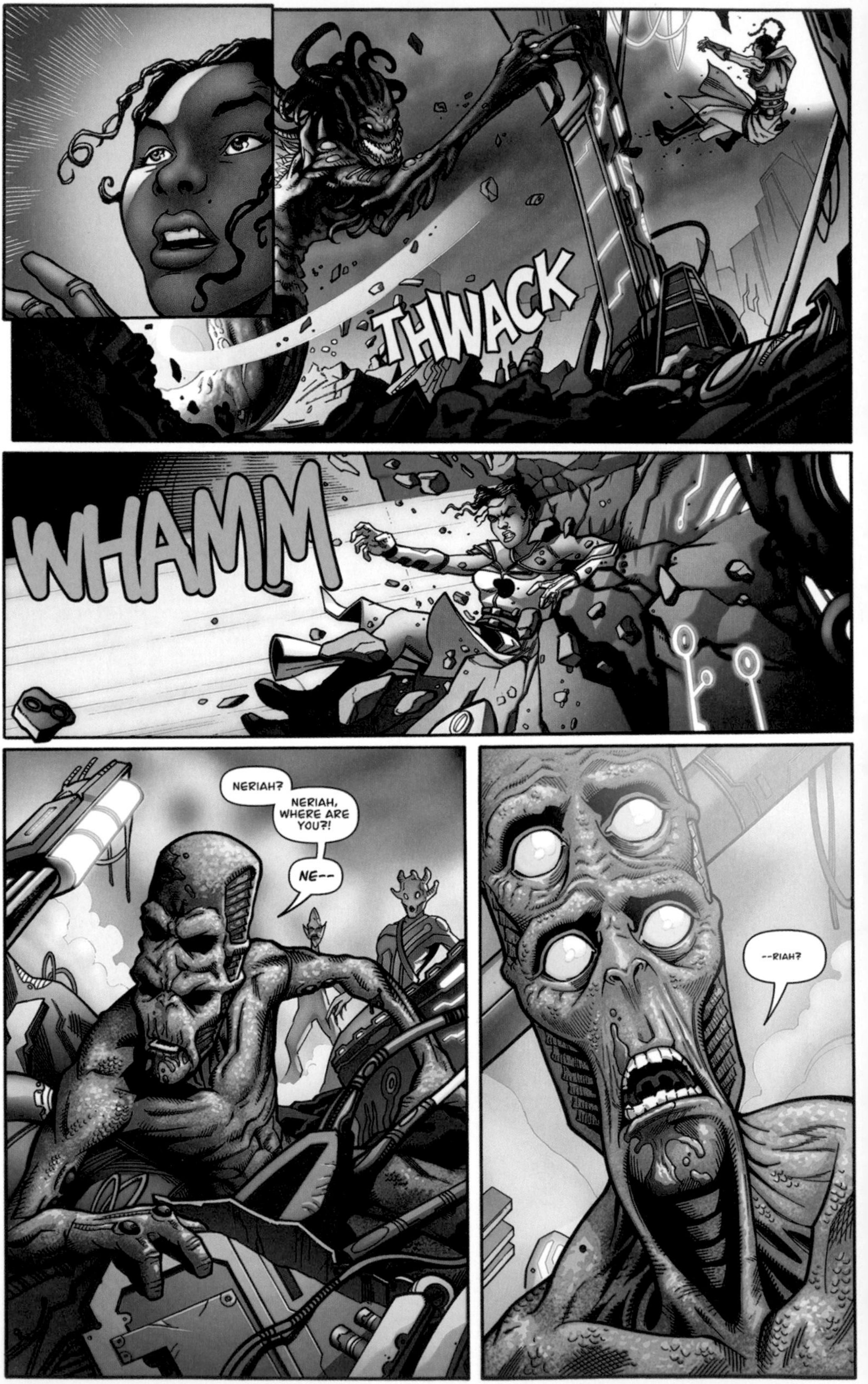
THWACK
WHAMM
NERIAH?
NERIAH, WHERE ARE YOU?!
NE--
--RIAH?

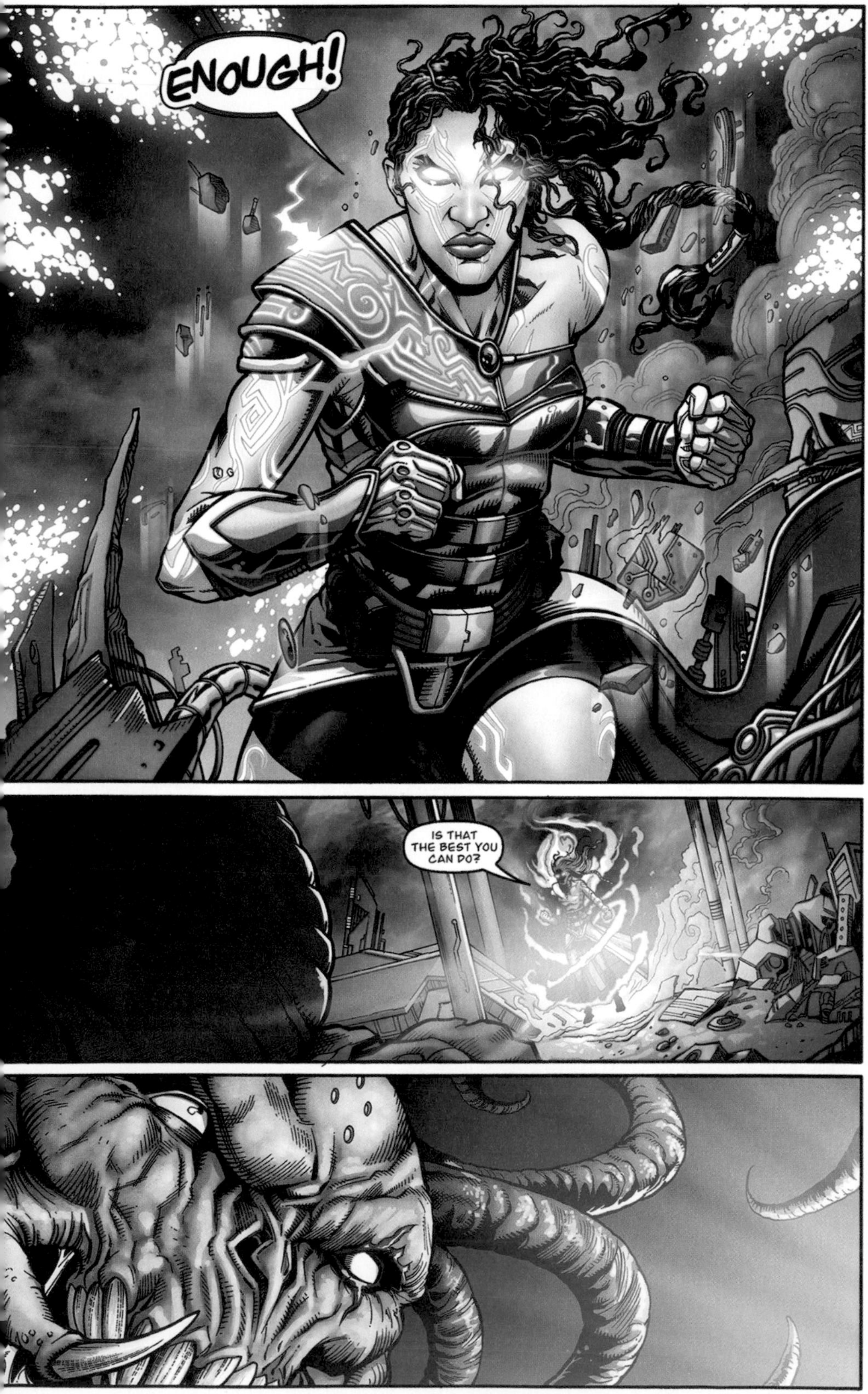
ENOUGH!
IS THAT THE BEST YOU CAN DO?

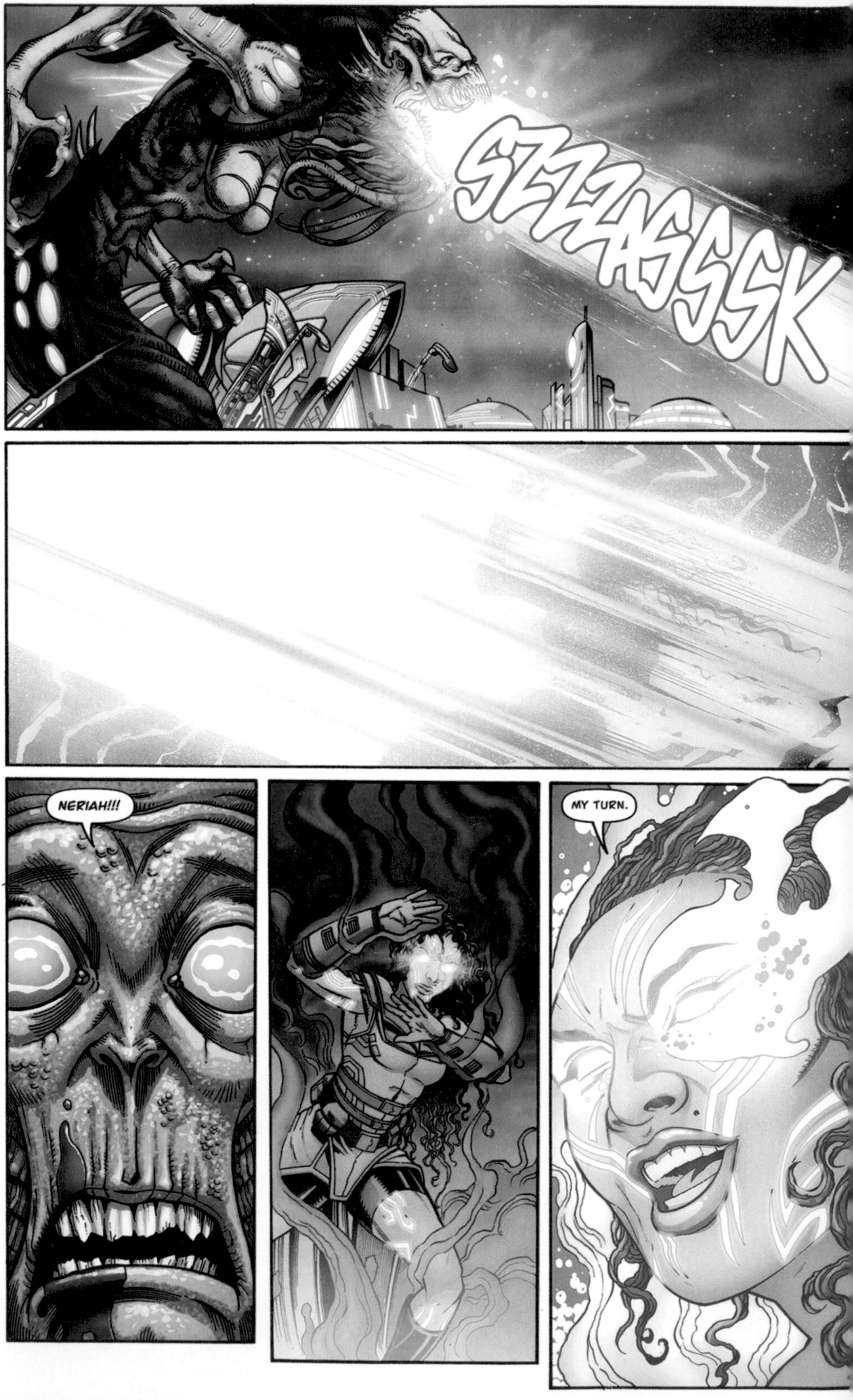
SZZZASSSK
NERIAH!!!
MY TURN.

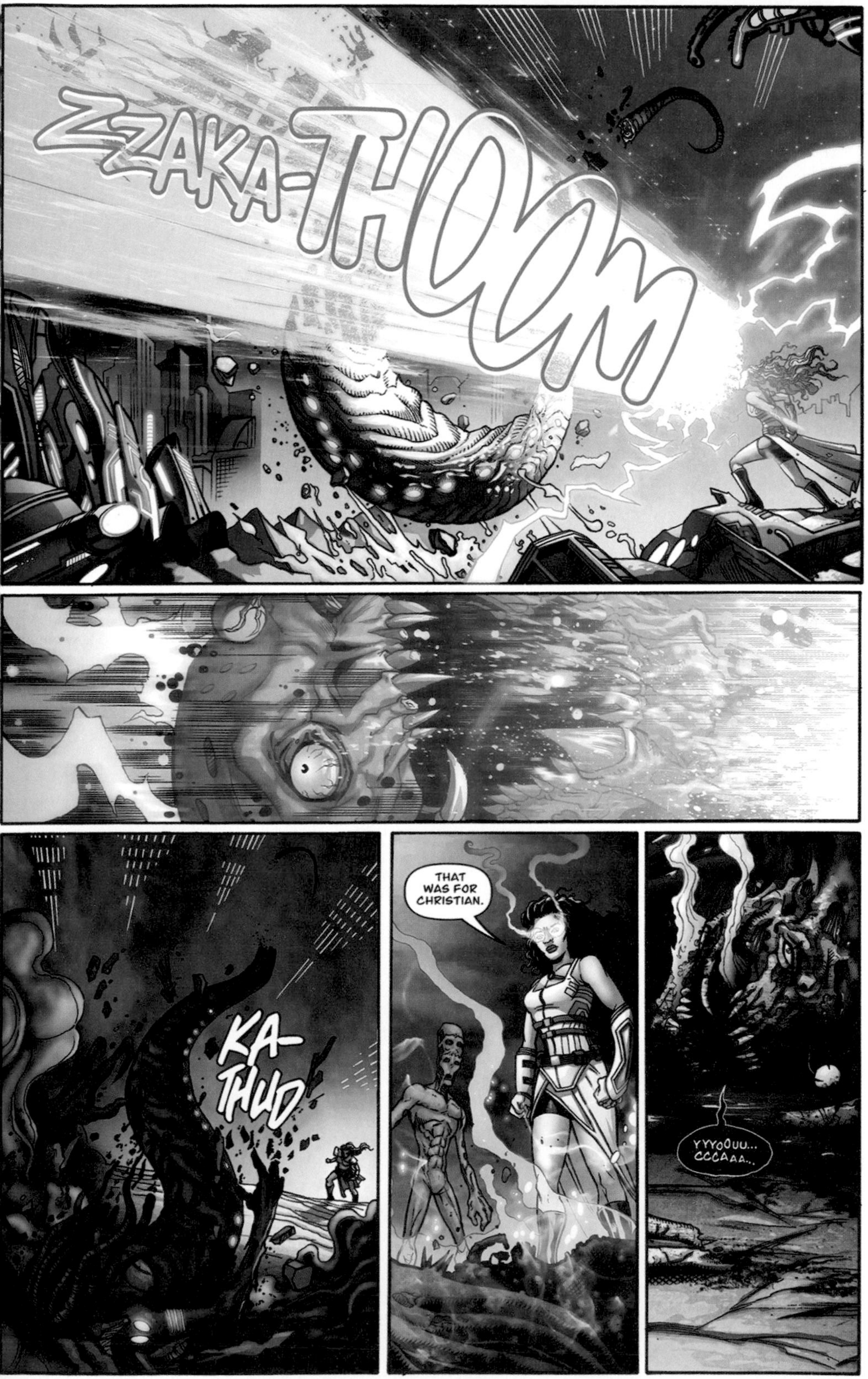
ZZAKA-THOOM
KA-THUD
THAT WAS FOR CHRISTIAN.
YYYOOUU... CCCAAA...

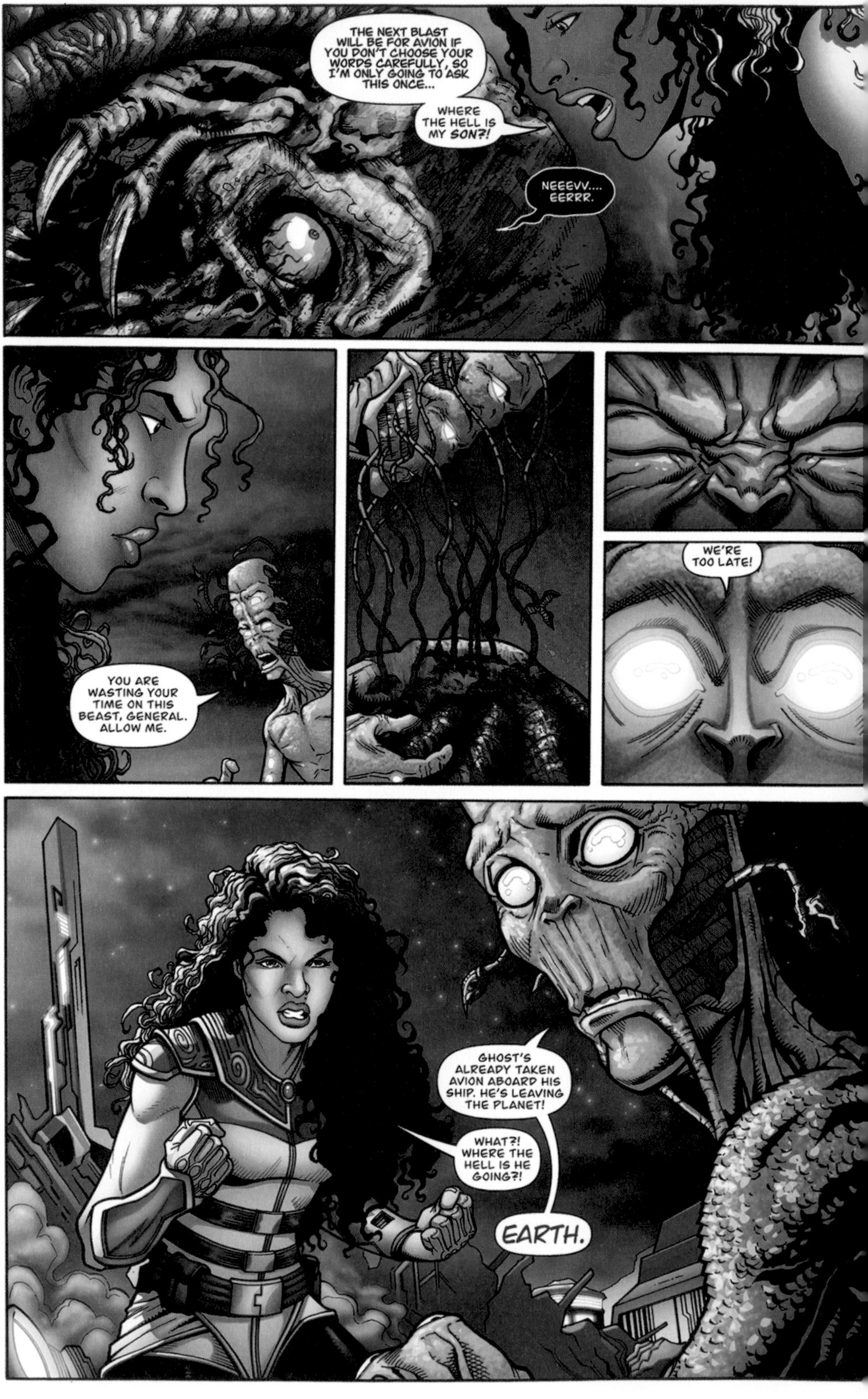
THE NEXT BLAST WILL BE FOR AVION IF YOU DON'T CHOOSE YOUR WORDS CAREFULLY, SO I'M ONLY GOING TO ASK THIS ONCE...
WHERE THE HELL IS MY SON?!
NEEEVV.... EERRR.
YOU ARE WASTING YOUR TIME ON THIS BEAST, GENERAL. ALLOW ME.
WE'RE TOO LATE!
GHOST'S ALREADY TAKEN AVION ABOARD HIS SHIP. HE'S LEAVING THE PLANET!
WHAT?! WHERE THE HELL IS HE GOING?!
EARTH.

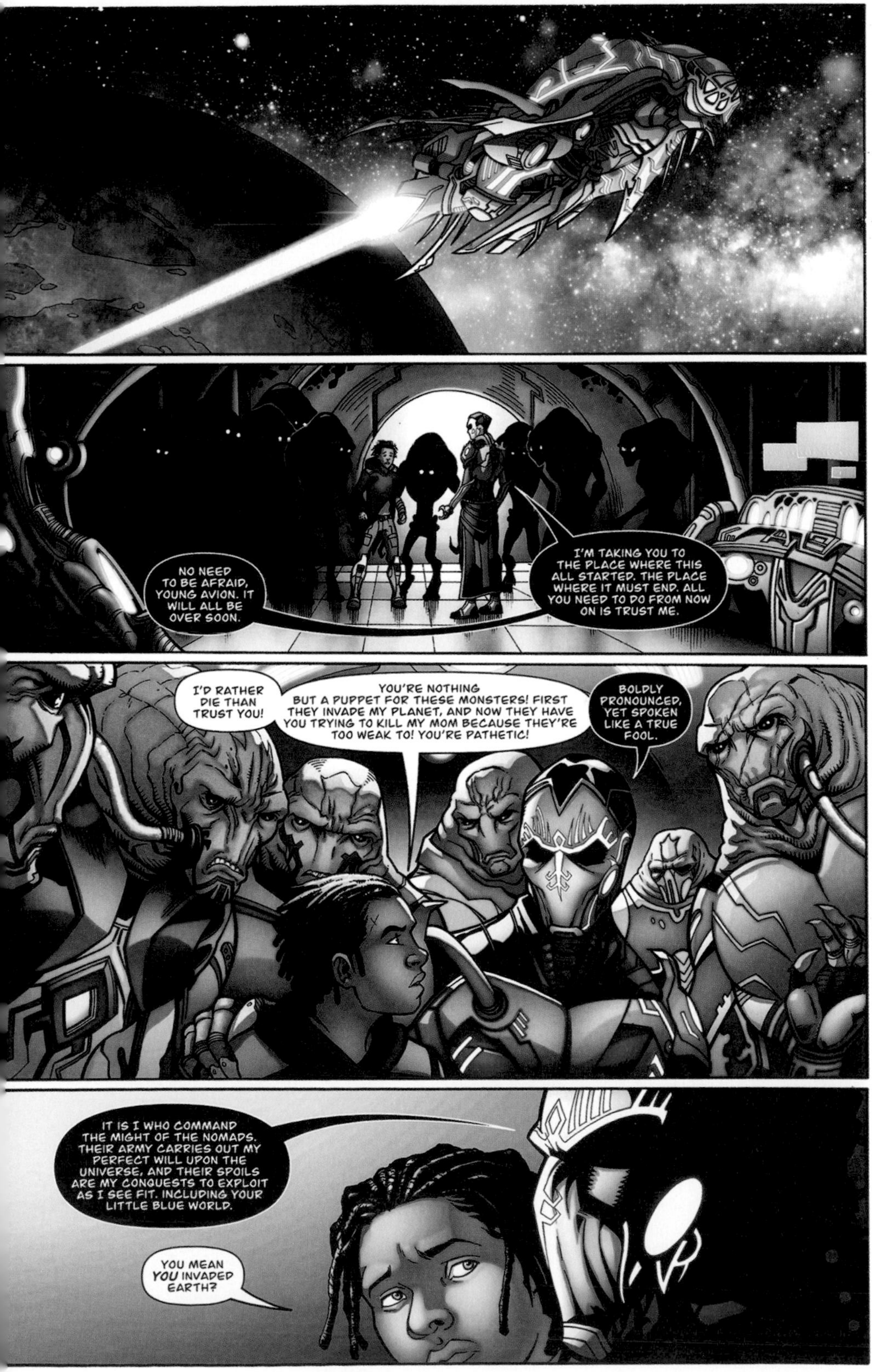
NO NEED TO BE AFRAID, YOUNG AVION. IT WILL ALL BE OVER SOON.
I'M TAKING YOU TO THE PLACE WHERE THIS ALL STARTED. THE PLACE WHERE IT MUST END. ALL YOU NEED TO DO FROM NOW ON IS TRUST ME.
I'D RATHER DIE THAN TRUST YOU!
YOU'RE NOTHING BUT A PUPPET FOR THESE MONSTERS! FIRST THEY INVADE MY PLANET, AND NOW THEY HAVE YOU TRYING TO KILL MY MOM BECAUSE THEY'RE TOO WEAK TO! YOU'RE PATHETIC!
BOLDLY PRONOUNCED, YET SPOKEN LIKE A TRUE FOOL.
IT IS I WHO COMMAND THE MIGHT OF THE NOMADS. THEIR ARMY CARRIES OUT MY PERFECT WILL UPON THE UNIVERSE, AND THEIR SPOILS ARE MY CONQUESTS TO EXPLOIT AS I SEE FIT. INCLUDING YOUR LITTLE BLUE WORLD.
YOU MEAN *YOU* INVADED EARTH?

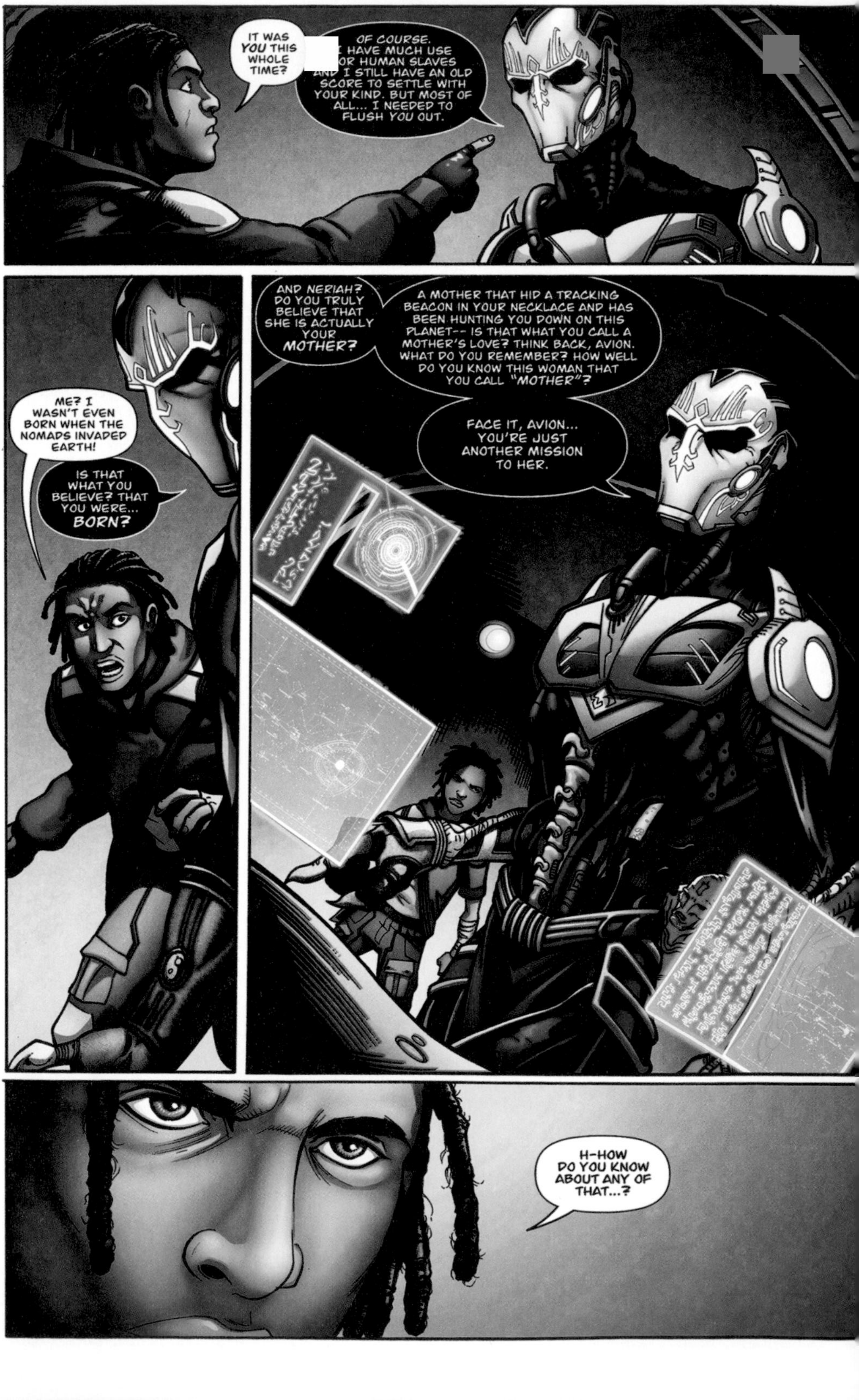
IT WAS YOU THIS WHOLE TIME?
OF COURSE. I HAVE MUCH USE FOR HUMAN SLAVES AND I STILL HAVE AN OLD SCORE TO SETTLE WITH YOUR KIND. BUT MOST OF ALL... I NEEDED TO FLUSH YOU OUT.
ME? I WASN'T EVEN BORN WHEN THE NOMADS INVADED EARTH!
IS THAT WHAT YOU BELIEVE? THAT YOU WERE... BORN?
AND NERIAH? DO YOU TRULY BELIEVE THAT SHE IS ACTUALLY YOUR MOTHER?
A MOTHER THAT HID A TRACKING BEACON IN YOUR NECKLACE AND HAS BEEN HUNTING YOU DOWN ON THIS PLANET-- IS THAT WHAT YOU CALL A MOTHER'S LOVE? THINK BACK, AVION. WHAT DO YOU REMEMBER? HOW WELL DO YOU KNOW THIS WOMAN THAT YOU CALL "MOTHER"?
FACE IT, AVION... YOU'RE JUST ANOTHER MISSION TO HER.
H-HOW DO YOU KNOW ABOUT ANY OF THAT...?

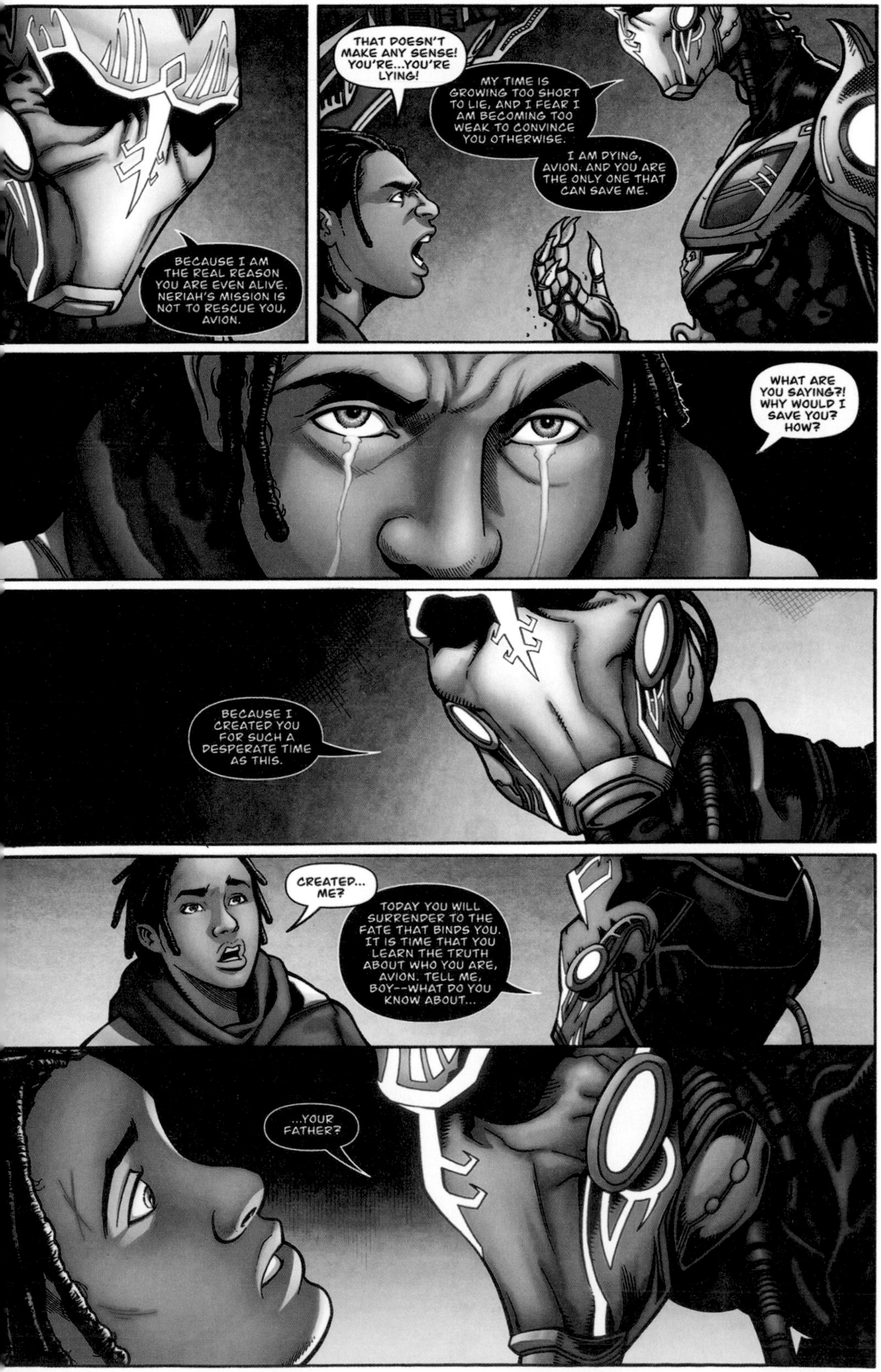
BECAUSE I AM THE REAL REASON YOU ARE EVEN ALIVE. NERIAH'S MISSION IS NOT TO RESCUE YOU, AVION.
THAT DOESN'T MAKE ANY SENSE! YOU'RE...YOU'RE LYING!
MY TIME IS GROWING TOO SHORT TO LIE, AND I FEAR I AM BECOMING TOO WEAK TO CONVINCE YOU OTHERWISE.
I AM DYING, AVION. AND YOU ARE THE ONLY ONE THAT CAN SAVE ME.
WHAT ARE YOU SAYING?! WHY WOULD I SAVE YOU? HOW?
BECAUSE I CREATED YOU FOR SUCH A DESPERATE TIME AS THIS.
CREATED... ME?
TODAY YOU WILL SURRENDER TO THE FATE THAT BINDS YOU. IT IS TIME THAT YOU LEARN THE TRUTH ABOUT WHO YOU ARE, AVION. TELL ME, BOY--WHAT DO YOU KNOW ABOUT...
...YOUR FATHER?

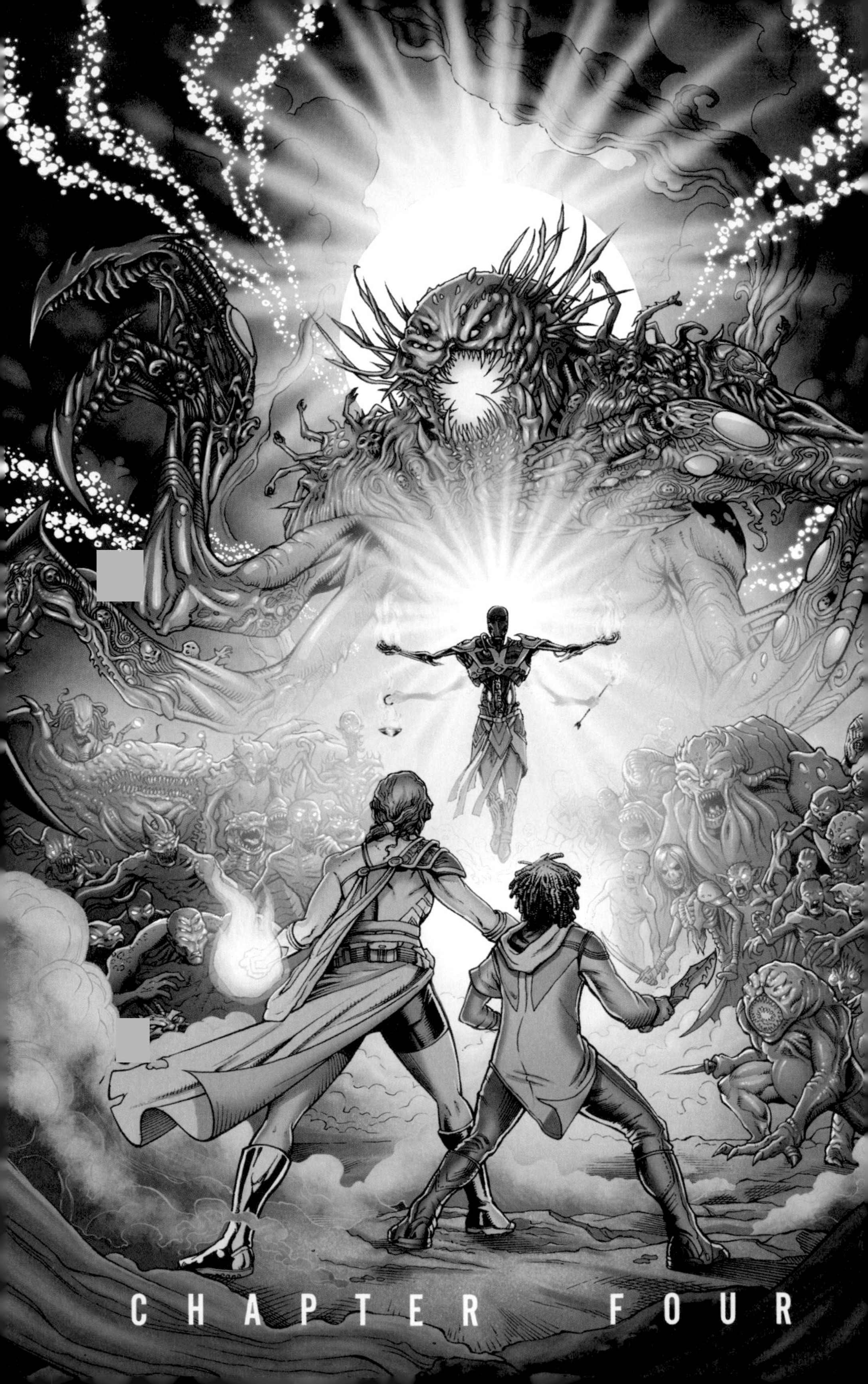

CHAPTER FOUR

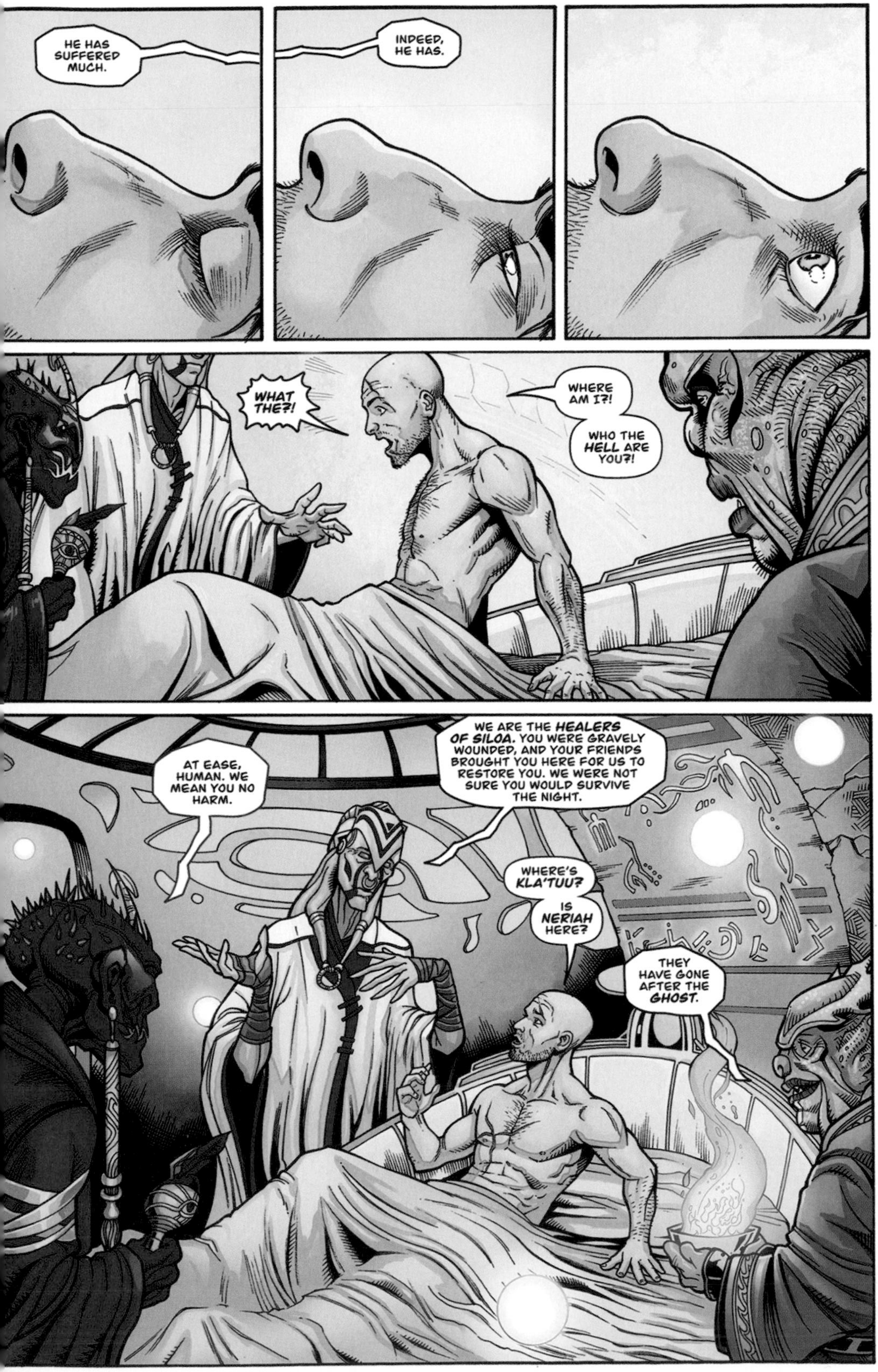
HE HAS SUFFERED MUCH.
INDEED, HE HAS.
WHAT THE?!
WHERE AM I?!
WHO THE HELL ARE YOU?!
AT EASE, HUMAN. WE MEAN YOU NO HARM.
WE ARE THE HEALERS OF SILOA. YOU WERE GRAVELY WOUNDED, AND YOUR FRIENDS BROUGHT YOU HERE FOR US TO RESTORE YOU. WE WERE NOT SURE YOU WOULD SURVIVE THE NIGHT.
WHERE'S KLA'TUU?
IS NERIAH HERE?
THEY HAVE GONE AFTER THE GHOST.

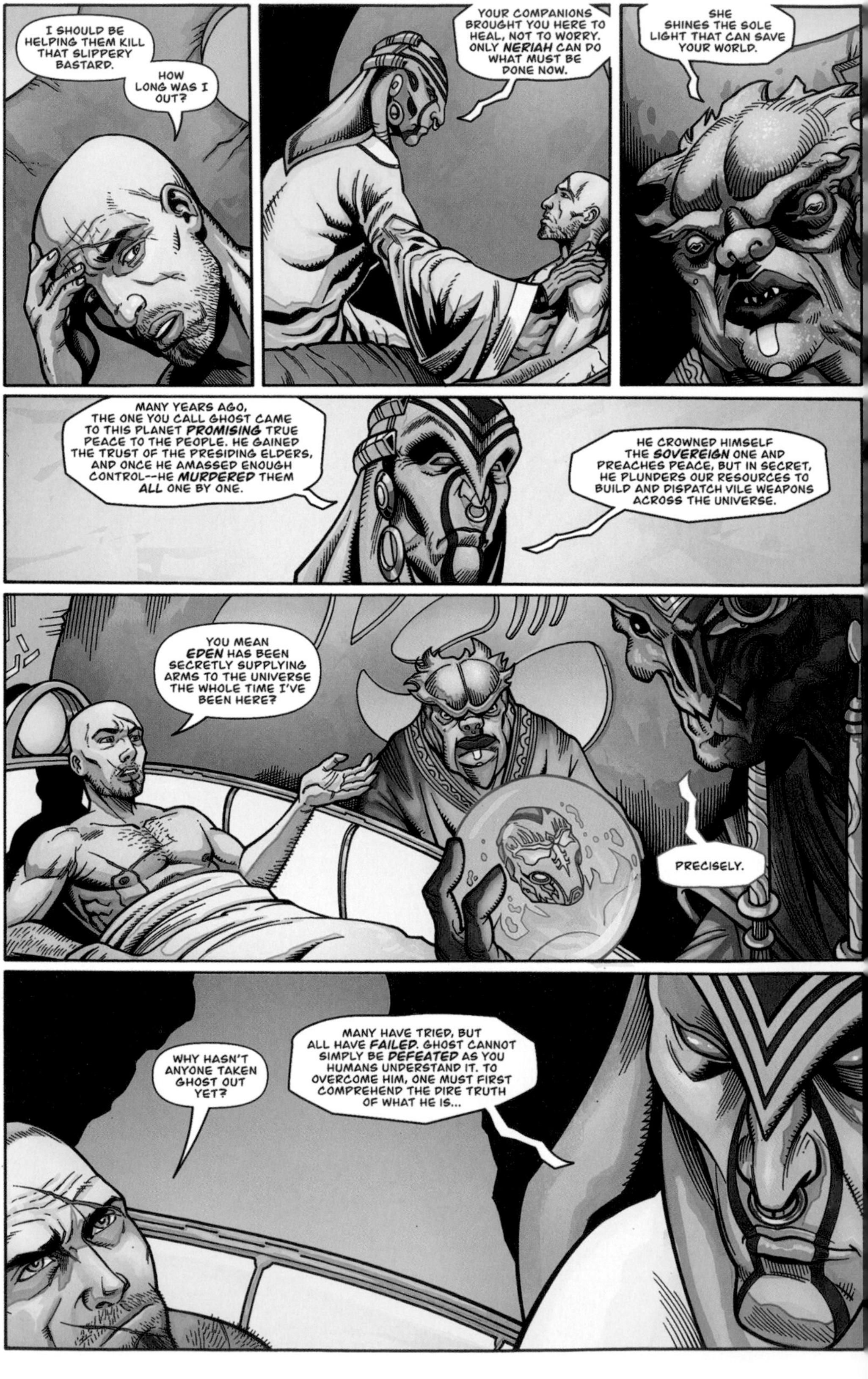
I SHOULD BE HELPING THEM KILL THAT SLIPPERY BASTARD.
HOW LONG WAS I OUT?
YOUR COMPANIONS BROUGHT YOU HERE TO HEAL, NOT TO WORRY. ONLY NERIAH CAN DO WHAT MUST BE DONE NOW.
SHE SHINES THE SOLE LIGHT THAT CAN SAVE YOUR WORLD.
MANY YEARS AGO, THE ONE YOU CALL GHOST CAME TO THIS PLANET PROMISING TRUE PEACE TO THE PEOPLE. HE GAINED THE TRUST OF THE PRESIDING ELDERS, AND ONCE HE AMASSED ENOUGH CONTROL--HE MURDERED THEM ALL ONE BY ONE.
HE CROWNED HIMSELF THE SOVEREIGN ONE AND PREACHES PEACE, BUT IN SECRET, HE PLUNDERS OUR RESOURCES TO BUILD AND DISPATCH VILE WEAPONS ACROSS THE UNIVERSE.
YOU MEAN EDEN HAS BEEN SECRETLY SUPPLYING ARMS TO THE UNIVERSE THE WHOLE TIME I'VE BEEN HERE?
PRECISELY.
WHY HASN'T ANYONE TAKEN GHOST OUT YET?
MANY HAVE TRIED, BUT ALL HAVE FAILED. GHOST CANNOT SIMPLY BE DEFEATED AS YOU HUMANS UNDERSTAND IT. TO OVERCOME HIM, ONE MUST FIRST COMPREHEND THE DIRE TRUTH OF WHAT HE IS...

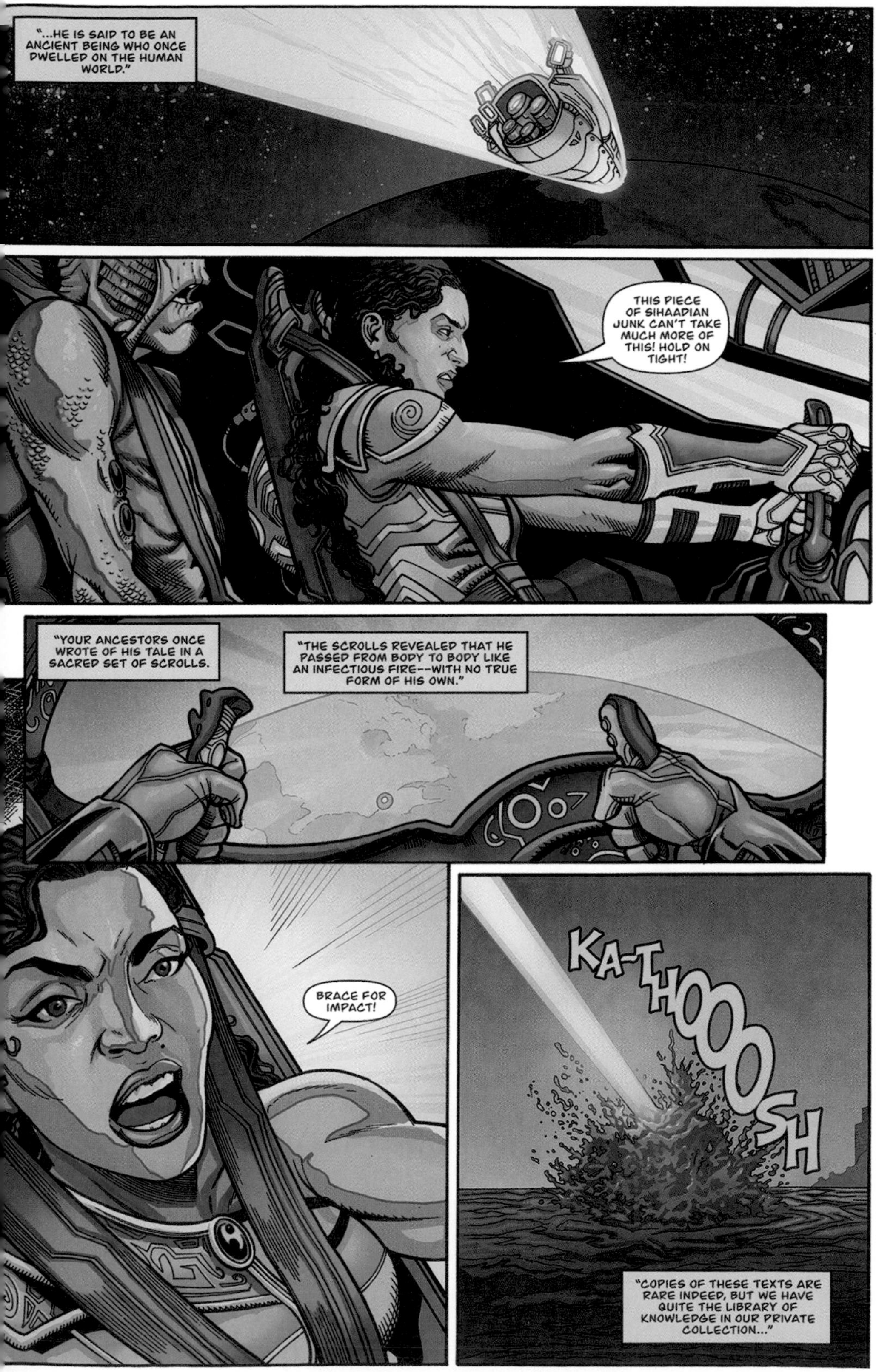
"...HE IS SAID TO BE AN ANCIENT BEING WHO ONCE DWELLED ON THE HUMAN WORLD."
THIS PIECE OF SIHAADIAN JUNK CAN'T TAKE MUCH MORE OF THIS! HOLD ON TIGHT!
"YOUR ANCESTORS ONCE WROTE OF HIS TALE IN A SACRED SET OF SCROLLS.
"THE SCROLLS REVEALED THAT HE PASSED FROM BODY TO BODY LIKE AN INFECTIOUS FIRE--WITH NO TRUE FORM OF HIS OWN."
BRACE FOR IMPACT!
KA-THOOOOSH
"COPIES OF THESE TEXTS ARE RARE INDEED, BUT WE HAVE QUITE THE LIBRARY OF KNOWLEDGE IN OUR PRIVATE COLLECTION..."

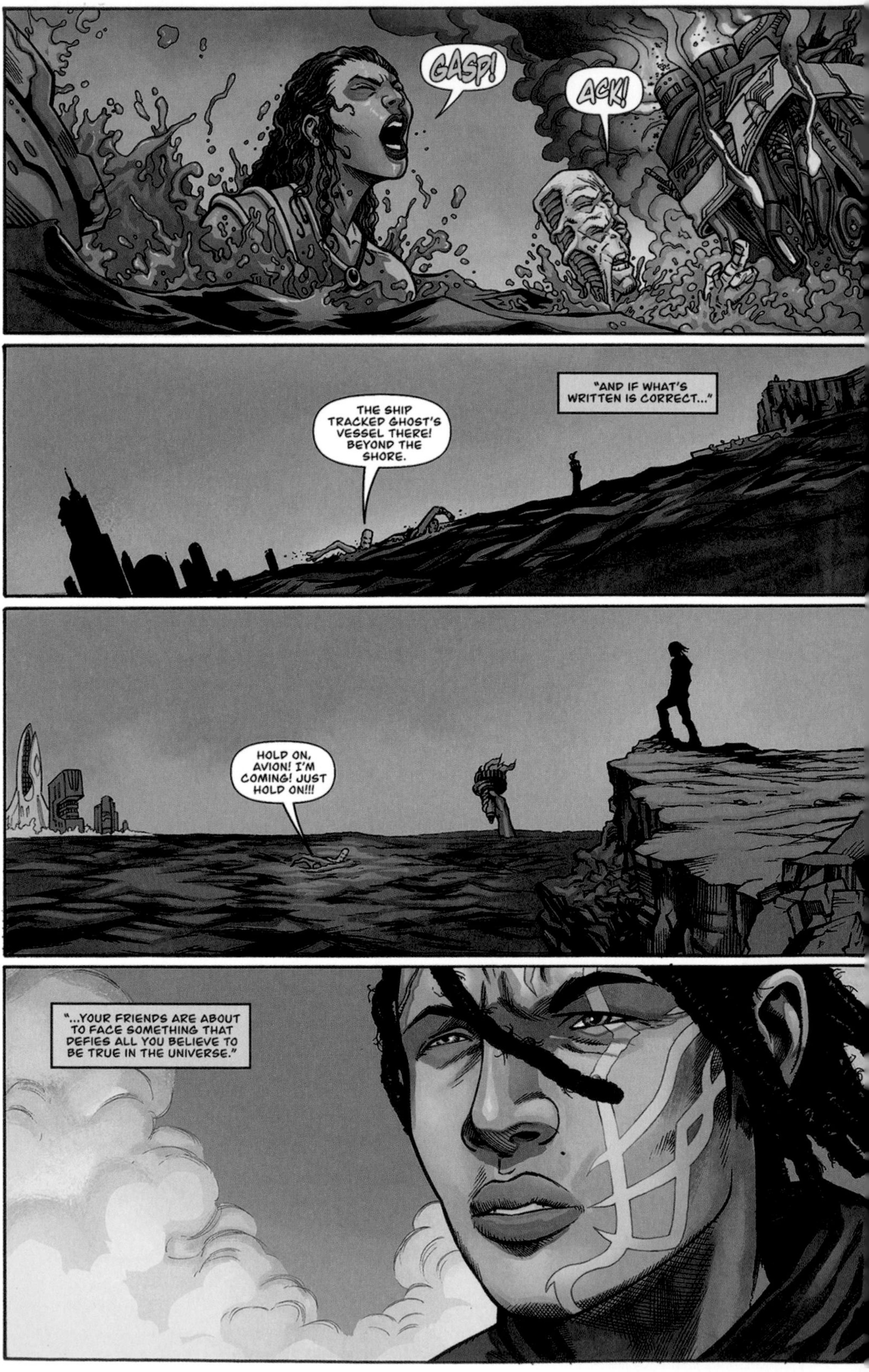
GASP!
ACK!
"AND IF WHAT'S WRITTEN IS CORRECT..."
THE SHIP TRACKED GHOST'S VESSEL THERE! BEYOND THE SHORE.
HOLD ON, AVION! I'M COMING! JUST HOLD ON!!!
"...YOUR FRIENDS ARE ABOUT TO FACE SOMETHING THAT DEFIES ALL YOU BELIEVE TO BE TRUE IN THE UNIVERSE."

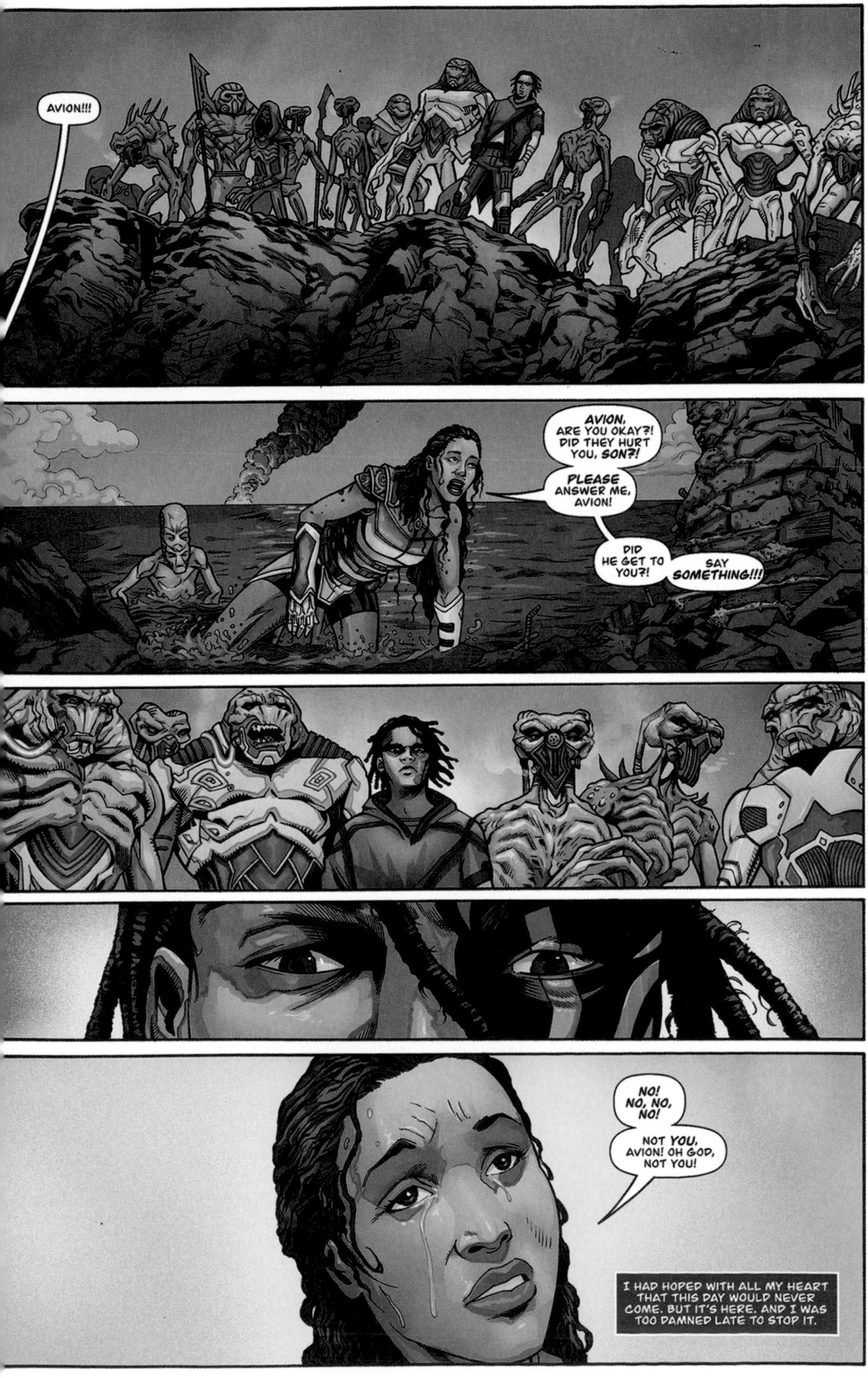
AVION!!!
AVION, ARE YOU OKAY?! DID THEY HURT YOU, SON?!
PLEASE ANSWER ME, AVION!
DID HE GET TO YOU?!
SAY SOMETHING!!!
NO! NO, NO, NO!
NOT YOU, AVION! OH GOD, NOT YOU!
I HAD HOPED WITH ALL MY HEART THAT THIS DAY WOULD NEVER COME. BUT IT'S HERE. AND I WAS TOO DAMNED LATE TO STOP IT.

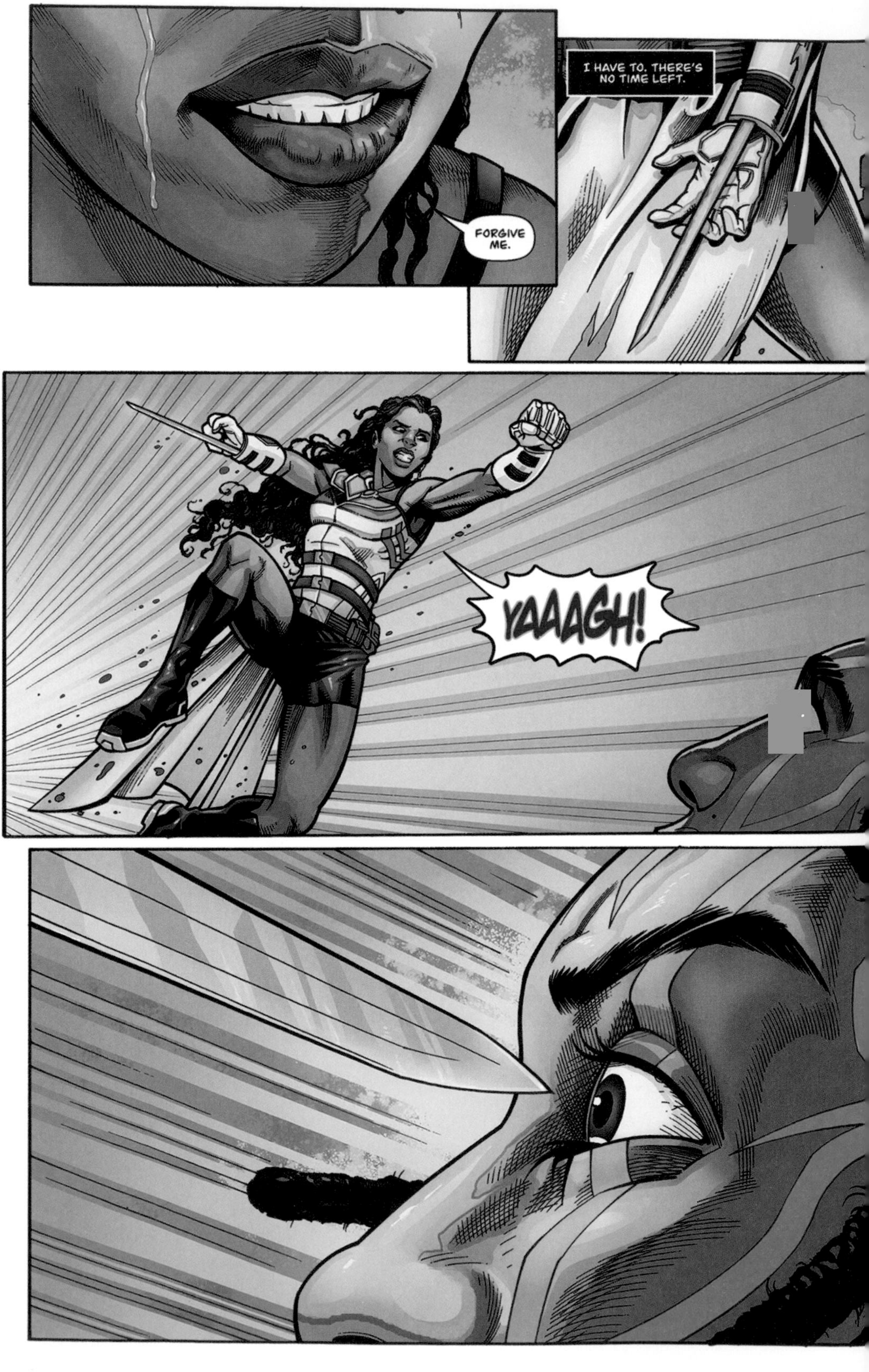
FORGIVE ME.
I HAVE TO. THERE'S NO TIME LEFT.
YAAAGH!

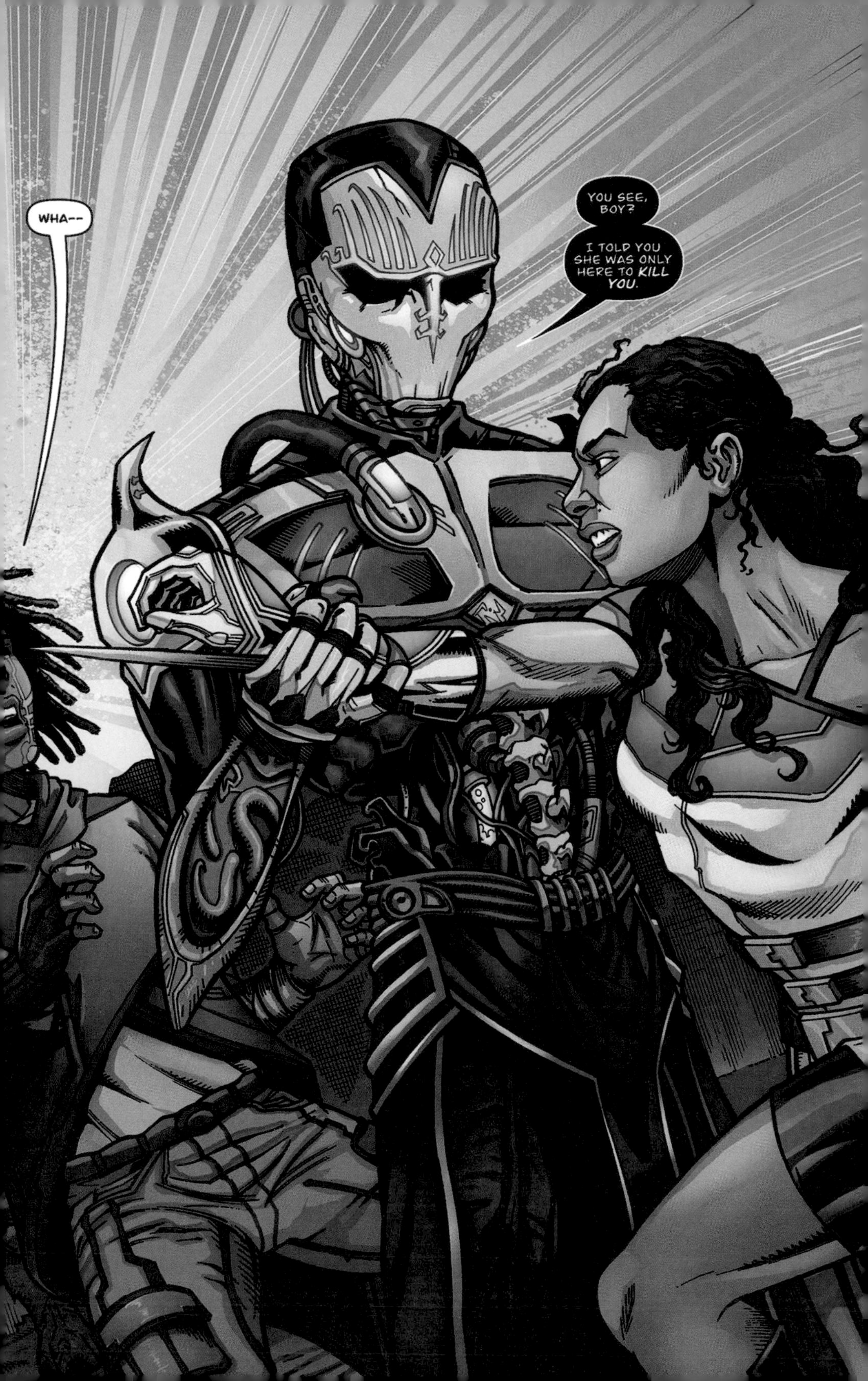
WHA--
YOU SEE, BOY?
I TOLD YOU SHE WAS ONLY HERE TO KILL YOU.

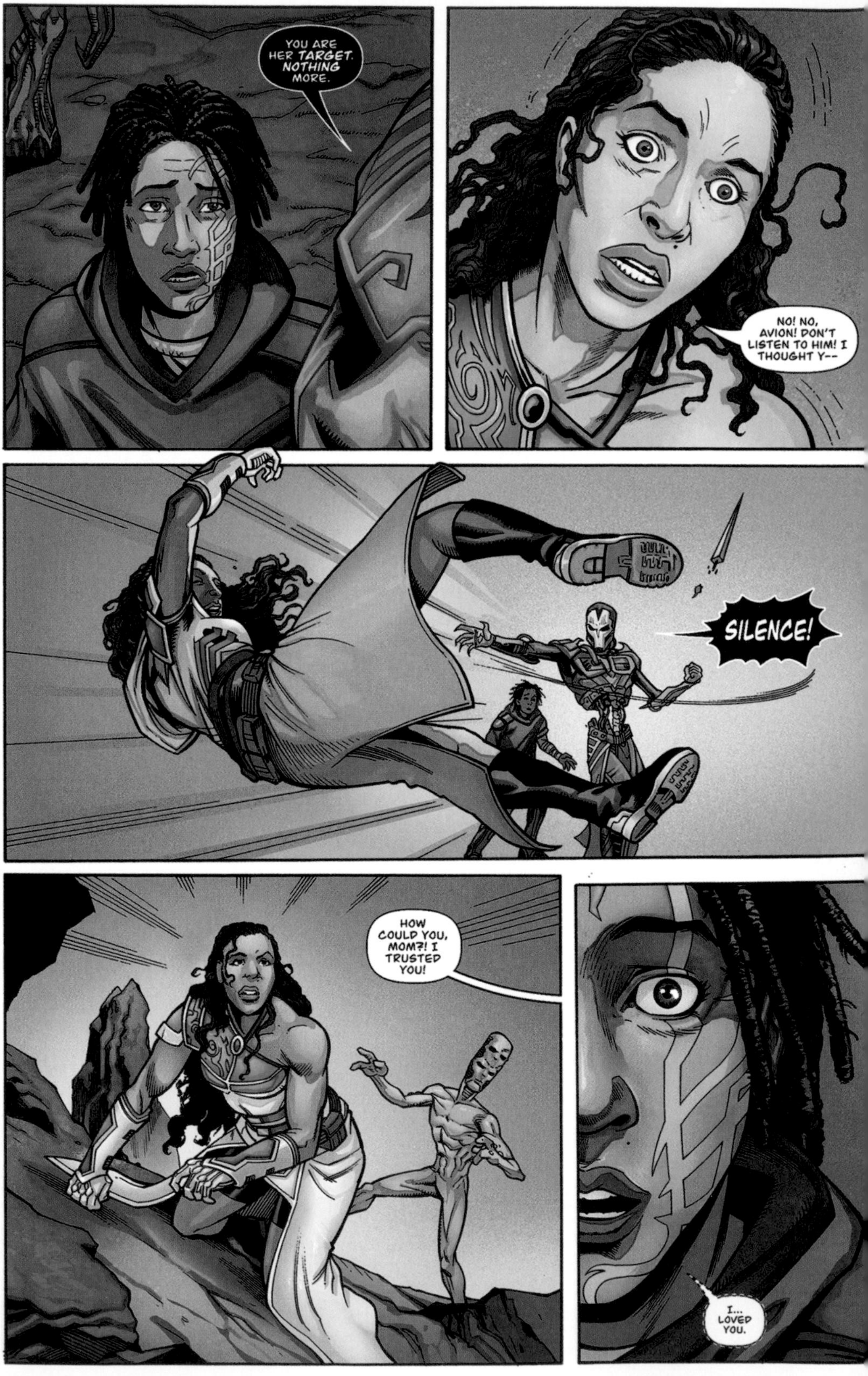
YOU ARE HER TARGET. NOTHING MORE.
NO! NO, AVION! DON'T LISTEN TO HIM! I THOUGHT Y--
SILENCE!
HOW COULD YOU, MOM?! I TRUSTED YOU!
I... LOVED YOU.

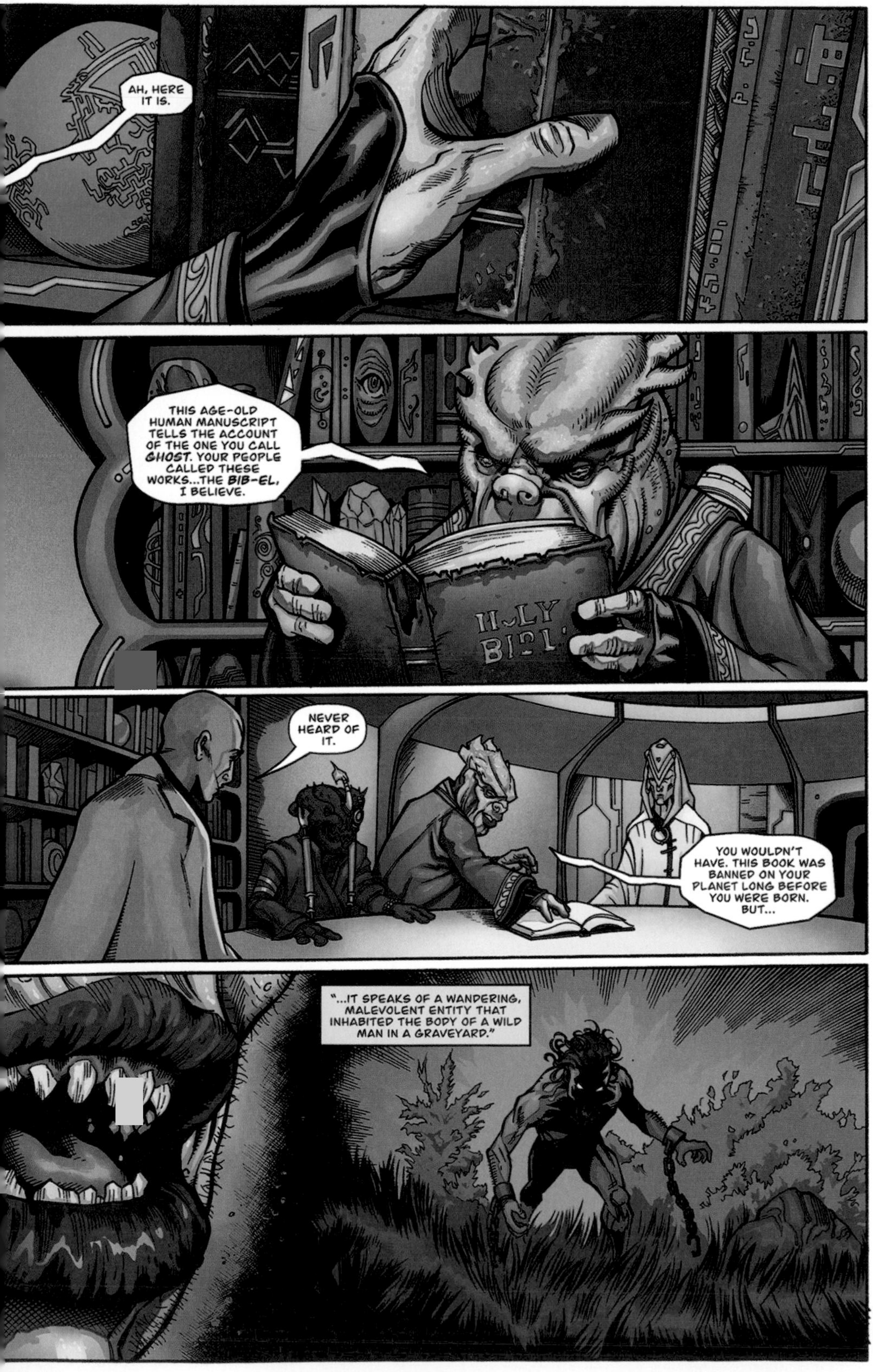
AH, HERE IT IS.
THIS AGE-OLD HUMAN MANUSCRIPT TELLS THE ACCOUNT OF THE ONE YOU CALL GHOST. YOUR PEOPLE CALLED THESE WORKS...THE BIB-EL, I BELIEVE.
NEVER HEARD OF IT.
YOU WOULDN'T HAVE. THIS BOOK WAS BANNED ON YOUR PLANET LONG BEFORE YOU WERE BORN. BUT...
"...IT SPEAKS OF A WANDERING, MALEVOLENT ENTITY THAT INHABITED THE BODY OF A WILD MAN IN A GRAVEYARD."

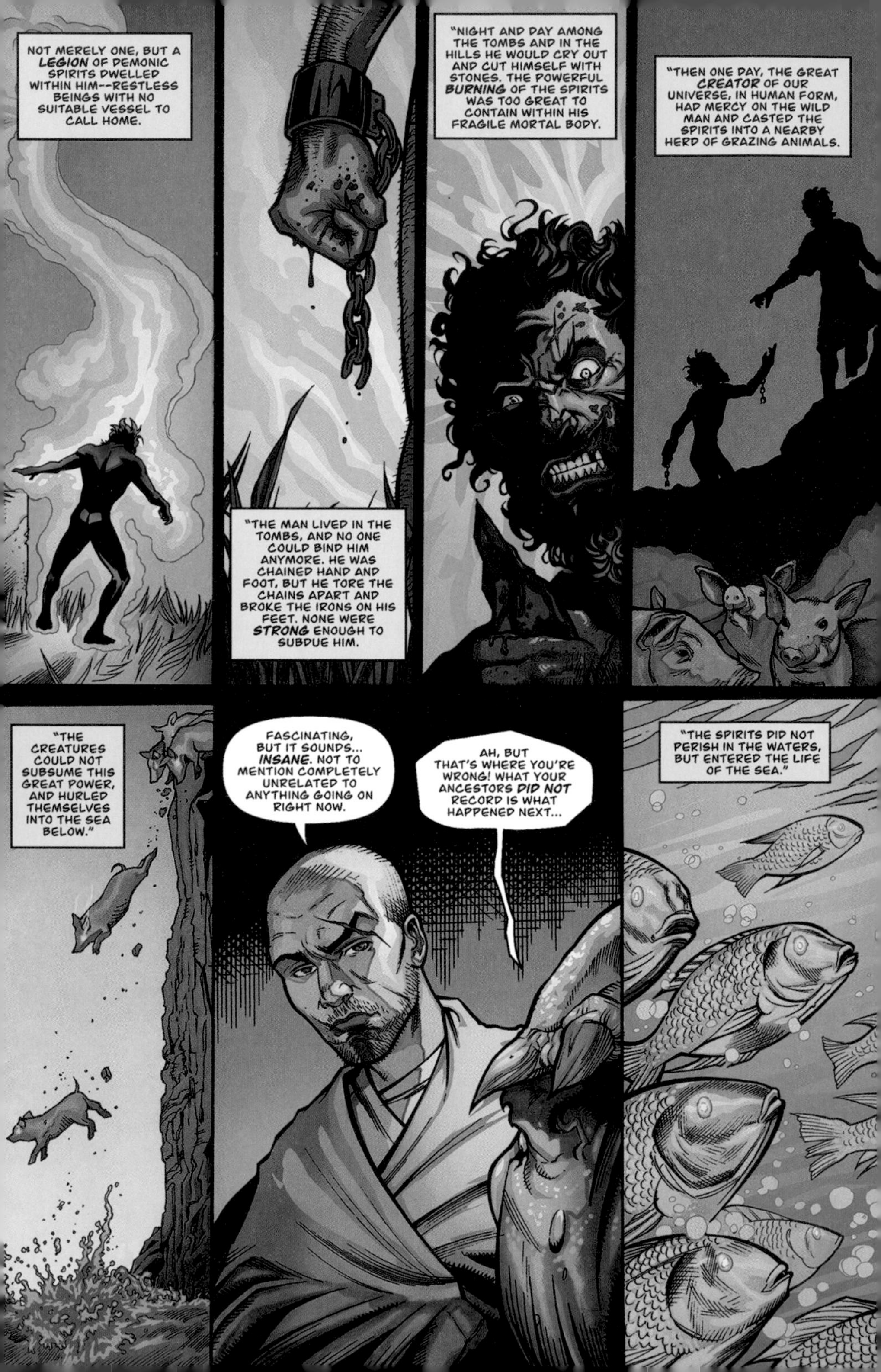
NOT MERELY ONE, BUT A LEGION OF DEMONIC SPIRITS DWELLED WITHIN HIM--RESTLESS BEINGS WITH NO SUITABLE VESSEL TO CALL HOME.
"THE MAN LIVED IN THE TOMBS, AND NO ONE COULD BIND HIM ANYMORE. HE WAS CHAINED HAND AND FOOT, BUT HE TORE THE CHAINS APART AND BROKE THE IRONS ON HIS FEET. NONE WERE STRONG ENOUGH TO SUBDUE HIM.
"NIGHT AND DAY AMONG THE TOMBS AND IN THE HILLS HE WOULD CRY OUT AND CUT HIMSELF WITH STONES. THE POWERFUL BURNING OF THE SPIRITS WAS TOO GREAT TO CONTAIN WITHIN HIS FRAGILE MORTAL BODY.
"THEN ONE DAY, THE GREAT CREATOR OF OUR UNIVERSE, IN HUMAN FORM, HAD MERCY ON THE WILD MAN AND CASTED THE SPIRITS INTO A NEARBY HERD OF GRAZING ANIMALS.
"THE CREATURES COULD NOT SUBSUME THIS GREAT POWER, AND HURLED THEMSELVES INTO THE SEA BELOW."
FASCINATING, BUT IT SOUNDS... INSANE. NOT TO MENTION COMPLETELY UNRELATED TO ANYTHING GOING ON RIGHT NOW.
AH, BUT THAT'S WHERE YOU'RE WRONG! WHAT YOUR ANCESTORS DID NOT RECORD IS WHAT HAPPENED NEXT...
"THE SPIRITS DID NOT PERISH IN THE WATERS, BUT ENTERED THE LIFE OF THE SEA."

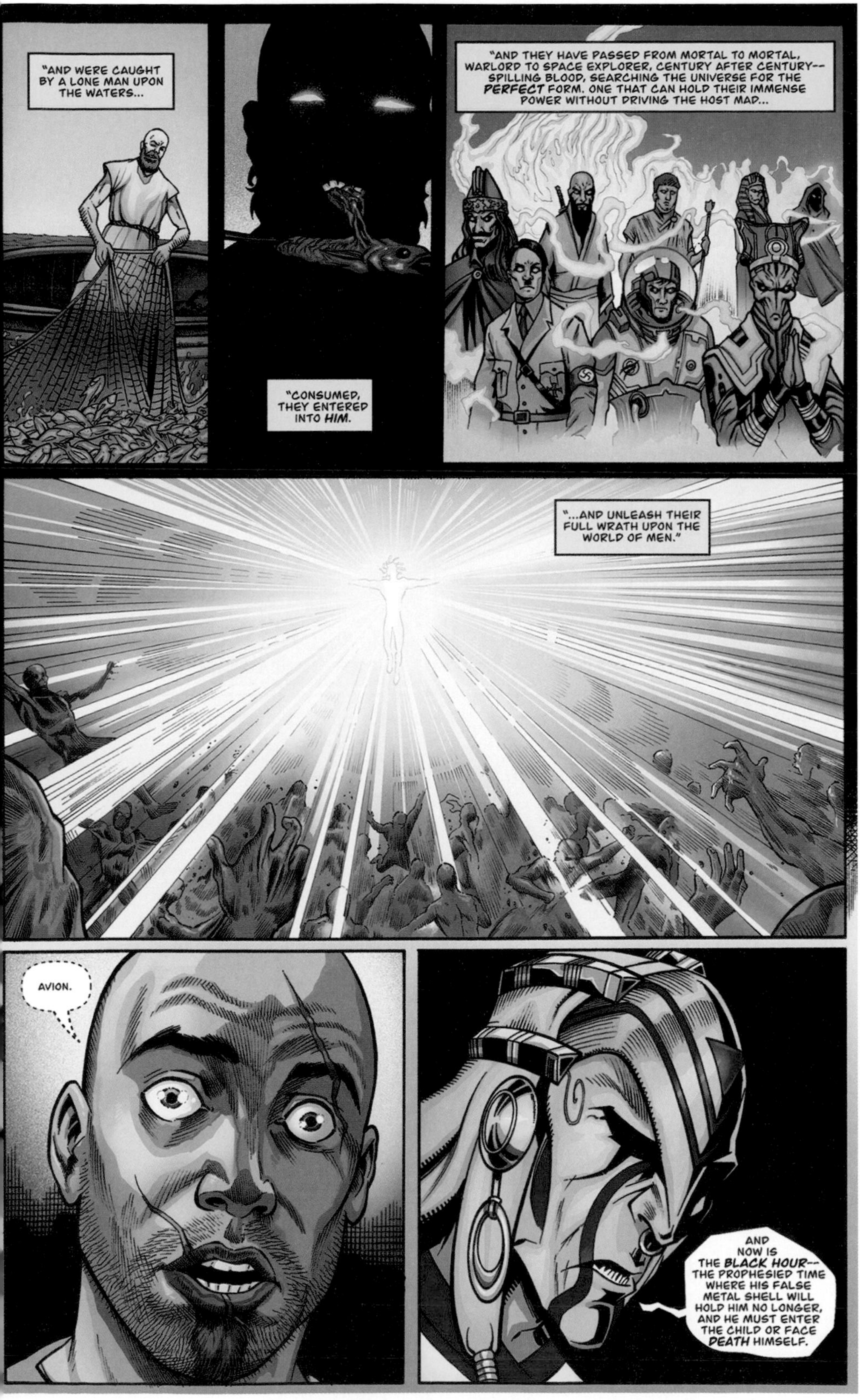
"AND WERE CAUGHT BY A LONE MAN UPON THE WATERS...
"CONSUMED, THEY ENTERED INTO *HIM*.
"AND THEY HAVE PASSED FROM MORTAL TO MORTAL, WARLORD TO SPACE EXPLORER, CENTURY AFTER CENTURY--SPILLING BLOOD, SEARCHING THE UNIVERSE FOR THE *PERFECT* FORM. ONE THAT CAN HOLD THEIR IMMENSE POWER WITHOUT DRIVING THE HOST MAD...
"...AND UNLEASH THEIR FULL WRATH UPON THE WORLD OF MEN."
AVION.
AND NOW IS THE *BLACK HOUR*-- THE PROPHESIED TIME WHERE HIS FALSE METAL SHELL WILL HOLD HIM NO LONGER, AND HE MUST ENTER THE CHILD OR FACE *DEATH* HIMSELF.

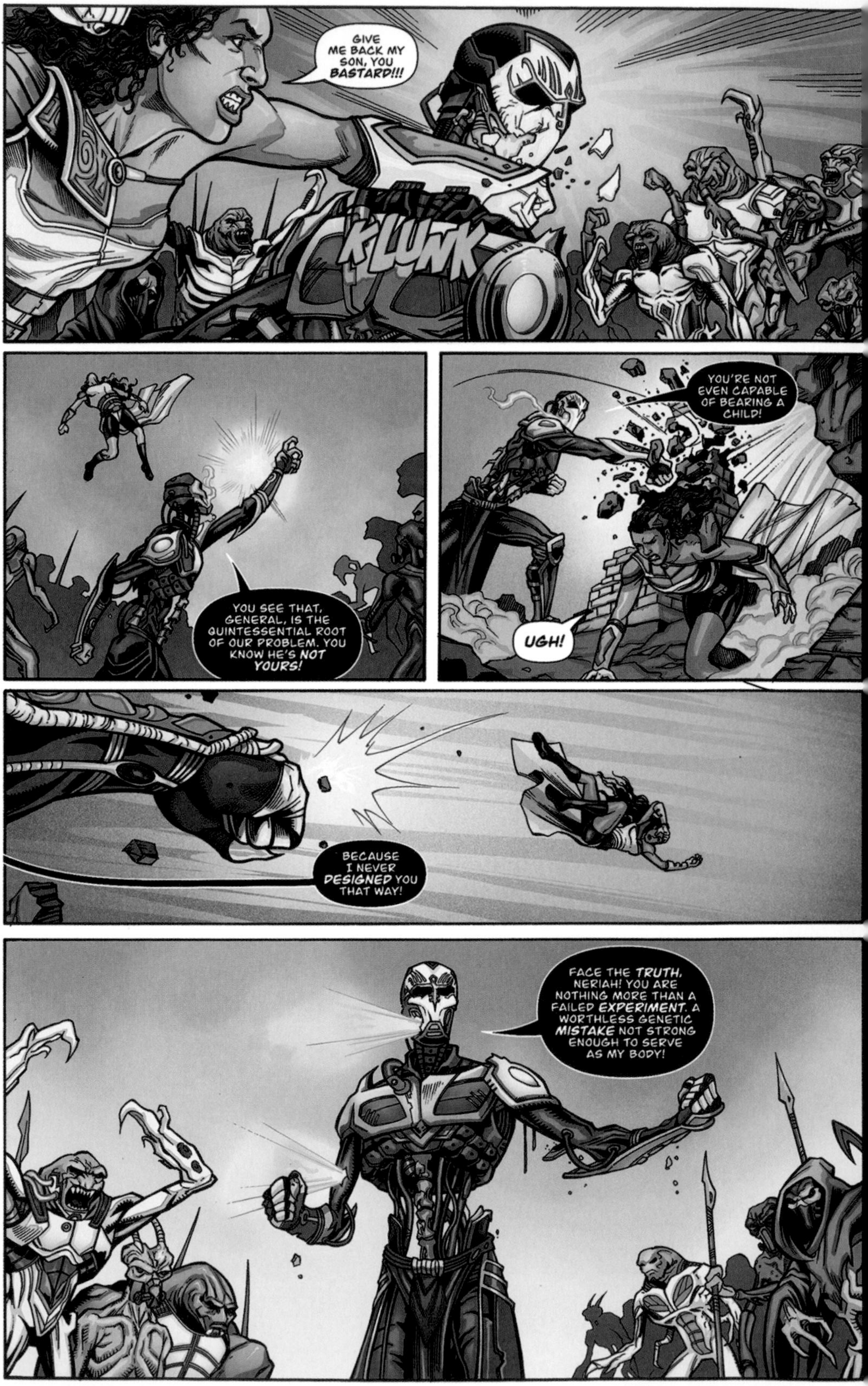
GIVE ME BACK MY SON, YOU BASTARD!!!
KLUNK
YOU SEE THAT, GENERAL, IS THE QUINTESSENTIAL ROOT OF OUR PROBLEM. YOU KNOW HE'S NOT YOURS!
YOU'RE NOT EVEN CAPABLE OF BEARING A CHILD!
UGH!
BECAUSE I NEVER DESIGNED YOU THAT WAY!
FACE THE TRUTH, NERIAH! YOU ARE NOTHING MORE THAN A FAILED EXPERIMENT. A WORTHLESS GENETIC MISTAKE NOT STRONG ENOUGH TO SERVE AS MY BODY!

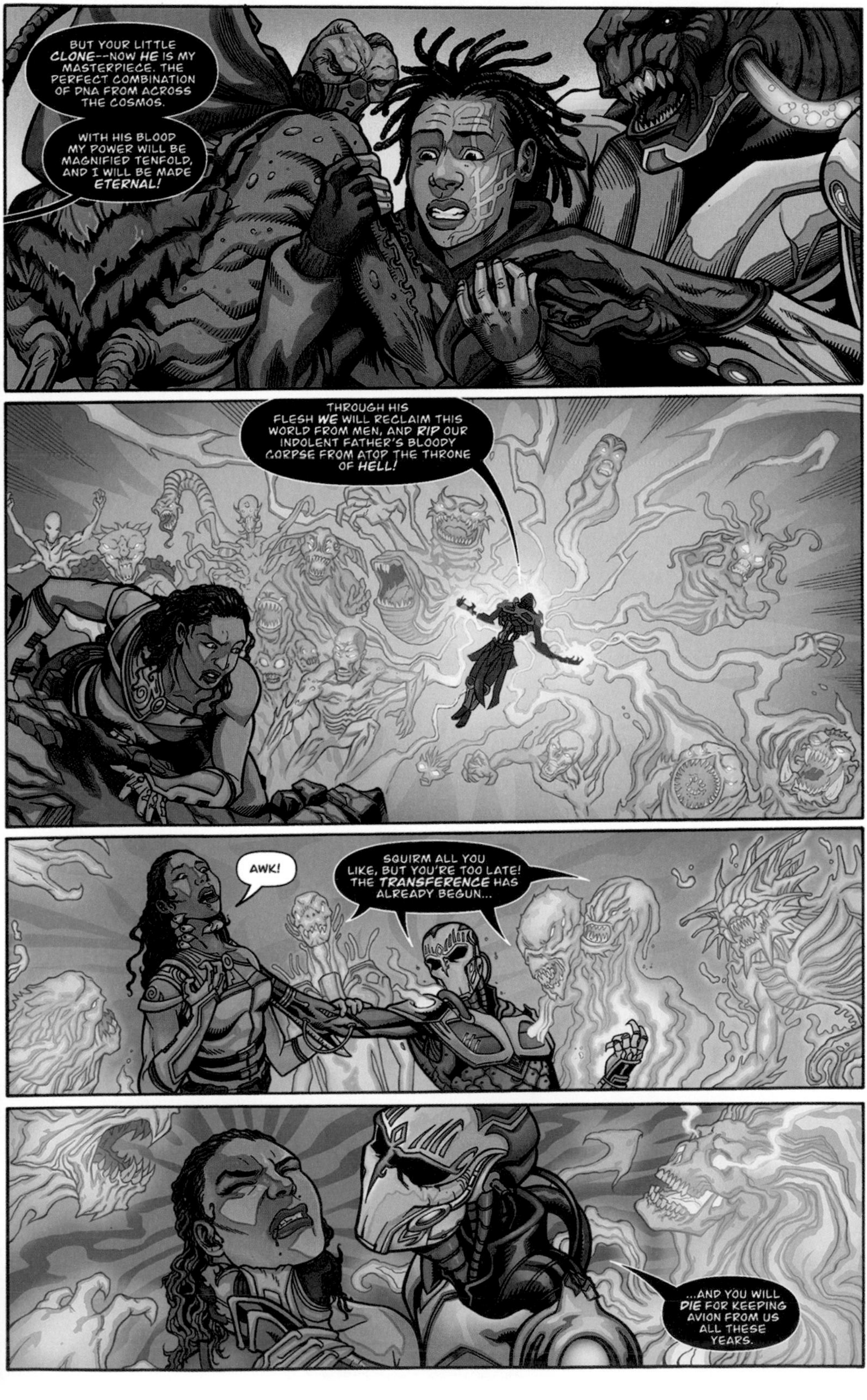
BUT YOUR LITTLE CLONE--NOW HE IS MY MASTERPIECE. THE PERFECT COMBINATION OF DNA FROM ACROSS THE COSMOS.
WITH HIS BLOOD MY POWER WILL BE MAGNIFIED TENFOLD, AND I WILL BE MADE ETERNAL!
THROUGH HIS FLESH WE WILL RECLAIM THIS WORLD FROM MEN, AND RIP OUR INDOLENT FATHER'S BLOODY CORPSE FROM ATOP THE THRONE OF HELL!
AWK!
SQUIRM ALL YOU LIKE, BUT YOU'RE TOO LATE! THE TRANSFERENCE HAS ALREADY BEGUN...
...AND YOU WILL DIE FOR KEEPING AVION FROM US ALL THESE YEARS.

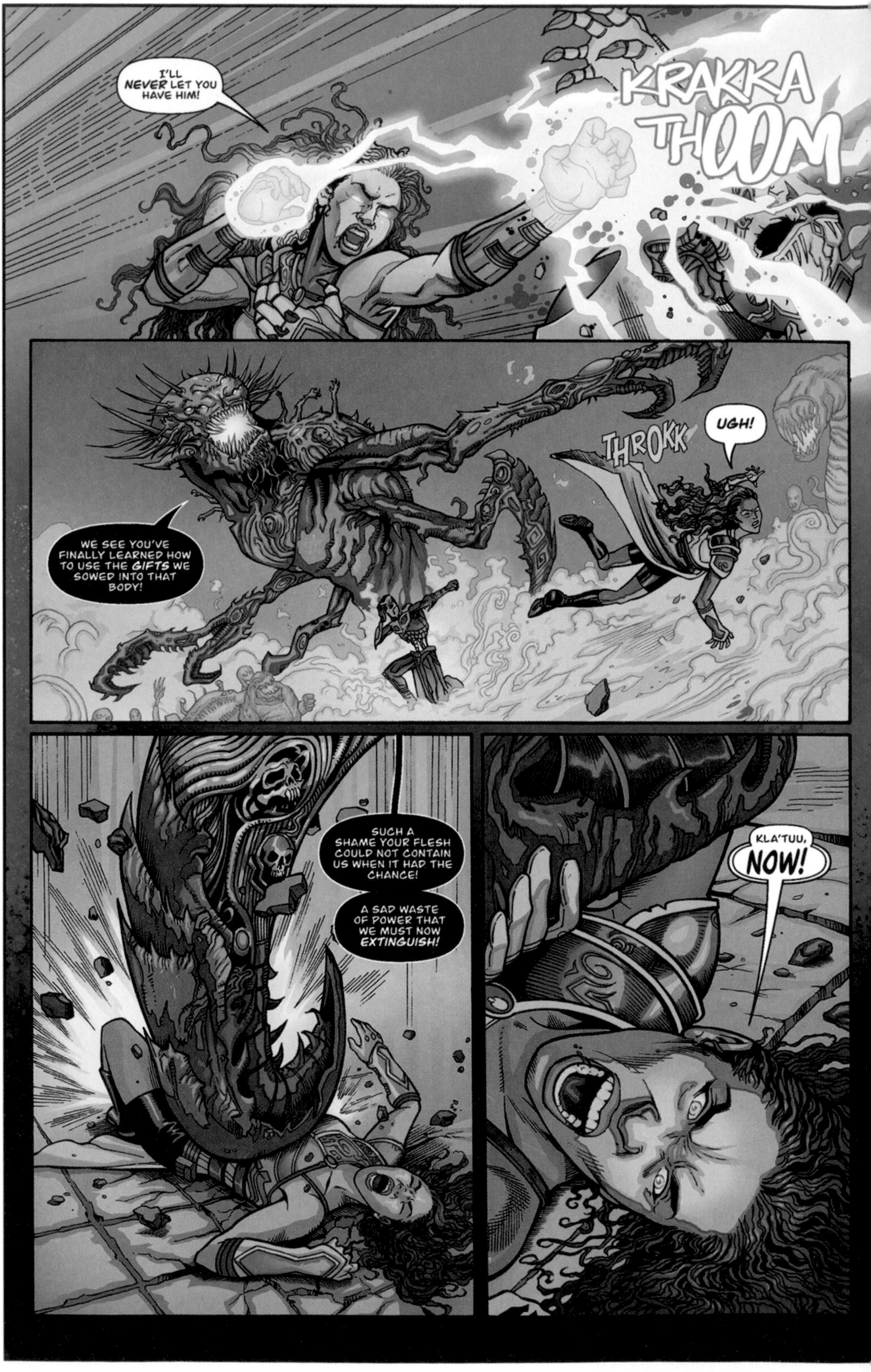
I'LL NEVER LET YOU HAVE HIM!
KRAKKA THOOM
UGH!
THROKK
WE SEE YOU'VE FINALLY LEARNED HOW TO USE THE GIFTS WE SOWED INTO THAT BODY!
SUCH A SHAME YOUR FLESH COULD NOT CONTAIN US WHEN IT HAD THE CHANCE!
A SAD WASTE OF POWER THAT WE MUST NOW EXTINGUISH!
KLA'TUU, NOW!

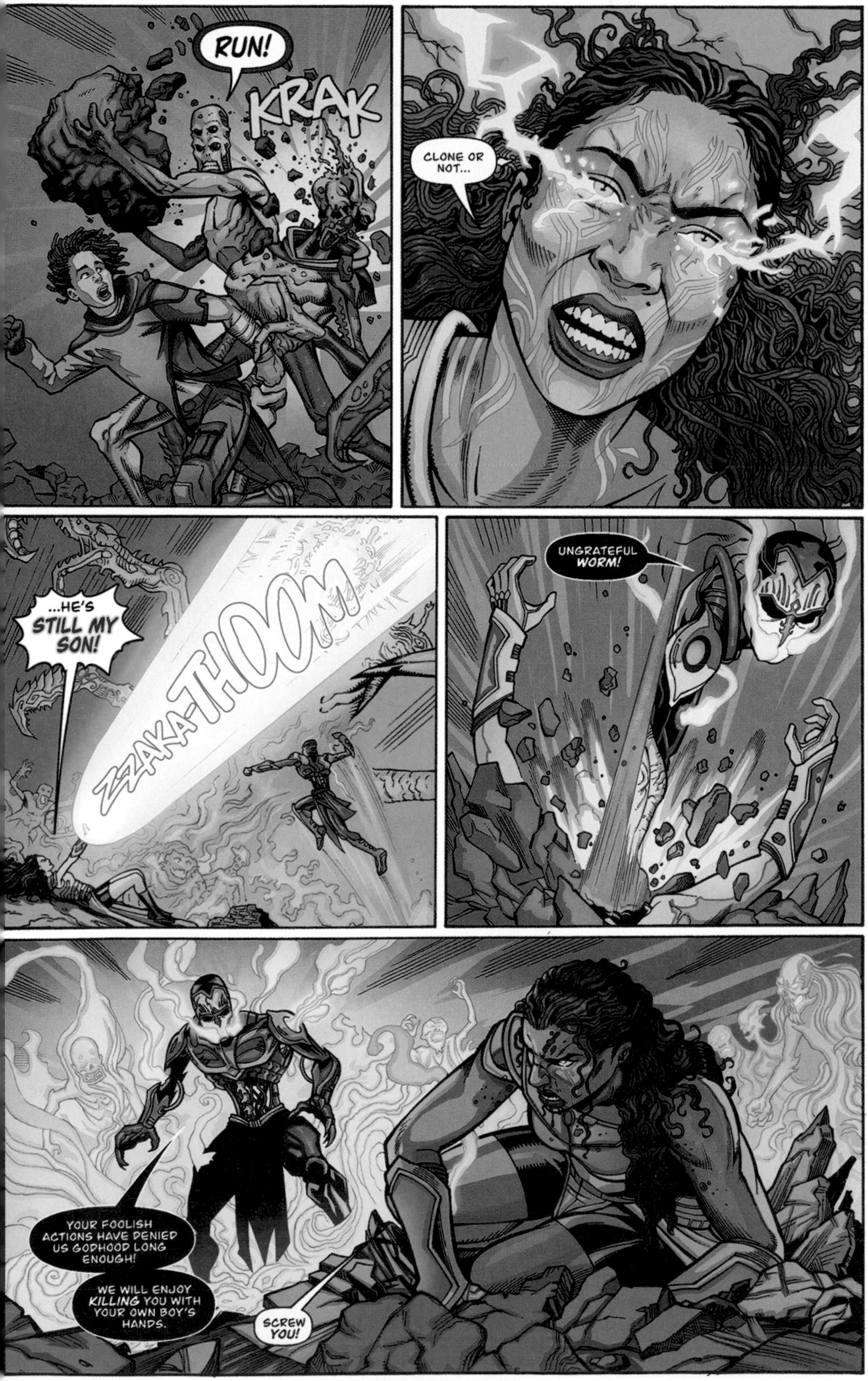
RUN!
KRAK
CLONE OR NOT...
...HE'S STILL MY SON!
ZZAKA-THOOM
UNGRATEFUL WORM!
YOUR FOOLISH ACTIONS HAVE DENIED US GODHOOD LONG ENOUGH!
WE WILL ENJOY KILLING YOU WITH YOUR OWN BOY'S HANDS.
SCREW YOU!

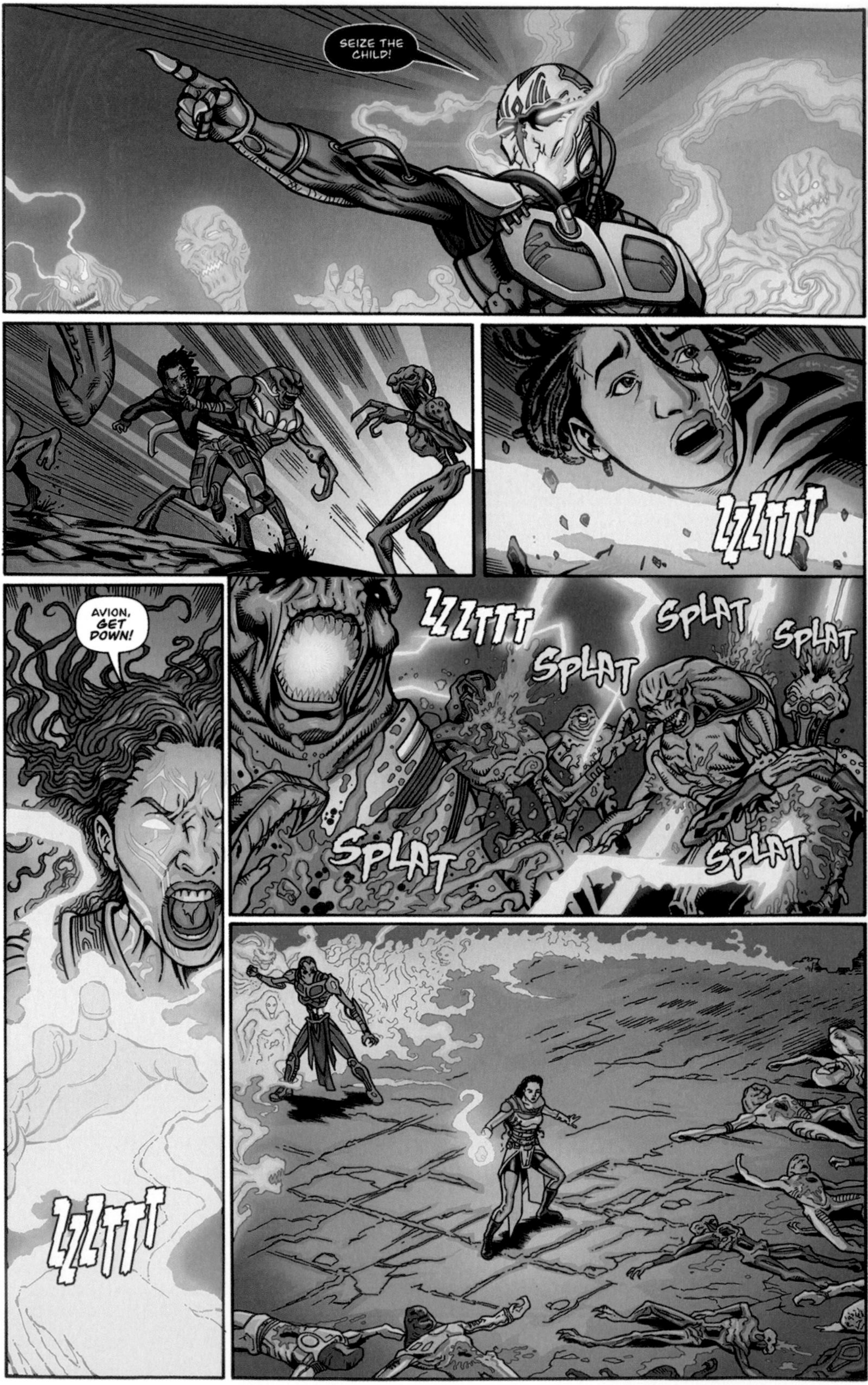
SEIZE THE CHILD!
ZZZTTT
AVION, GET DOWN!
ZZZTTT
ZZZTTT
SPLAT
SPLAT
SPLAT
SPLAT
SPLAT
SPLAT

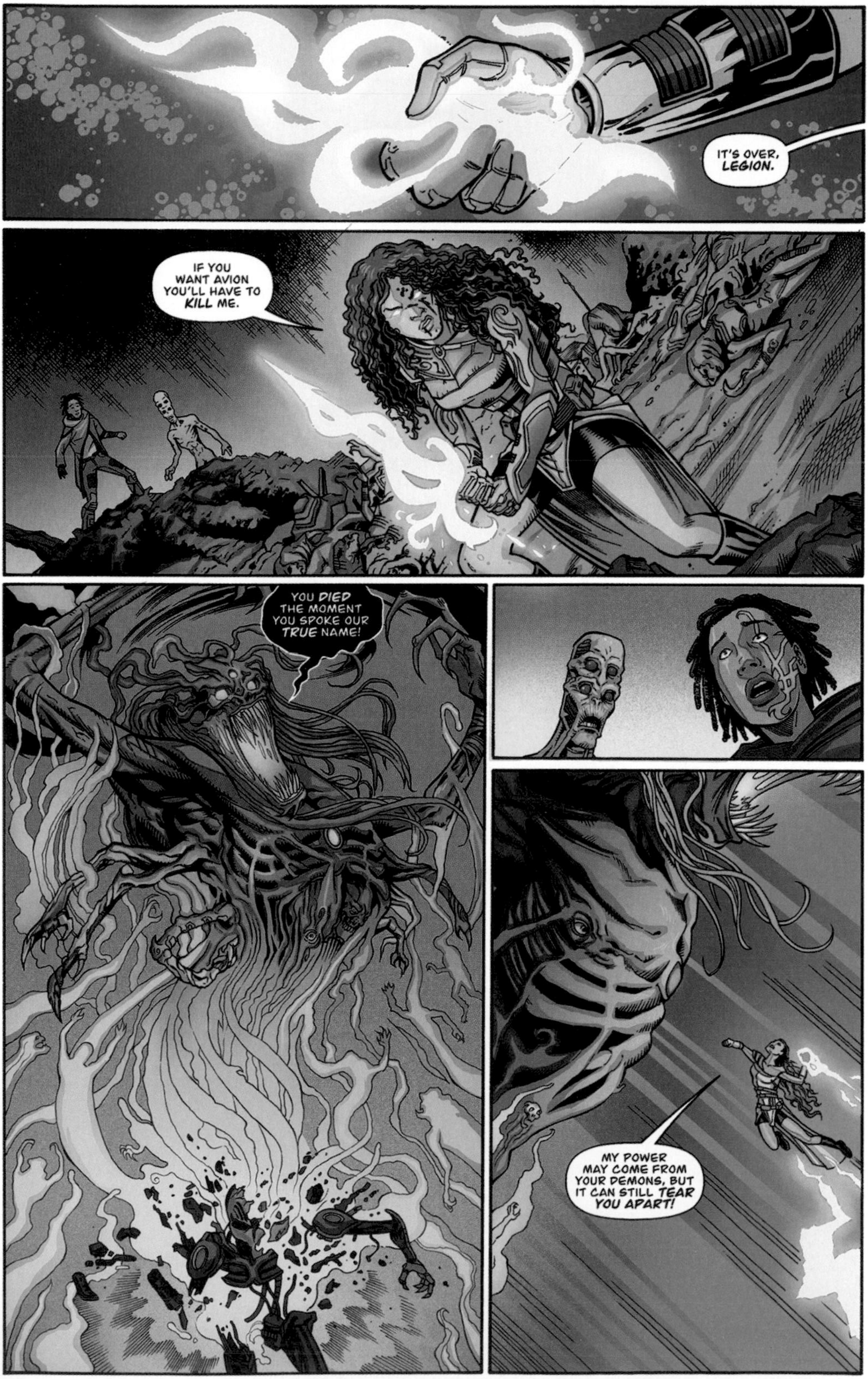
IT'S OVER, LEGION.
IF YOU WANT AVION YOU'LL HAVE TO KILL ME.
YOU DIED THE MOMENT YOU SPOKE OUR TRUE NAME!
MY POWER MAY COME FROM YOUR DEMONS, BUT IT CAN STILL TEAR YOU APART!

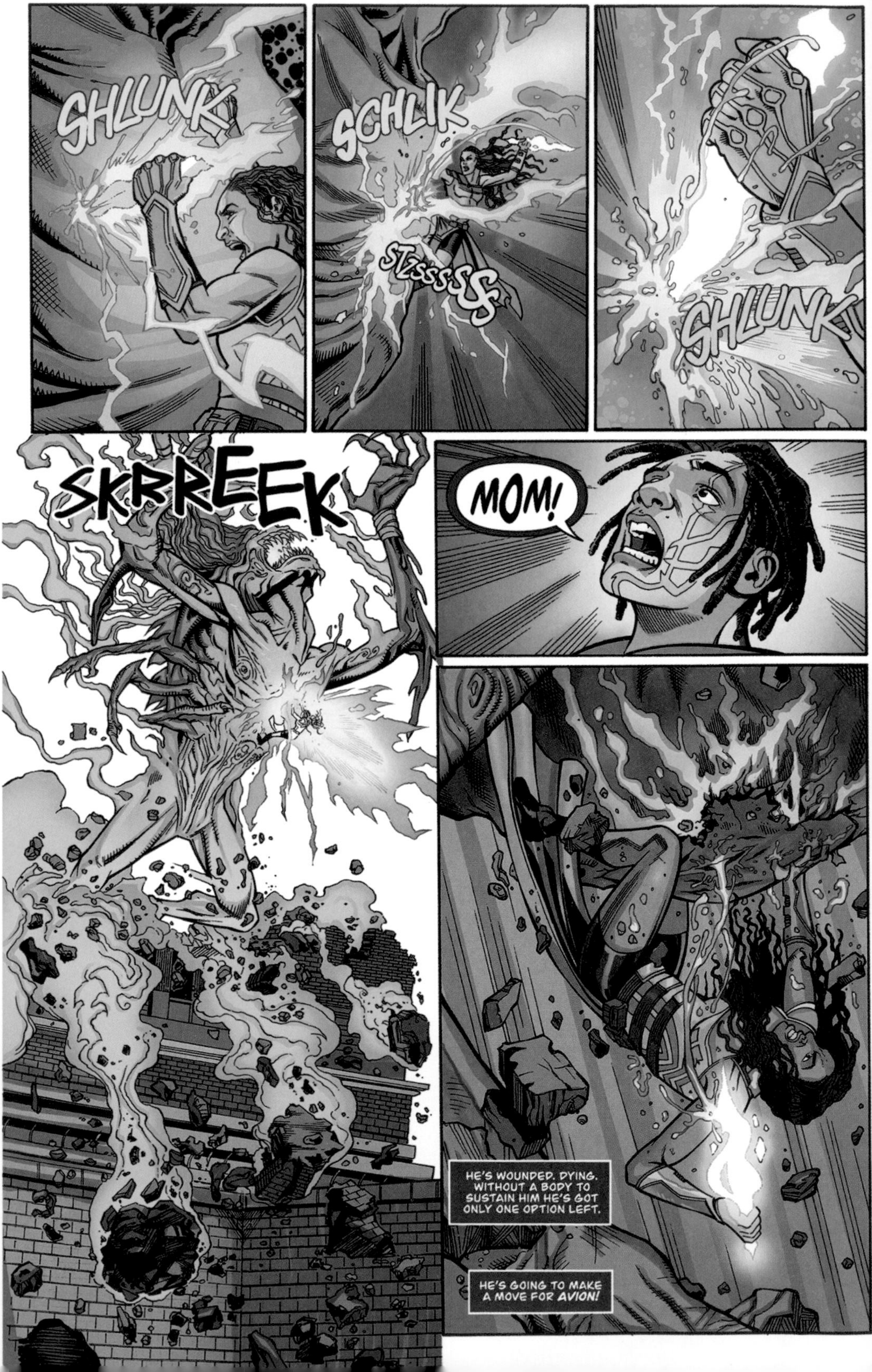
SHLUNK
SCHLIK
STZSSSSSS
SHLUNK
SKRREEK
MOM!
HE'S WOUNDED. DYING. WITHOUT A BODY TO SUSTAIN HIM HE'S GOT ONLY ONE OPTION LEFT.
HE'S GOING TO MAKE A MOVE FOR AVION!

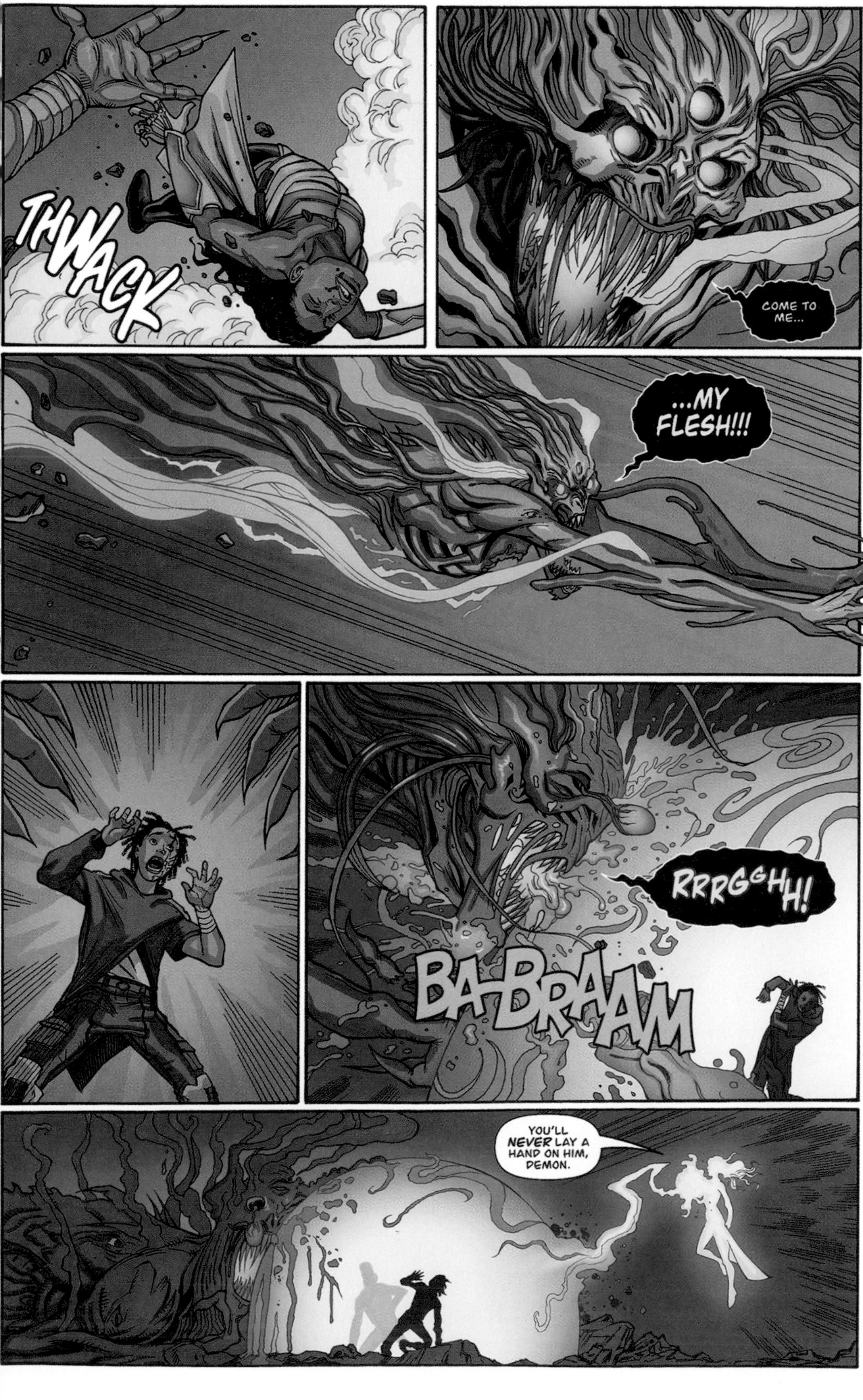
THWACK
COME TO ME...
...MY FLESH!!!
RRRGGHH!
BA-BRAAM
YOU'LL NEVER LAY A HAND ON HIM, DEMON.

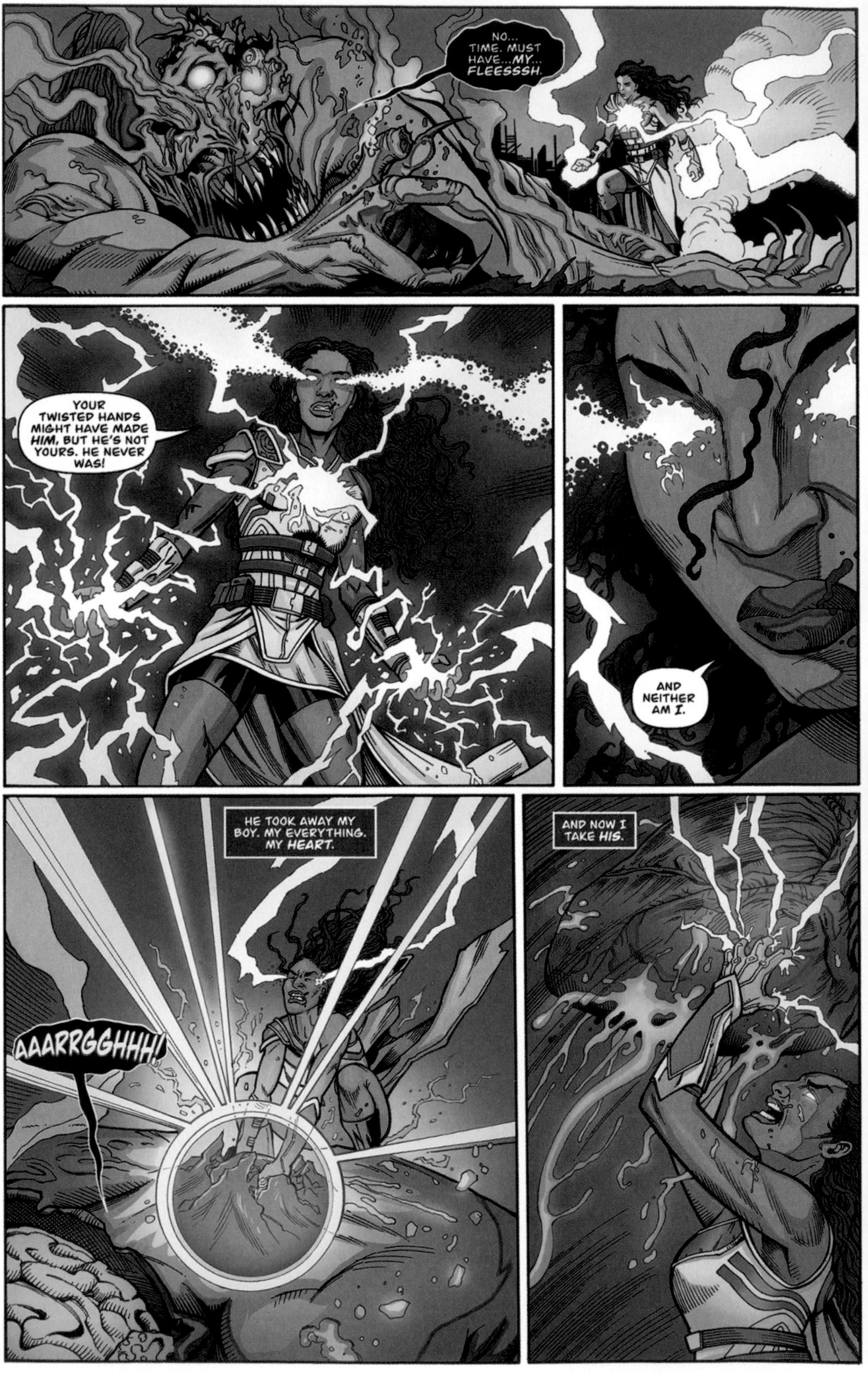
NO... TIME. MUST HAVE...MY... FLEESSSH.
YOUR TWISTED HANDS MIGHT HAVE MADE HIM, BUT HE'S NOT YOURS. HE NEVER WAS!
AND NEITHER AM I.
HE TOOK AWAY MY BOY. MY EVERYTHING. MY HEART.
AAARRGGHHH!
AND NOW I TAKE HIS.

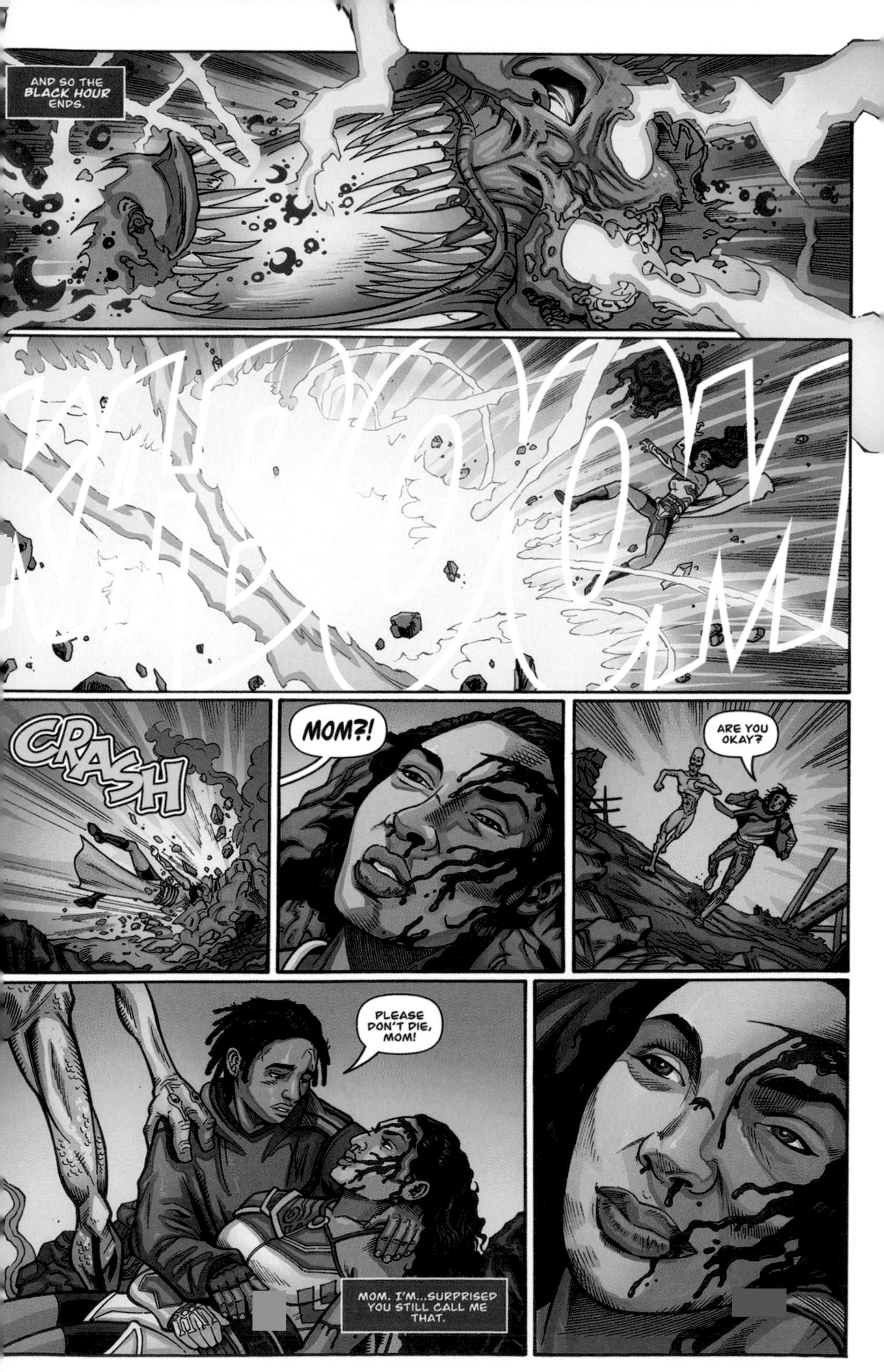
AND SO THE BLACK HOUR ENDS.
CRASH
MOM?!
ARE YOU OKAY?
PLEASE DON'T DIE, MOM!
MOM. I'M...SURPRISED YOU STILL CALL ME THAT.

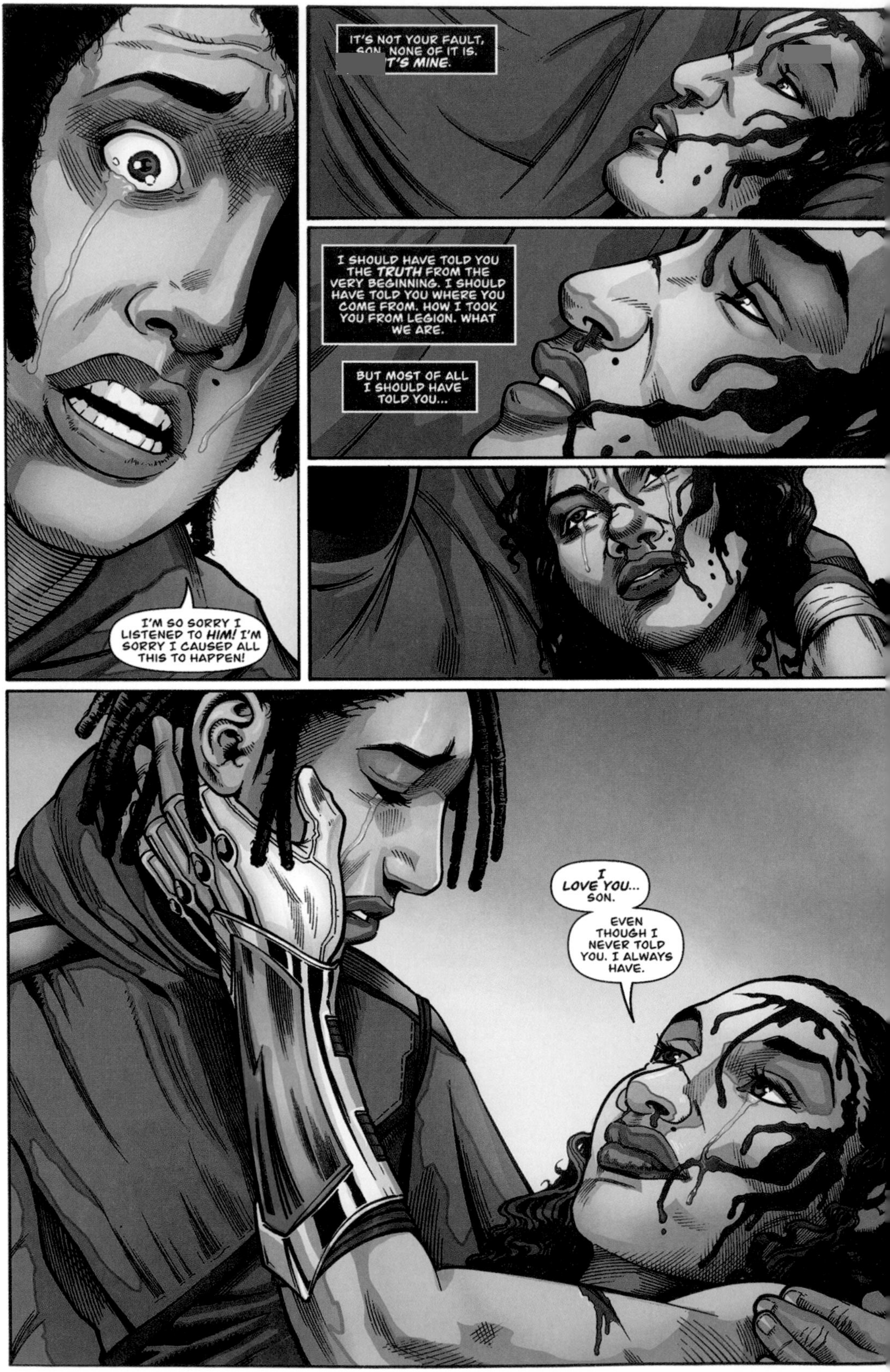
I'M SO SORRY I LISTENED TO ***HIM!*** I'M SORRY I CAUSED ALL THIS TO HAPPEN!
IT'S NOT YOUR FAULT, SON. NONE OF IT IS. [redacted]T'S ***MINE.***
I SHOULD HAVE TOLD YOU THE ***TRUTH*** FROM THE VERY BEGINNING. I SHOULD HAVE TOLD YOU WHERE YOU COME FROM. HOW I TOOK YOU FROM LEGION. WHAT WE ARE.
BUT MOST OF ALL I SHOULD HAVE TOLD YOU...
I LOVE YOU... SON.
EVEN THOUGH I NEVER TOLD YOU. I ALWAYS HAVE.

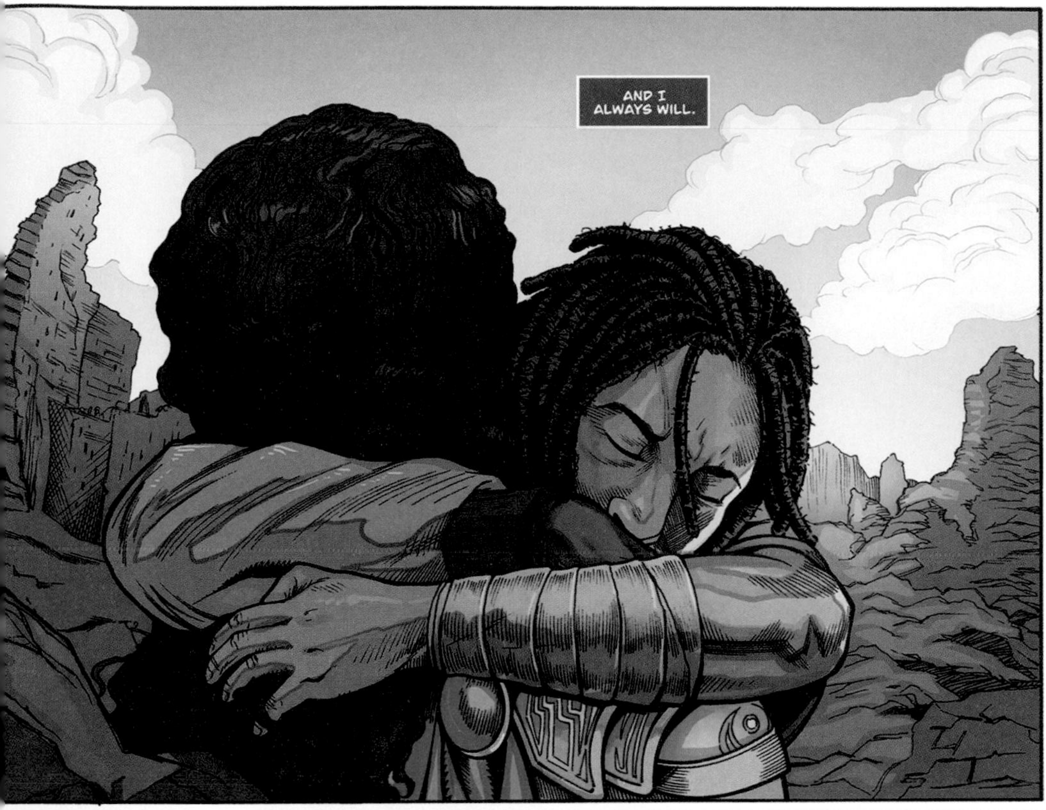
AND I
ALWAYS WILL.

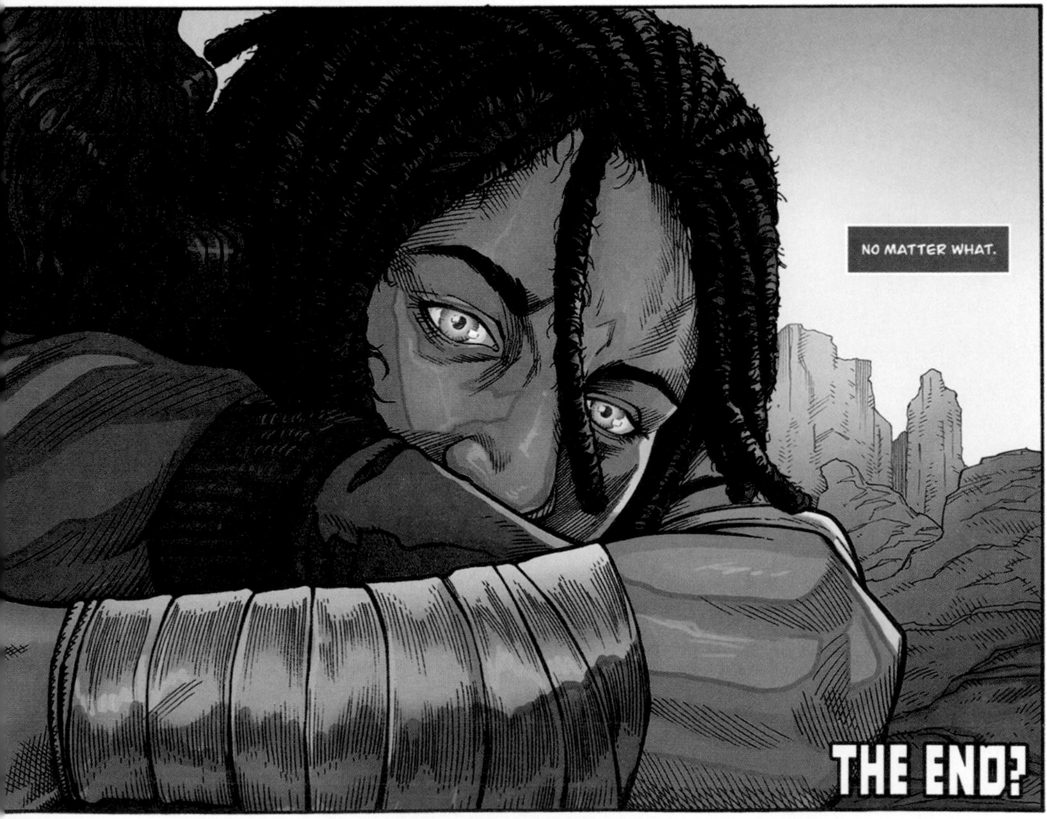
NO MATTER WHAT.
THE END?

ERIC HENSON'S EDEN™ ART GALLERY

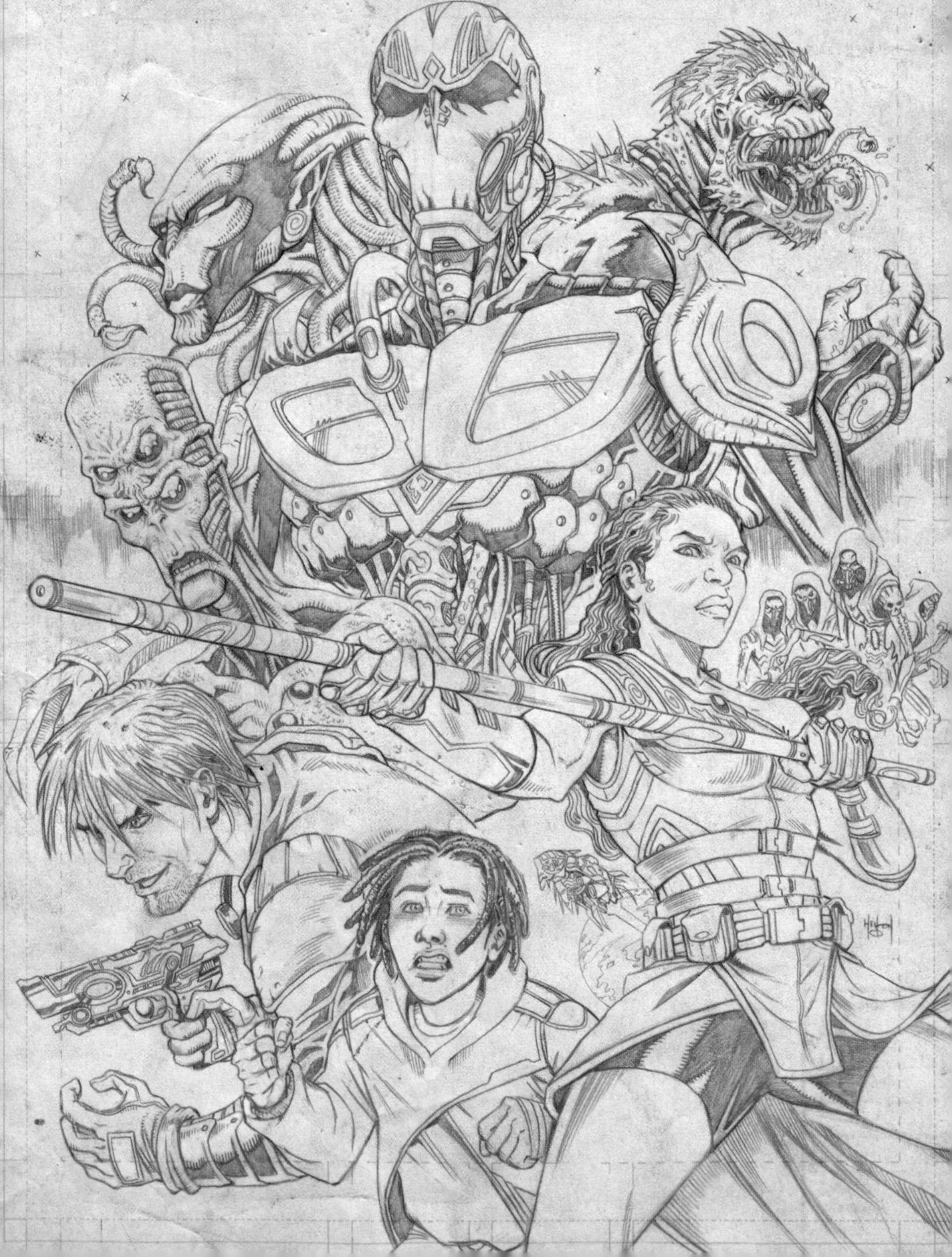

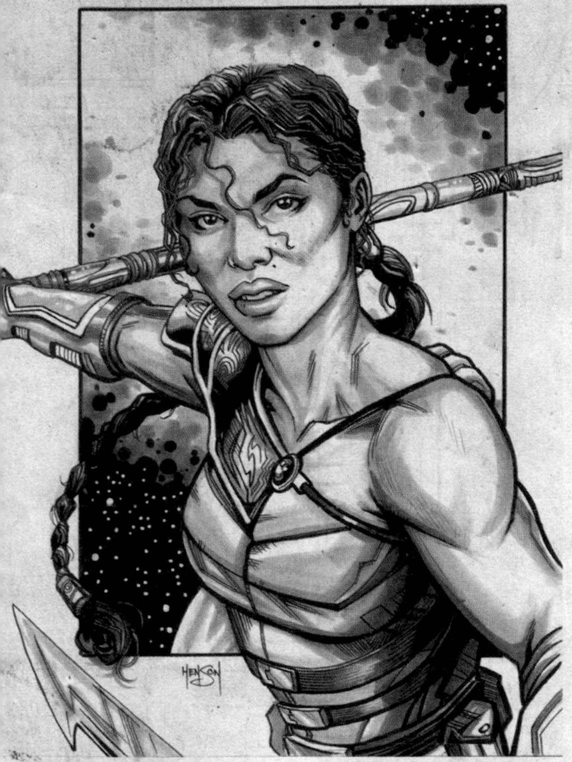

NERIAH

When I began to sketch ideas for Neriah, the goal was to make her convey a sense of militaristic strength, but also motherly compassion.

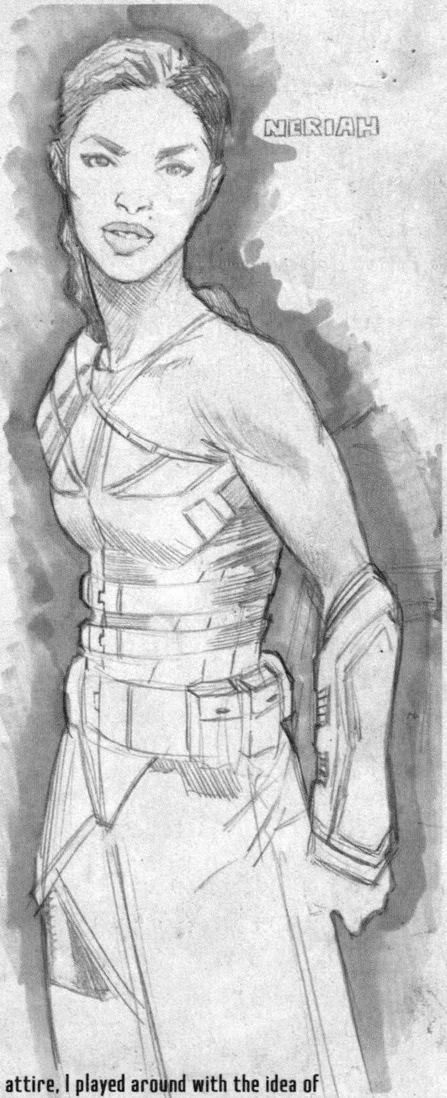
NERIAH

I initially based her off of my youngest daughter of the same name—with her physique clearly reflecting a more warrior-like background.

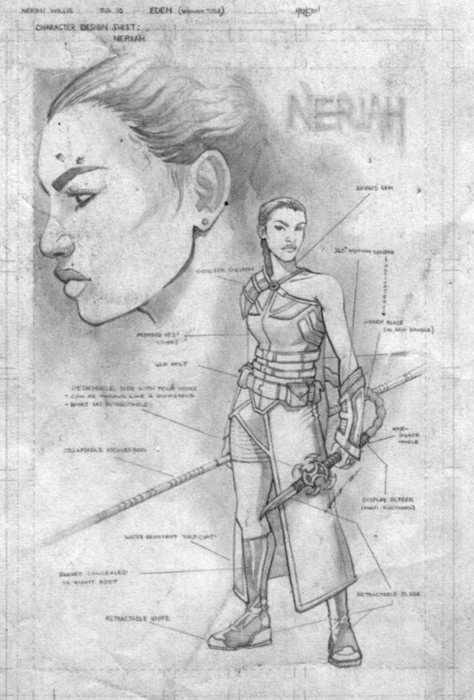
EDEN
CHARACTER DESIGN SHEET:
NERIAH
NERIAH

For her attire, I played around with the idea of using asymmetrical cuts and military uniform elements from various eras and cultures. This futuristic patchwork of samurai garb and knightly gear led to a bizarre balance of something both sleek and utilitarian. Similarly, her primary weapon is a mixture of old and new—with the idea being to update an antiquated style of weaponry (bo) to have modern, transmuting properties.

KLA'TUU

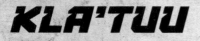

The toughest challenge in designing Kla'Tuu was finding a way to make him different than the other "big-eyed" alien creatures out there.

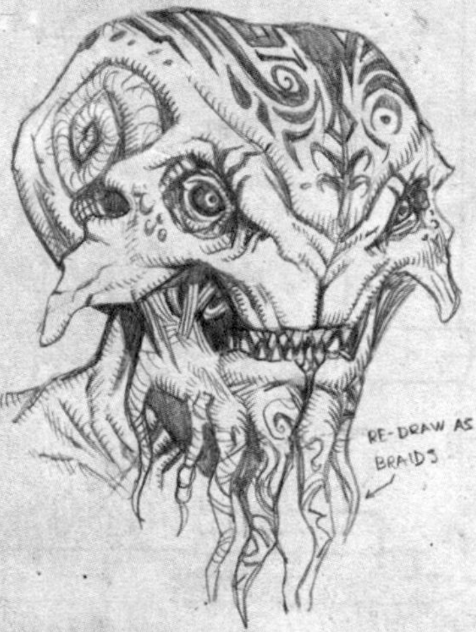
RE-DRAW AS BRAIDS

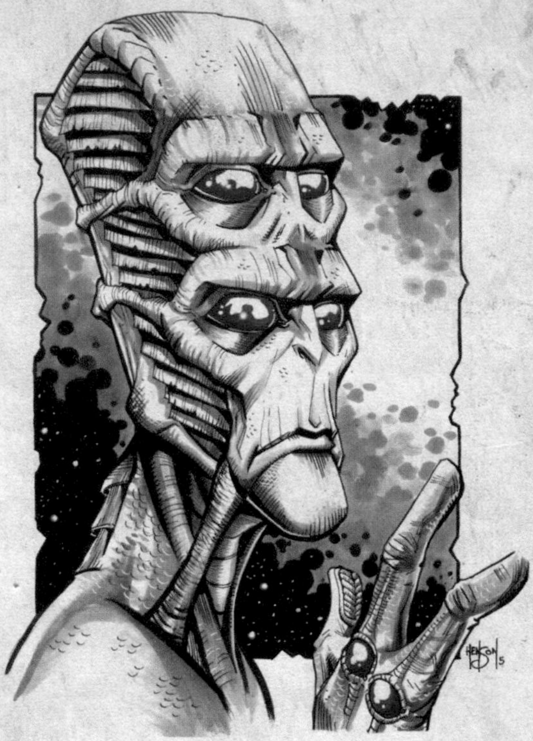

Some of my earlier designs were a bit too intimidating for his peaceful personality, so I eventually started leaning in a more amiable direction.

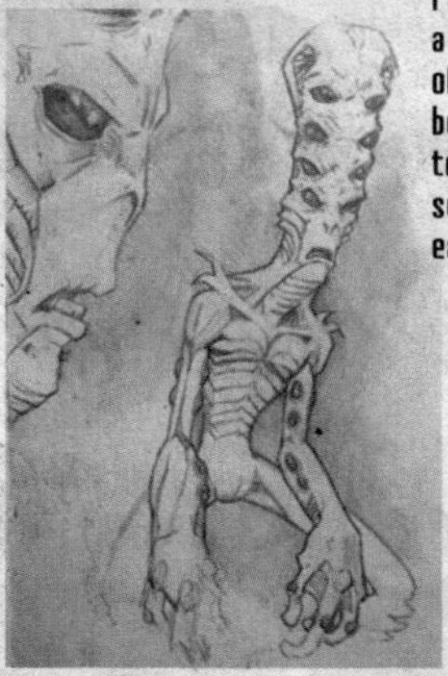

I began to settle on a version of him that was a bit more bug-like and equipped with about 15 pairs of eyes all over his body. As unique as that may have been, however, it would have been a total nightmare to draw over and over, so I toned it down to just 6 sets of eyes and a shorter cranium that was much easier to fit into a comic book panel.

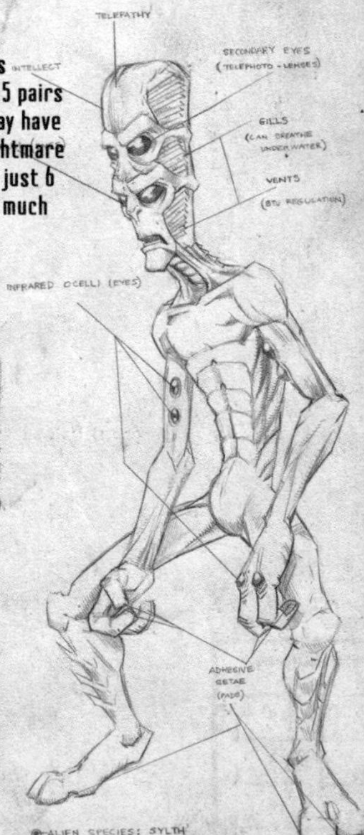
TELEPATHY
INTELLECT
SECONDARY EYES
(TELEPHOTO - LENSES)
GILLS
(CAN BREATHE UNDERWATER)
VENTS
(BTU REGULATION)
INFRARED OCELLI (EYES)
ADHESIVE SETAE (PADS)
ALIEN SPECIES: SYLTH

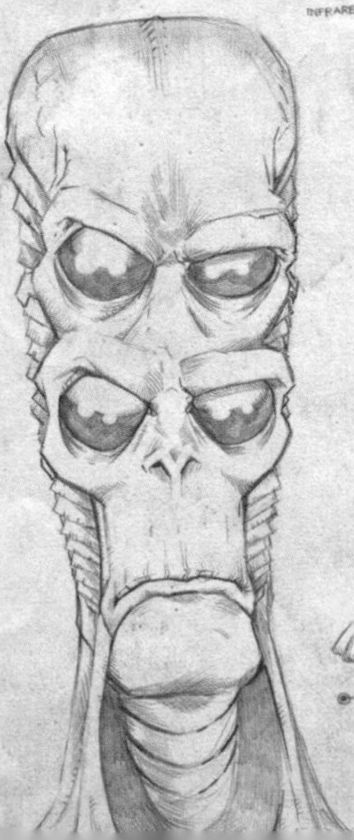

While there were lots of more complex ideas for his form early on, the final design for Kla'Tuu ended up being a really simple humanoid blend of a salamander, fish and jumping spider. Sometimes simple is better.

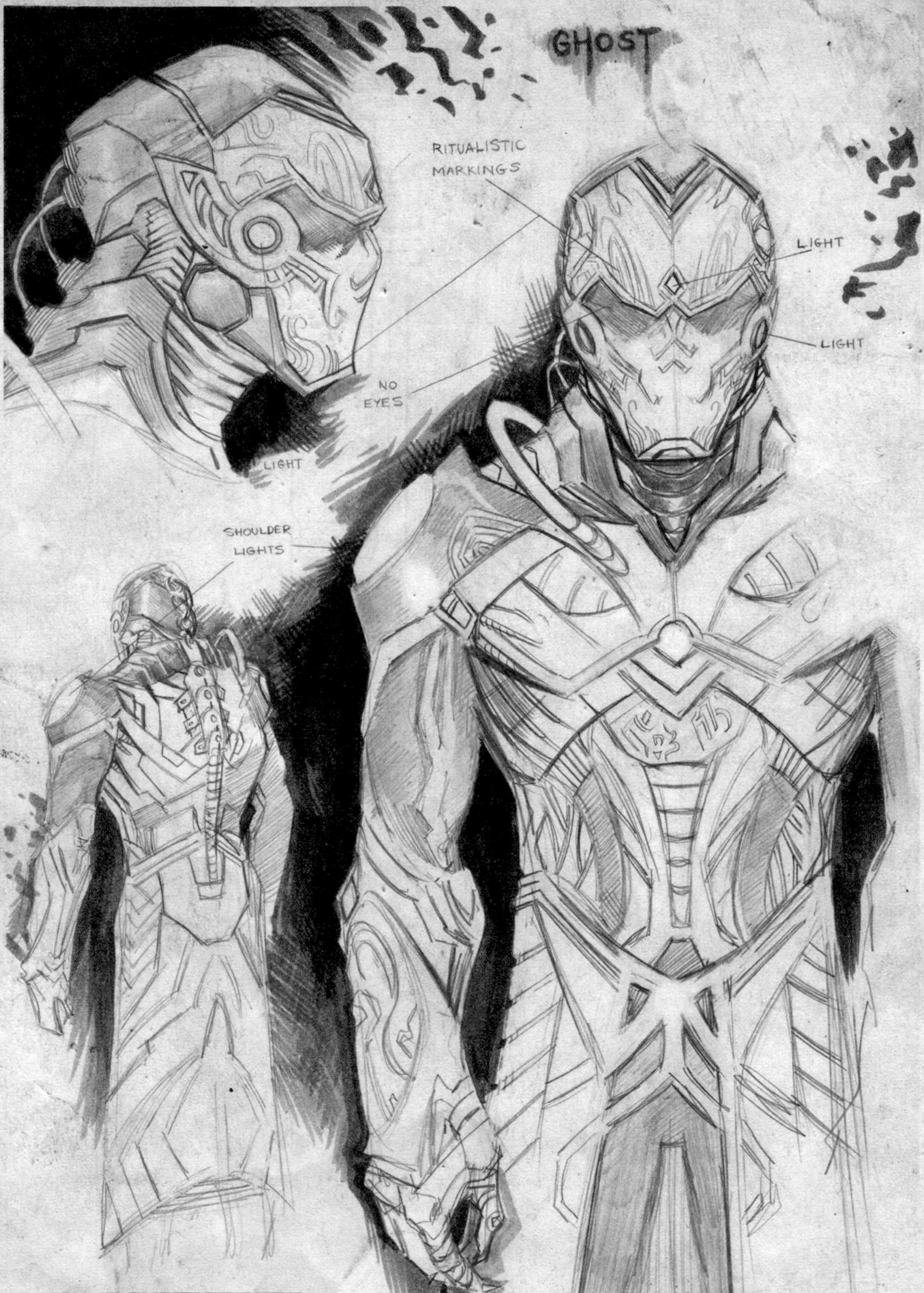

GHOST
RITUALISTIC MARKINGS
LIGHT
LIGHT
NO EYES
LIGHT
SHOULDER LIGHTS

GHOST

The main idea behind Ghost's armor was to look futuristic, but also worn and cracked. I knew I didn't want any eyes or other facial features because I thought it would make him creepier and more mysterious. His armor also needed to look alien and it had to be multilayered because he needed to be able to change out the plates as they weakened.

OTHER DESIGNS

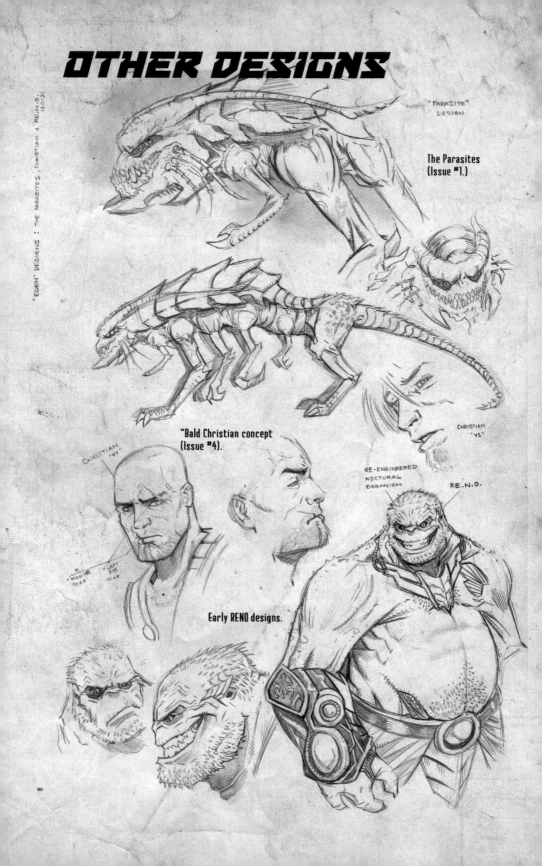

"PARASITE" DESIGN

The Parasites
(Issue #1.)

"EDEN" DESIGNS : THE PARASITES, CHRISTIAN & R.E.N.O. (2013)

"Bald Christian concept
(Issue #4).

CHRISTIAN "V1"

CHRISTIAN "V2"

MOUTH SCAR

LEFT EYE SCAR

RE-ENGINEERED NOCTURNAL ORGANISM

R.E.N.O.

Early RENO designs.

OTHER DESIGNS

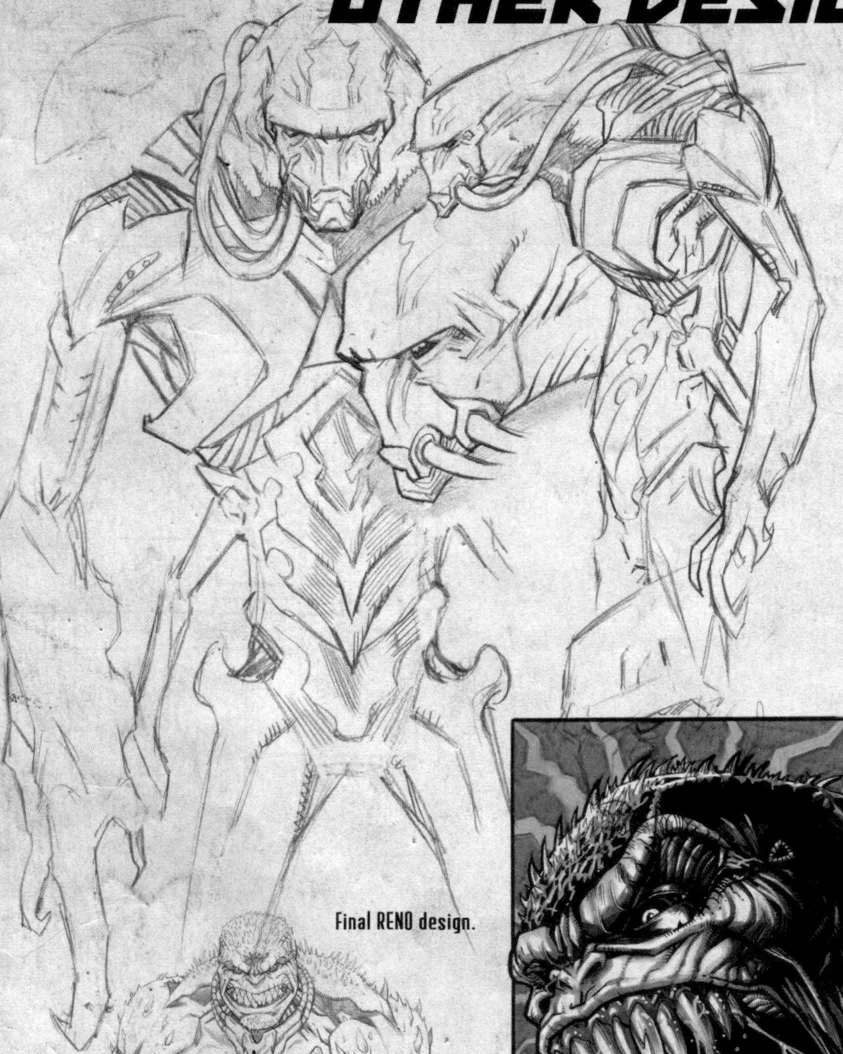

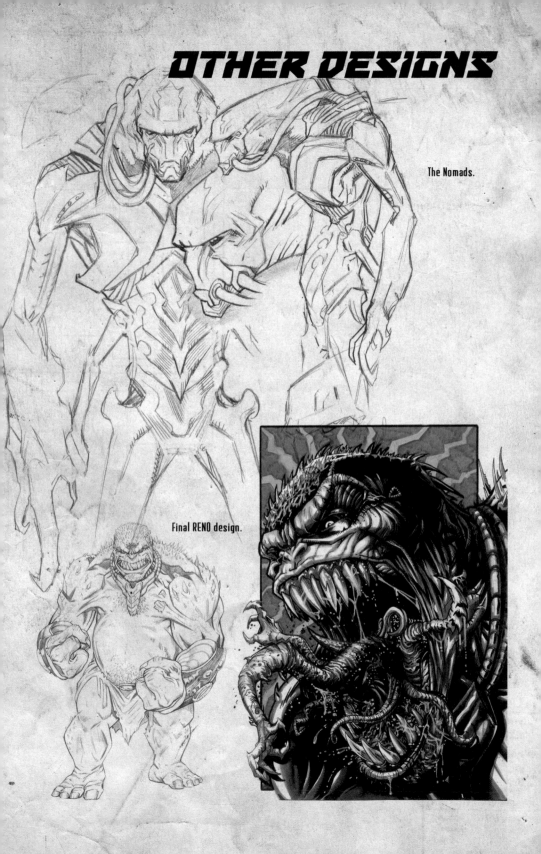

The Nomads.

Final RENO design.

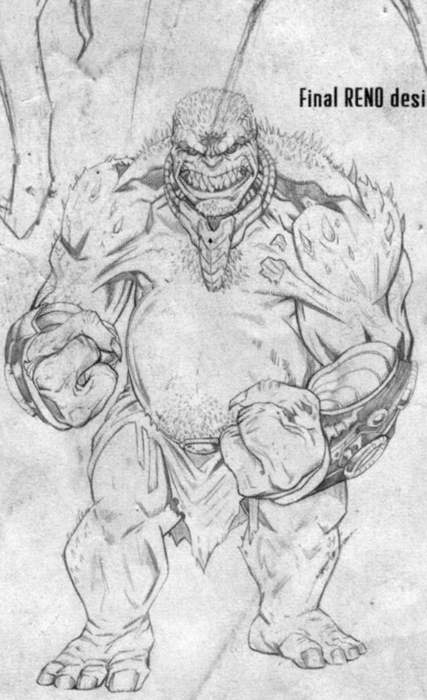

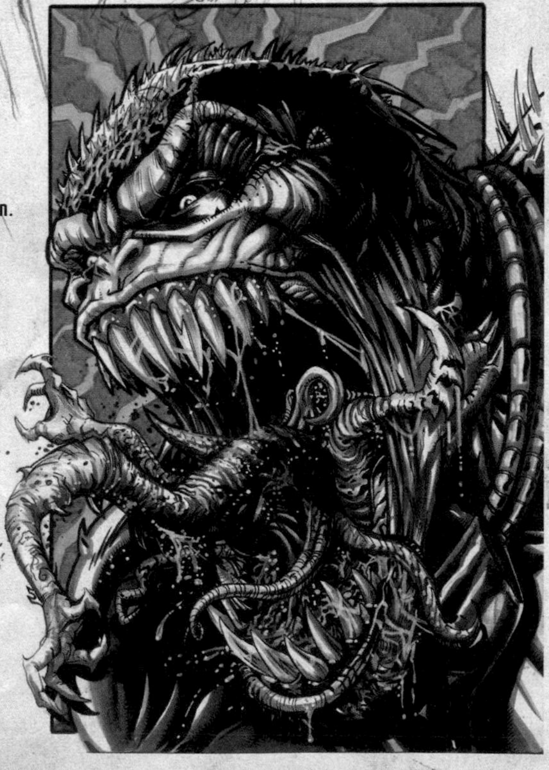

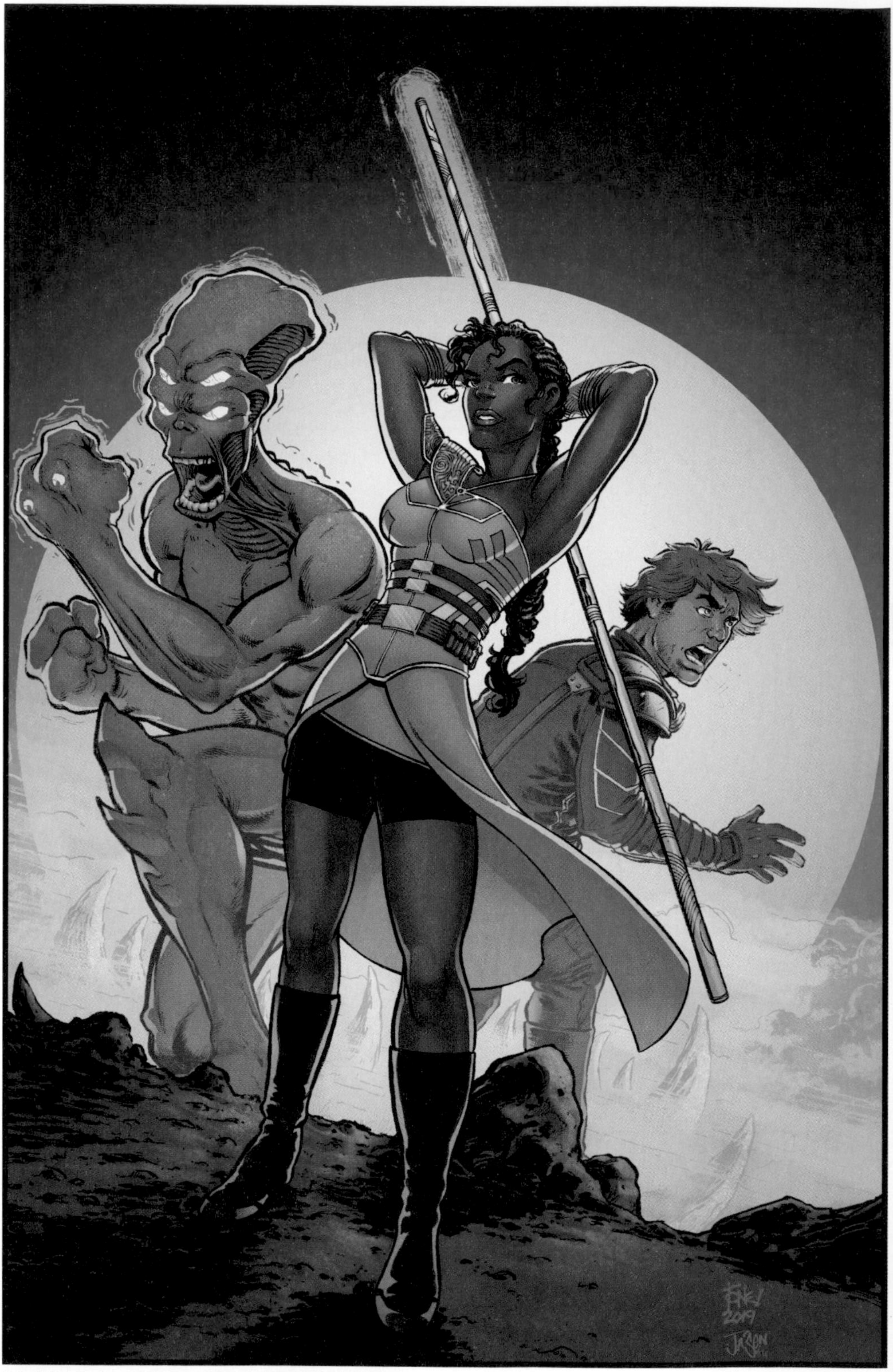

KLA'TUU, NERIAH & CHRISTIAN
ART BY TONE RODRIGUEZ / COLORS BY JASEN SMITH

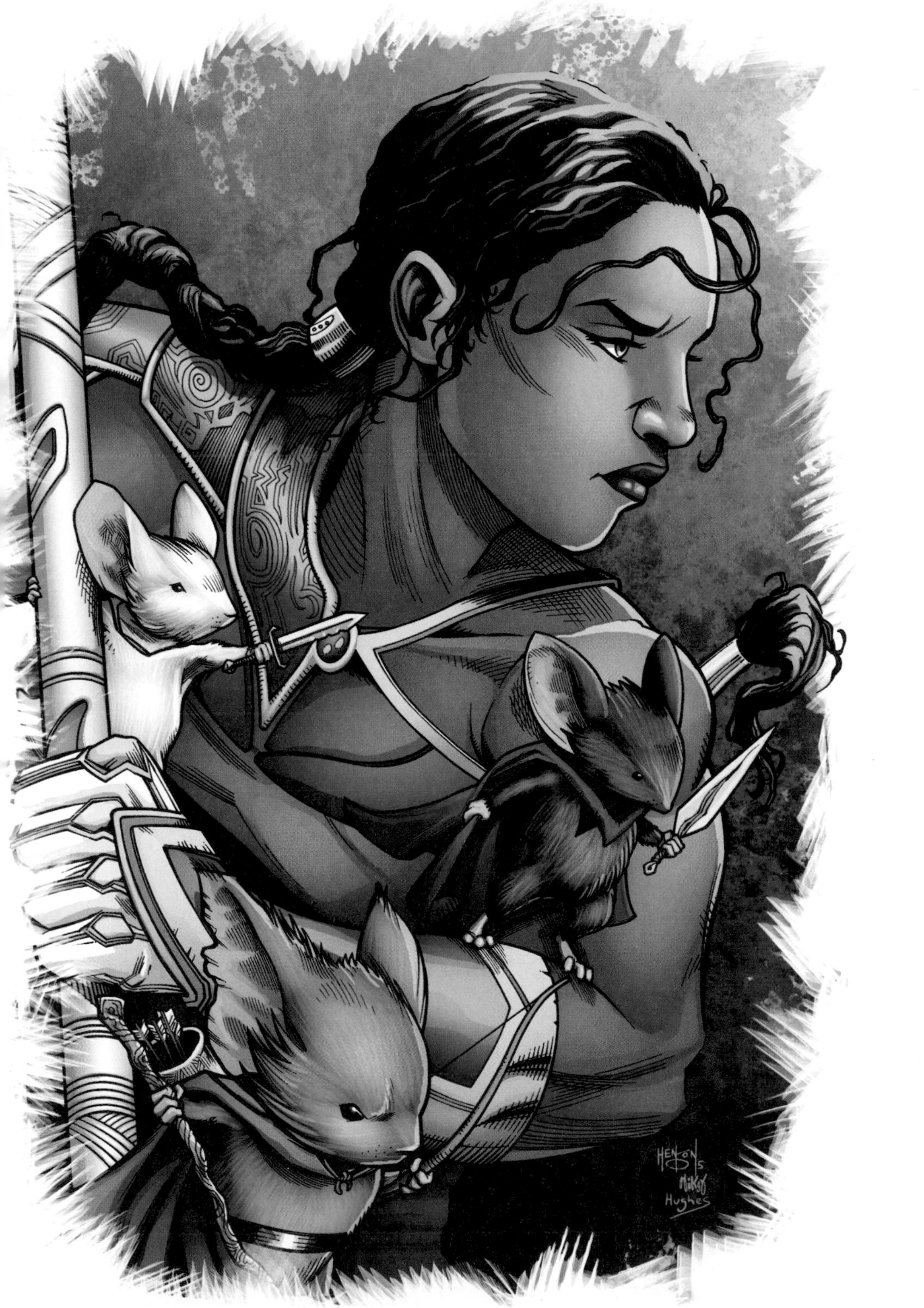

NERIAH/MOUSEGUARD TEAM-UP

PENCILS BY ERIC HENSON / INKS BY MICHAEL BABINSKI / COLORS BY ROSS HUGHES

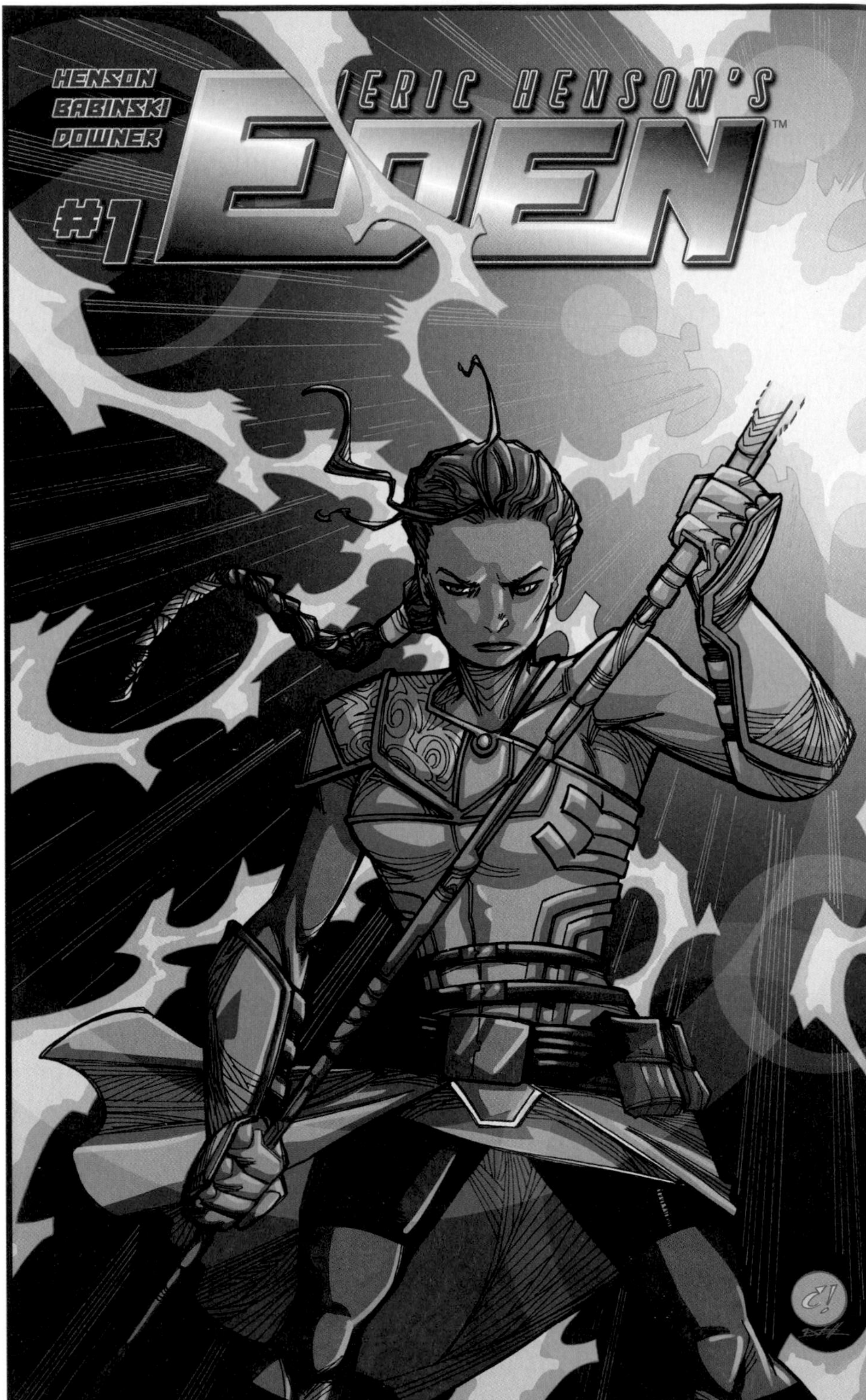
HENSON
BABINSKI
DOWNER
#1
ERIC HENSON'S
EDEN
TM

EDEN #1: VARIANT COVER
ART BY CRAIG ROUSSEAU / COLORS BY NATE LOVETT